RACING POST
ANNUAL 2018

Racing Post Floor 7, The Podium, South Bank Tower Estate, 30 Stamford Street, London, SE1 9LS. 0203 034 8900
Irish Racing Post The Capel Building, Mary's Abbey, Dublin 7. 01 828 7450

Editor Nick Pulford
Art editor David Dew
Cover design Jay Vincent
Other design Peter Gomm
Chief photographers Edward Whitaker, Patrick McCann
Other photography Alain Barr, Debbie Burt, Mark Cranham, Steve Davies, Getty, John Grossick, Roger Harris, Caroline Norris, Louise Pollard
Picture editor David Cramphorn
Graphics Nathan Bines, Samanatha Creedon, Shane Tetley
Picture artworking Nigel Jones, Stefan Searle
Feature writers Scott Burton, David Carr, Steve Dennis, Alastair Down, Katherine Fidler, Richard Forristal, Nicholas Godfrey, Jack Haynes, Daniel Hill, David Jennings, Jon Lees, Keith Melrose, Lee Mottershead, Julian Muscat, Maddy Playle, Lewis Porteous, Nick Pulford, Colin Russell, Brian Sheerin, Mark Storey, Alan Sweetman, Peter Thomas, Kitty Trice, Zoe Vicarage
Contributors Mark Bowers, Paul Curtis, John Randall, Martin Smethurst, Sam Walker

Advertisement Sales
Racing Post: Floor 7, The Podium, South Bank Tower Estate, 30 Stamford Street, London, SE1 9LS. 0203 034 8900. Cheryl Bartley, cheryl.bartley@racingpost.com

Archant Dialogue
Advertising Sales
Gary Stone, 01603 772463, gary.stone@archantdialogue.co.uk
Advertising Production Manager
Kay Brown, 01603 772522, kay.brown@archantdialogue.co.uk
Prospect House, Rouen Road, Norwich NR1 1RE. 01603 772554
archantdialogue.co.uk

Distribution/availability
01933 304858 help@racingpost.com

Published by Racing Post Books
27 Kingfisher Court, Hambridge Road, Newbury, Berkshire RG14 5SJ

Copyright © Racing Post 2017

ISBN 978-1-910497-09-8 [UK]
ISBN 978-1-910497-10-4 [Ireland]

Printed in Great Britain by Buxton Press. Every effort has been made to fulfil requirements with regard to copyright material. The author and publisher will be glad to rectify any omissions at the earliest opportunity.

www.racingpost.com/shop

WELCOME to the seventh edition of the Ra such a firm favourite in our growing stable

Once again it is our pleasure to bring you has been so much to choose from, over ju an incredible year it has been just by recall... Might Bite's RSA Chase, the Eclipse, the Gold Cup at Royal Ascot, the Derby, the Nunthorpe, the Punchestown Gold Cup . . .

On the Flat one horse never needed to be involved in any close finishes simply because she was so much better than her opponents. Enable started the season with an official rating of 84 but less than six months later she was the queen of Europe after a string of dominant performances.

The brilliant filly's official rating soared to 128 and records tumbled as she became the first British-trained filly to win the Prix de l'Arc de Triomphe and the first female name on a select list who have won the King George and the Arc in the same year.

Her only rival as horse of the year on the Flat was housed near her in John Gosden's Clarehaven yard in Newmarket. Cracksman did not compile a string of big-race wins like Enable but his grand finale to the season in the Champion Stakes rivalled his stablemate's romp to Arc victory for sheer class and authority.

Others also had the hallmark of quality. The sprint division especially featured some electrifying performers – Harry Angel, Battaash, Lady Aurelia, Marsha, Caravaggio – in a summer that was often gloomy weather-wise but illuminated so brightly on the track.

The Flat's theme of new stars emerging from unlikely beginnings was mirrored over jumps as Sizing John turned from Douvan's punchbag over two miles to a champion in the Gold Cups engraved with Cheltenham, Irish and Punchestown. Buveur D'Air, meanwhile, went chasing briefly and then came back to claim the Champion Hurdle, while the novice chasing scene instead was lit up by his stablemate Altior as well as Thistlecrack.

These stories of equine achievement were, of course, directed by some remarkable people and there were heartwarming comebacks to the biggest stages for Jessica Harrington, Robbie Power and Sir Michael Stoute, an unlikely Derby hero in Padraig Beggy, and more awe-inspiring accomplishments by giants such as Aidan O'Brien, Ruby Walsh, Nicky Henderson, Frankie Dettori, Willie Mullins and Gordon Elliott.

Best of all as we look back on a great year is that many of the stars will take another bow in 2018. Within ten days of her Arc victory came the news that Enable will stay in training as a four-year-old and Cracksman, along with ace sprinters Harry Angel and Battaash, will be back too.

Most of the top jumpers of 2017 will return as well and the most exciting aspect is that many of them are so young. Sizing John, Altior, Douvan, Buveur D'Air, Fox Norton, Our Duke and Native River are just some of the big-race winners from last season who will be no older than eight by the time of the next Cheltenham Festival.

That gives us so much to look forward to, as well as plenty to look back on.

Nick Pulford

Nick Pulford, Editor

CONTENTS

50

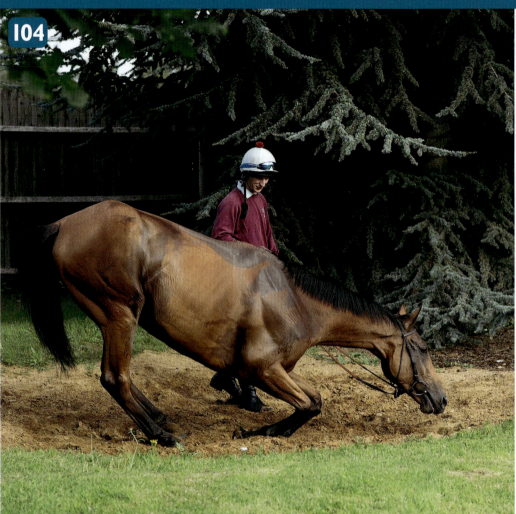

104

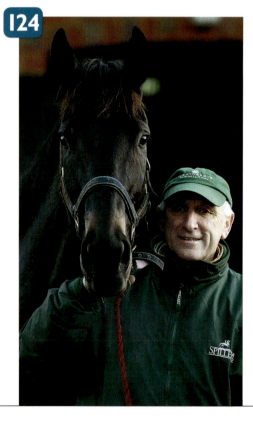

124

118

140

174

FINAL FURLONG

202

READY WILLING ENABLE

Khalid Abdullah's brilliant filly rose to every challenge with five Group 1 triumphs including the Arc, King George and two Classics – and she will be back in 2018

By Julian Muscat

THE hallmark of outstanding racehorses is their ability to tear up the script. They go boldly where none has gone before, breaching frontiers that were deemed impassable. It also helps when trainers are attuned to the brilliance in their midst. In that respect Enable and John Gosden make the perfect couple.

They are even compatible physically. Both are tall and rangy, yet with obvious core strength. Gosden used to hurl the discus at Cambridge University; by the season's end Enable could have hurled herself through a brick wall. She did just that, metaphorically speaking, in the Prix de l'Arc de Triomphe.

To watch the three-year-old filly power to Arc victory was to witness the seemingly preordained. Enable's tour de force was governed by subtle nuances, yet the simple truth is that outstanding racehorses make it look easy. Arcs do not come more easily than by a geared-down two and a half lengths, with the outcome assured from the moment Enable swung for home.

It was a triumph of powerful grace. More than that, it was a triumph the like of which had never come to pass in 95 previous runnings. No filly trained in Britain or Ireland had won Europe's signature race. As Enable

▸ Continues page 6

quickened to the front, that curse was screaming at her in the face. She repelled it with a casual flick of her long ears.

The Arc had brought to heel a feminine who's who of the Turf. Among three-year-old fillies in the last 35 years, the vanquished include Diminuendo, Ouija Board, Taghrooda, Salsabil, Sun Princess and User Friendly. That sextet brought a combined haul of 12 Classic triumphs into the race. All to no avail.

This collective failure underlined the magnitude of a task Enable would accomplish with casual disdain for her 17 opponents. From Frankie Dettori's standpoint, however, there was nothing casual about it. Trainer and jockey rehearsed their options incessantly in the preamble, yet come the moment and there were artistic overtures to Dettori's flourish from the saddle.

This was a time for precise draftsmanship over sweeping brushstrokes. With five Aidan O'Brien-trained runners, there was bound to be a tactical slant to Ballydoyle's assault. Dettori was ready and waiting, so when Idaho strode forward from the gates the Italian was happy to station Enable on his tail.

One aspect of Chantilly's tricky

RIDE INTO HISTORY

In his own words, Frankie Dettori on how he won a record-breaking fifth Prix de l'Arc de Triomphe

Before the race I was toying with the idea of making the running, but I was aware Idaho, Capri and Order Of St George are good stayers. There's a little tower by the 2,000-metre mark and that was my first marker. I said to John [Gosden]: "I have 400 metres to really find out what's going to happen."

I went to make the running but I saw Idaho was running free, so I let him slot in. Then I could see Order Of St George breathing down my quarters, so I checked behind him and there was plenty of room. I managed to drag her back and get behind Order Of St George.

At that moment I was exactly where I wanted her to be, with free air on my left. It got to the point where I was running away around the bend. I was striking Order Of St George's heels, I was going that well, and I could see distress signals from the one in front.

I thought at York I perhaps went a little too soon, so I counted to ten. I couldn't wait to get to the 400-metre mark and when I got there I asked her to go and she flew. She's got a burst of three or four lengths and then sustains it. When we plateaued at that speed I was just counting the furlong discs – it was so smooth and so effortless.

Enable deserves all the credit. She's the best filly I've ever ridden and John is a genius. He kept her at absolutely top shape all year. I'm the first jockey to get to five Arc wins and I'm very proud.

DETTORI'S RECORD ARC HAUL

Year	Horse	Trainer
1995	Lammtarra	Saeed Bin Suroor
2001	Sakhee	Saeed Bin Suroor
2002	Marienbard	Saeed Bin Suroor
2015	Golden Horn	John Gosden
2017	Enable	John Gosden

topography is that there is plenty of room on the inside for the first two furlongs, by which time most races take their shape. At that very point, however, Dettori became aware of an imminent danger as Order Of St George, another from the Ballydoyle team, advanced on his outer under Donnacha O'Brien.

O'Brien tried to outmanoeuvre Dettori. He wanted to pin Enable against the far rail, in behind Idaho, and thus with nowhere to go. Dettori responded in the blink of an eye, reining Enable back behind Order Of St George and then switching to the latter's outside. It was a demonstration of instinctive saddle-craft that assured Enable a clear passage thereafter. It was all she would require.

"Usually in an Arc something happens but it was so smooth and so effortless," Dettori said. "I was quite shocked but I was able to enjoy it because it happened so easily."

Enable in full flight is a sight to behold. She is of a different hue to

▸▸ Crowning glory: Enable powers home at Chantilly for a historic win in the Arc; (left) the Racing Post's front page the next day

Dancing Brave, Khalid Abdullah's other iconic winner of the Arc in 1986. Dancing Brave was the rapier, lunging fast and late at his prey. Enable resembles water tumbling down the side of a hill, increasing in velocity until it becomes a torrent. The six horses engulfed in Enable's immediate wake at Chantilly were all Group 1 winners.

As for Dettori, his almost imperceptible change of tack amplified why he remains among the global elite at the age of 46. It was the sort of race-winning move he has made countless times on the big occasion and it brought him a record fifth victory in the Arc. Four years earlier, however, he must have despaired of ever returning to the summit.

Rides – any old rides – were hard to come by in May 2013, when Dettori resumed after a six-month ban for failing a drugs test. He was sliding anonymously towards enforced retirement when Sheikh Joaan

Al-Thani's retainer brought him back from the brink. When, the following year, William Buick left Gosden to ride for Godolphin, the trainer turned to Dettori. The jockey's rehabilitation was complete, although on those dark days he could scarcely have envisaged steering Golden Horn to victory in the 2015 Arc – much less repeating the feat aboard Enable two years later.

For Gosden, Enable's Arc triumph represented his finest hour in a career that has now reached the drawbridge of excellence. As with Golden Horn two years earlier, Gosden was as sure as he could be that a busy season had not overtly depleted Enable's reserves.

"She'll tell me what to do," the trainer said during the Arc build-up. "Horses always tell you if you watch and listen. Where and when she runs is more her idea than mine sometimes."

These were revelatory words. Most trainers bow to precedent, sticking with tried-and-trusted staging posts towards races like the Arc. Rarely is an

▸ Continues page 8

ENABLE ENCORE?

History is against Enable winning the Arc in 2018, as Treve is the only one of the previous 12 Arc-winning three-year-old fillies to follow up at four. Nine of the 12 were kept in training, with Pearl Cap, Akiyda and Zarkava all being retired.

Of the other eight, six failed in their Arc defence. Samos was fifth in 1936, Coronation 11th in 1950, La Sorellina outside the first ten in 1954, San San 12th in 1973 and Three Troikas fourth in 1980, beaten less than a length by Detroit, who herself finished 20th in her defence in 1981. Nikellora (1946) and Danedream (2012) raced on at four but did not run in the Arc again. Danedream, who won the King George at four, missed the Arc because of a swamp fever ban in Germany.

Corrida is the only filly or mare apart from Treve (2013-14) to win the Arc twice, and she did so at the ages of four and five (1936-37).

John Randall

Arc prospect asked to win the King George in midsummer, as Enable did – much less take in that race just two weeks after the Irish Oaks, which Enable won by five and a half lengths.

"It was never the original plan to run her in the King George," Gosden said after the race. "They geared it up

ENABLE'S RAPID RISE: FROM NEWCASTLE TO CHANTILLY

Nov 28, 2016	**Apr 21, 2017**	**May 10, 2017**	**Jun 2, 2017**	**Jul 15, 2017**	**Jul 29, 2017**	**Aug 24, 2017**	**Oct 1, 2017**
Enable has her only run as a two-year-old in a 1m fillies' maiden on the Newcastle all-weather and wins by three and three-quarter lengths under Rab Havlin *RPR 83*	Ridden by William Buick, she is third in a 1m2f Newbury conditions race won by Shutter Speed, also owned by Khalid Abdullah and trained by John Gosden *RPR 103*	Frankie Dettori, having preferred Shutter Speed at Newbury, rides Enable for the first time and they land the Cheshire Oaks by a length and three-quarters from Alluringly *RPR 112*	Rhododendron is 8-11 favourite for the Oaks but proves no match for Enable, who forges clear to beat her by five lengths with Alluringly another six lengths adrift in third *RPR 123*	Favourite for the first time in her career, she confirms herself the top middle-distance filly in winning the Irish Oaks by five and a half lengths from Rain Goddess *RPR 121*	Up against males and the older generation in the King George, Enable justifies 5-4 favouritism as she powers four and a half lengths clear of Eclipse winner Ulysses *RPR 128*	A fourth Group 1 success in 12 weeks, by a total of 20 lengths, as she goes back against her own sex and takes the Yorkshire Oaks by five lengths from Coronet *RPR 124*	The biggest test of the year as she lines up against 17 rivals in the Arc but she produces her best yet to score by two and a half lengths from Cloth Of Stars *RPR 129*

RACING & EQUESTRIAN CLUB   QATAR PRIX DE L'ARC DE TRIOMPHE

plenty early on and then, going into the bend, they really went for home. It was a tough race. All in that [good to soft] ground too."

It should, by any account, have been just as Gosden told it, but Enable was only limbering up. She raced prominently and keenly under Dettori at Ascot as Maverick Wave set demanding early fractions. When Enable took it up more than two furlongs out she was stalked by Ulysses, who appeared full of running. It was an optical illusion.

Ulysses duly accelerated but the response from Enable carried far more authority. She was clear in a few strides, gone beyond recall as she galloped away from a colt who had just won the Eclipse and would cruise to victory in the International Stakes on his next start.

With most horses, such exertions on testing ground would have warranted a rest. Less than four weeks later Gosden saddled Enable to win the Yorkshire Oaks by five lengths. The Knavesmire can be a graveyard of champions – Golden Horn, remember, came unstuck there at odds of 4-9 – but for her it was just another step on the road to greatness.

A welcome footnote to the King George was the presence at Ascot of Abdullah's eldest son, Prince Ahmed Bin Khalid. Speculation has surrounded the future of Juddmonte Farms beyond the life of its founder, who has now entered his ninth decade. Rumours of a dispersal of one of the finest breeding models anywhere in the world surface from time to time, largely on the premise that none of Abdullah's sons was said to be committed to taking Juddmonte forward. Prince Ahmed's presence at Ascot, and his evident delight at Enable's triumph, suggested otherwise.

"I promised my father I would bring the trophy back," the beaming prince said. "I told John [Gosden], 'Please don't make a liar out of me.' The last time I was at Ascot was 1986, when Dancing Brave won the King George, but Enable was very, very impressive. I think this is the best filly we've ever owned."

Enable was a third King George winner for Gosden and the first of them, Nathaniel, was pivotal to him

▶▶ Taking it easy: Enable (main picture, right) makes her way back to John Gosden's Clarehaven stables with Rab Havlin after working on the gallops before her winning run at Chantilly; (top, from left to right) her sequence of five consecutive Group 1 victories in the Oaks, Irish Oaks, King George, Yorkshire Oaks and Prix de l'Arc de Triomphe

taking possession of Enable in the first place. Enable is by Nathaniel. But for that, she would likely have been sent to Andre Fabre's stable in France.

"Andre has developed most of the [female] family on the racecourse," said Simon Mockridge, stud director at Abdullah's Juddmonte Farms in Europe. "It's a family he knows very well. He trained Apogee, who is the granddam of Enable and Flintshire – whom Andre also trained. One of the main reasons for John getting Enable was that he trained Nathaniel."

It also helped that Enable was very much in Nathaniel's mould. A tall,

SUPER SEVEN

Enable became the seventh horse to win the King George and Arc in the same year and the first filly to do so

Ribot 1956

Ballymoss 1958

Mill Reef 1971

Dancing Brave 1986

Lammtarra 1995

Dylan Thomas 2007

Enable 2017

angular filly in her younger days, she needed time to furnish her powerful frame. "When she first came to us [as a yearling in December 2015] you saw straight away that she had this incredible body," Gosden said. "She had real depth of girth – space for an engine room, or heart room. When they're like that you have the chance that they have a seriously powerful cardio-vascular system."

It was some time before Gosden put his theory to the test. When Enable made her racecourse debut last winter all the talk was of Colin Tizzard's

▶▶ Continues page 10

NATURE AND NURTURE

On February 12, 2014, the bay filly by Nathaniel who had just been foaled tipped the scales at 125lb. This was greeted with nods of approval at Banstead Manor Stud, near Newmarket, the European nerve centre of Juddmonte Farms.

"We have noticed over the years that most of our better racehorses tend to weigh in at between 121lb and 126lb at birth," reflects Juddmonte's stud director, Simon Mockridge. "I like to see that at foaling. She was at the upper end of where we like them to be."

It's the sort of detail that matters at Prince Khalid Abdullah's nurseries. Studious attention is paid to what other breeders might feel is superfluous information. In the case of this filly, who would be named Enable, it would prove portentous. She would evolve into the formidable runner who dominated the 2017 Flat season.

Within the rearing process, every new-born foal is given a rating out of ten. That rating is regularly updated during the (typically) 20-month period these horses are reared by Juddmonte before they are sent into training. All marks are hard earned.

"Enable was given a seven when she was born," Mockridge says. "She had great big ears on her, which is always nice to see. She was very deep through her girth, she had a lot of quality and she walked well."

It was no great surprise that Enable was unable to sustain that rating as she grew. "She had got very tall when she was going through the weaning process," Mockridge continues. "She got a bit angular through her body and quarters, which is normal for a tall, stretchy filly like her, so her rating was downgraded to 6.5. At five or six months they can just lose their way a bit until they start regrouping physically."

At that point Enable was transferred to New Abbey Stud in Ireland for the winter, and from there to the nearby Ferrans Stud in April of her yearling year. "She got stronger as she started to develop as a yearling," Mockridge says.

"She caught up with herself, her quarters developed and she went up to seven again, then up to 7+. She went through her teenage phase [in human terms] but she always remained very attractive, scopey and well balanced, and always a good walker."

Ferrans was run by Rory Mahon until he retired in January. Mahon, who was succeeded by his son Barry, had overseen Juddmonte's breaking-in process for more than 30 years. He, too, was taken by Enable as he put her through her paces.

"One thing Rory always said about Enable when she was cantering and being broken was that she always moved well," Mockridge says. "She was always easy to deal with, and the stronger she got, the sweeter he became on her before she was allocated to John Gosden in December 2015."

Enable's exploits under Gosden's expert tutelage have promoted a feeling of pride in Juddmonte's employees, particularly at Banstead Manor Stud, where she spent the early part of her life.

"It has been exhilarating for the staff," Mockridge says. "She's very special, let's be honest. For her to come so hard on the heels of Frankel and Kingman, sometimes you have to pinch yourself. It's been a long time since we had a filly of this extreme quality in Europe. Midday was probably the last one."

Despite Midday's notable exploits, Enable is almost certainly the best filly Juddmonte has ever bred. Her Racing Post Rating of 129 exceeds the 124 posted by Midday at her best, when she won the 2010 Nassau Stakes at Goodwood. And there may be more to come.

▶▶ A star is born: Enable at two weeks old (left) after being foaled on February 12, 2014 Picture: JUDDMONTE FARMS

apparent stranglehold on the Cheltenham Gold Cup. Cue Card had just won the Betfair Chase, while on November 26 Thistlecrack initiated a stable double that was completed by Native River in the Hennessy Gold Cup.

To no fanfare, Enable stepped out for the first time at Newcastle two days later. She won easily enough, yet when she reappeared at three she was overlooked by Dettori, who rode her stablemate, Shutter Speed, to a comfortable victory at Newbury. Enable fared well enough in finishing third, albeit with little portent of what was to come.

Her profile started to take shape when she stepped up in trip to engage Alluringly in the Cheshire Oaks. Dettori propelled Enable to a decisive victory, in the process introducing us to her destructive rhythms. The race also served as a perfect springboard to the middle-distance Classics.

The Oaks was a seminal occasion in more ways than one. The biblical thunderstorm that engulfed Epsom was in itself a harbinger. Gosden later described it as "straight out of Hollywood". It was a description befitting of Enable's triumph, too, as the bay galloped Rhododendron, the 1,000 Guineas runner-up, into a state of exhaustion.

It was a visceral triumph, especially when Enable's male contemporaries failed to make much impact in the following day's Derby. It prompted the suggestion that Enable might be a match for any of them. In the end she was a mismatch for males of all ages.

A vivid memory from Oaks day was Enable's appearance in the paddock. It was no easy decision to choose the pick of the fillies until we realised we had only been looking at eight of the nine runners. Enable was by some way the last to reach the paddock. When she did, she dominated through the

GOSDEN ON . . .

Her character She's a charming filly, a playful one. If she worked here she would always walk into the yard humming a tune. She enjoys life, enjoys her exercise and likes to please, but when she gets her tack on she's very assertive

Her racing style She can cruise and then put in a massive turn of foot. Her acceleration kills off a field. She's a majestic queen of a filly

An unlikely fan Ryan [Moore] told me he was very impressed with our filly when she beat him at Chester. He said, 'Boy, she quickened and then quickened again'. It isn't often Ryan compliments someone else's horse. he's quite tight with that sort of thing

The Arc It's been hellish [in the build-up]. You watch the filly every moment and are in danger of wearing down a path from your back door to her box. It's the expectation, so when she wins like that it's a relief and you can really enjoy it

Her ranking I think she's the best filly I've trained. Royal Heroine in America, Taghrooda and her are fabulous fillies. Then there's The Fugue and Dar Re Mi. I love great fillies to train. They're a pleasure to be around

Next year It's good news for racing that a quality racemare like her will be around next year. She's only really had ten months of racing and she would be a bit of a crowd-puller

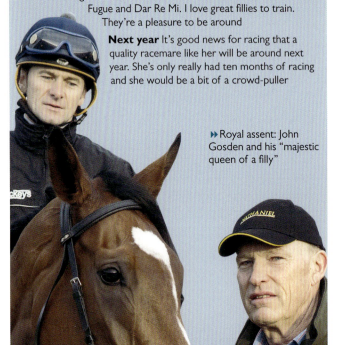

▶▶ Royal assent: John Gosden and his "majestic queen of a filly"

visually arresting combination of her physical strength and a fleetness of foot at the walk. She was a behemoth in ballet shoes.

Best of all, however, better than anything she has achieved to date, Enable stays in training as a four-year-old. Abdullah's willingness to explore the full range of her sublime talent gives rise to enticing possibilities, especially with Gosden calling the shots in his intuitive way.

This is a veritable gift to a sport that often compromises itself when attempting to diversify its audience. The 2018 campaign will start with an established totem that was desperately lacking in 2017 after the early misfortunes that beset Minding and Almanzor. A season of fits and starts found expression only in October when Enable plundered the Arc.

And there's the rub. Racing folk are entirely au fait with Enable's true merit. The imperative now is for her merit to be appreciated by a broader sporting audience, in the process illustrating the best of racing's virtues.

Enable has the potential to penetrate that audience in the manner of Frankel. What a treat it must be for Abdullah and his Juddmonte flagship to contemplate a second coming. What a treat, too, for racing fans to join him on the ride. It will be a winter of content.

There is another Juddmonte colour-bearer who imposed a similar dominance in his time, which wasn't all that long ago. For all his evident quality, however, his name does not trip off the tongue.

It might have been different had Kingman stayed in training at four. There may be valid reasons why that didn't happen, but Kingman's name will never be advanced when fans debate the best they have seen over a few beers at the races. Enable now has her chance to make the shortlist.

ARC WINNERS BY RACING POST RATINGS OVER THE LAST TEN YEARS

RACING POST		RACING POST		RACING POST		RACING POST	
Found (2016)					Zarkava (2008)		
Solemia (2012)		Treve (2014)	Golden Horn (2015)	Danedream (2011)	ENABLE (2017)	Workforce (2010)	Treve (2013)	See The Stars (2009)
RPR 124	125	126	127	128	129	130	131	132

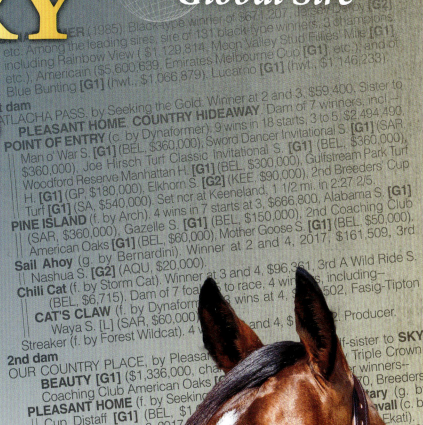

THE
BIGGER
PICTURE

Winx, the Australian wonder mare with a higher Racing Post Rating than Enable, takes a relaxing walk on Altona Beach, Melbourne, in October. The Chris Waller-trained six-year-old is top of the international wishlist for European racecourses in 2018, with Ascot, York and Leopardstown among those hoping to attract her to their showcase meetings
VINCE CALIGIURI (GETTY IMAGES)

By Nick Pulford

CRACKSMAN spent months and months trailing around in the shadow of Enable. For so long he tried but just wasn't able to match his superstar stablemate. She brought home all the major prizes to John Gosden's Clarehaven yard while he picked up place money or won much lesser races. Then, finally, he stepped forward with a glittering performance that was better than Enable had managed all season, the best of the year in Europe. He had cracked it at last.

A big run was expected when Cracksman lined up in the Qipco Champion Stakes at Ascot in October – he was 13-8 favourite after all – but not in the manner he produced. Frankie Dettori took the race by the scruff of the neck at the top of the straight and quickly strangled the life out of it as Cracksman stormed clear in breathtaking fashion to win by seven lengths. Anthony Oppenheimer, the colt's owner-breeder, summed up the sense of astonishment that resounded around Ascot. "It was miles beyond what I had expected. He just took off, didn't he?" he said. "We're all suffering from shock."

The surprise stemmed from how far Cracksman went beyond anything he had done before. He had always seemed capable of a top-level performance but went into the Champion Stakes with a Racing Post Rating of 123; he was good, but only joint-eighth among the European three-year-olds at all distances. He came out of the race on 131, an 8lb improvement that took him to the top of the rankings in one fell swoop.

Finally he was the champion he had promised to be for so long.

****

EVENTS often seemed to conspire against Cracksman, not least the emergence of Enable. Throughout the spring he was always ahead of her as Gosden's main Classic hope for Epsom but once they got to that time-honoured proving ground he slipped behind.

After Enable announced her Group 1 quality for the first time with a runaway win in the Oaks, Cracksman turned up at Epsom the following day as Derby favourite but fell short. He went before her at the Curragh and went close in the Irish Derby, but a fortnight later Enable secured another clear-cut Oaks success. Then he had to stay at home while she took on male rivals and beat them in the King George.

Oppenheimer's colt kept dropping hints that he was a top-quality performer despite the Classic setbacks but Enable always stayed one step ahead. Cracksman won the Group 2 Great Voltigeur at York by six lengths; the next day, Enable won the Yorkshire Oaks – a Group 1 – by five lengths, recording a higher RPR than her stablemate.

When it came to decision time for the Prix de l'Arc de Triomphe, Enable got the nod and Cracksman was left at Clarehaven again. Even after the Ascot annihilation in October, Gosden was confident he had made the right call. "In the Arc it was a difficult decision but I felt Enable was just more in the zone, just a bit more streetwise than him, and Chantilly is not like Longchamp. You've got to have tactical position and kick off that bend. It's not easy. I was happy with the decision we made and I think it was the right decision."

Cracksman had already won at Chantilly, in the Group 2 Prix Niel in September, but that Arc trial

Cracksman's first Group 1 win was worth the wait as he went past Enable to the top of the European rankings with an astonishing performance in the Champion Stakes at Ascot

TRUE CHAMPION

had only five runners and perhaps Gosden was right about his colt's suitability for the hustle and bustle created by 18 runners in the big race. Frankie Dettori had to be alive to Ballydoyle's tactical manoeuvres to keep Enable in the right place in the Arc, and the master jockey could not have ridden Cracksman as well.

Dettori had partnered Cracksman in the Derby, where the favourite had a far from straightforward run, and Gosden could cite that as evidence of the long-striding colt's lack of seasoning for a big-field test on Europe's most challenging tracks. Having only the third run of his career, Cracksman showed his inexperience and had to be niggled down the hill to Tattenham Corner

before picking up in the straight to finish third, beaten a length by Wings Of Eagles.

Gosden was disinclined to make excuses, giving credit to the 40-1 winner's ability to overcome his own troubles in running, but there was no doubt connections felt Cracksman could have done with another prep before Epsom. He had won on the course in April and gone round again at the Breakfast with the Stars event, but in between the weather had washed away plans to run him in the Dante at York. This time it was the weather, the great

uncontrollable, that had held back Cracksman.

The Irish Derby was a second chance of Classic glory and, on the more galloping expanse of the Curragh, Cracksman went much closer but fell a neck short of Capri at the line. On this occasion it was the Ballydoyle team who worked against his interests, pouring on the pace at the front while he again needed stoking to get into his

stride. He was closing with every stride but Capri had first run – and once again perhaps the crucial factor of more experience, with eight previous runs to Cracksman's three.

Pat Smullen, who had taken over
▸▸ Continues page 16

▶▶ Super man: (clockwise from left) Cracksman wins at Ascot; Frankie Dettori in the winner's enclosure; owner Anthony Oppenheimer; (below) Dettori dismounts

the ride on Cracksman from the injured Dettori, said: "He never really travelled as well as I'd hoped but he really got it together in the closing stages and my gut feeling is that we've yet to see the best of him. He should go on to better things in the coming months."

****

CRACKSMAN really did get it together after the Irish Derby and Smullen, for so long such a trusted judge for Dermot Weld, clearly knew what had passed through his hands at the Curragh. The ride went back to Dettori and he must have felt the difference when Cracksman returned from a seven-week break to pulverise the opposition in the Great Voltigeur on the same sort of good to soft ground at York that had been deemed too much for a Dante appearance. By now Cracksman was ready for the test and he made light of it, powering clear by six lengths in his most impressive performance yet.

Less than three weeks later – his shortest gap between races – he ran on soft in the Niel and again scored decisively, this time by three and a half lengths. With four consecutive runs over a mile and a half, and proof positive that he acted on soft ground, the Arc seemed a natural target but instead Gosden sent Enable and kept Cracksman in reserve.

The target was still premier league, though, and the mile and a quarter of

the Champion Stakes was a test Oppenheimer's colt had not faced at such a high level. He had won at the trip on his seasonal reappearance but in much lesser company at Epsom, and now he was up against rivals proven at the distance in top-quality races – Eclipse runner-up Barney Roy, French Derby winner Brametot, Irish Champion runner-up Poet's Word and Prince of Wales's winner Highland Reel.

Three and a half months had passed since Cracksman's last run in Group 1 company and Gosden assured everyone they would see a different horse. "He's a stronger horse now, about 16lb or 17lb heavier than he was in April," he said. "He's won over a mile and a quarter this year and is actually bred to be a miler." Ascot is another challenging track but tractability was not such an issue by now and, while Gosden had been concerned about getting a bad draw for the short run to the first bend, he was happy once he knew Cracksman was in stall four.

Now, on his seventh start, Cracksman was ready to show what he could really do. Ryan Moore, on Highland Reel, tried the tactic made famous by Willie Carson of racing under the trees on the far side of the track but Dettori – just as astute

Best RPRs in Europe in 2017

Cracksman 131
Enable 129
Battaash 128
Harry Angel 128
Ulysses 127
Cloth Of Stars 126
Ribchester 126
Churchill 125
Order Of St George 125

and riding at the top of his game after a record-breaking fifth Arc – preferred to stay with the main group, albeit away from the more churned-up ground near the rail.

When Moore tacked across on the home turn, he slotted in near Cracksman – but not for long. Just as he had in the Arc on Enable, Dettori pressed the button early in the straight and quickly settled the race, with Poet's Word seven lengths back in second and Highland Reel a neck third. In becoming his sire Frankel's first Group 1 winner in Europe, Cracksman packed such a punch that Gosden's post-race boxing analogy seemed entirely appropriate. "Cracksman seems to have got bigger and stronger, like a fighter weighing more. He started as a middleweight, he's now a light heavyweight."

Next year he will be a heavyweight, metaphorically if not literally, and Gosden will have a pair of them with Enable also staying in training.

Immediately after the Ascot win, the trainer said with a smile: "Enable and him would be fun. There's not much between them, is there?" Not now there isn't. Roll on next year.

Going from unruly juvenile to electrifying three-year-old, Battaash made a fast ascent to the top in a year of exciting sprinters – and he stays in training in 2018

WHOOSH

By Peter Thomas

THE sprinters of 2017 drew many words of wonderment throughout a truly vintage season, but for the trainer of a top sprinter there is only one word that truly matters, and that's 'speed'. Velocity, pace, boot: the raw material of the fastest horses in the game and a commodity possessed in bundles by Battaash, perhaps the most thrilling speedster of his generation

(although it wouldn't be advisable to say so in the earshot of Clive Cox and Harry Angel).

"I've never seen anything so fast on the gallops in my life," says an awestruck Charlie Hills, whose experience with Muhaarar, the four-time Group 1-winning champion sprinter of 2015, qualifies him to know a little about fast horses. "When he goes past, you just think 'oh my lord', and when you've seen it once you don't want to see it again, it's that unbelievably scary. It's like two

horses against one when he works – he can go past at double the speed of anything else."

It takes the breath away just listening to the trainer talk, but when Hills brings out his mobile phone and summons up a homemade video of the son of Dark Angel demolishing a strictly anonymous Group-winning stablemate on the Faringdon Place proving grounds in preparation for his seasonal debut at Sandown in June, the deed shows itself as even more mighty than the word.

Battaash's natural speed proved an almost unplayable asset in his three-year-old season, as he blitzed

his way from Listed class all the way to Group 1, fulfilling his video reputation with a blistering success at Sandown before putting himself alongside Harry Angel as the joint-fourth-best sprinter of the 21st century on Racing Post Ratings behind only Mozart, Oasis Dream and Dream Ahead.

It wasn't ever thus, mind you. Pace has never been a problem for the Sheikh Hamdan Al Maktoum-owned gelding, but in the days before he became a gelding he wasn't always focused on using it for the right reasons, and even after the operation he exhibited some of

▶ *Continues page 20*

the unfortunate tendencies inherited from his excitable mother.

John 'Bluey' Cannon has been at Faringdon Place forever, from the time of Barry Hills to the present day, so he has seen some top sprinters and some speedy yet wayward ones, and Anna Law was definitely from the second category. So when he saw her gifted son run choke-out as a juvenile before falling in an exhausted hole, he wasn't entirely surprised.

"She was only rated 45 but she could have been a lot better," he explains. "She had to be led down to the start and when the stalls opened it was vroom, but it was all cheap speed and she could never get home."

If Battaash's first run – when he started slowly before recording a ready four-length success in a Bath maiden – lulled anybody into a false sense of security, then all illusions were soon shattered. His remaining four runs as a two-year-old all ended in defeat and featured in-running comments such as "unruly and rearing in stalls . . . pulled hard, set strong pace and hung badly right . . . went right start and hung right throughout".

There was huge promise there, but as Cannon says, "we had to learn to keep a lid on it", and he, along with regular work rider Michael Murphy and Bob Grace, who also looked after Dark Angel, have worked the oracle with a horse who could just as easily have been lost as developed into the best sprinter of Hills's seven-year career, better even than Muhaarar.

"He's a very different horse to Muhaarar," explains the 38-year-old. "Muhaarar was just class, absolutely brilliant, his temperament was amazing, he never had any issues with his health and we never had a vet out to see him in all the time he was here. But this fellow is all about speed, proper speed, raw speed. There's an air of brilliance about him, true excitement, but he's learned to be straightforward and the continuity of the team here has helped a lot."

"He's so relaxed cantering, then you let him go and he's gone like a Ferrari from first to fifth in two seconds," enthuses Cannon, "but now he does it when you want him to."

That managed speed became increasingly evident as 2017

▶▶ Calming influence: Regular work rider Michael Murphy takes Battaash out for exercise at Faringdon Place

progressed. His opening Listed win from a poor draw over five furlongs at Sandown was followed by a repeat in Group 3 company at the same track under Dane O'Neill, in which he lowered the course record in spectacular fashion.

Any thoughts that this was a flash in the pan, a perfect sprinting storm from a favourable stall, were quickly dispelled when he teamed up with Jim Crowley – presumably forgiving Sheikh Hamdan's number one rider for passing him over in favour of the owner's Muthmir for the second of those Sandown wins – in Goodwood's Group 2 King George Stakes, where he took the rise in grade in his lightning-quick stride.

Taken down early that day, he showed all his dash from the gates but also admirable compliance that allowed Crowley to use the speed when he needed it. Tracking the leaders on ground that was officially soft, he swept to the front before the furlong pole and cleared away from

▶▶ *Continues page 22*

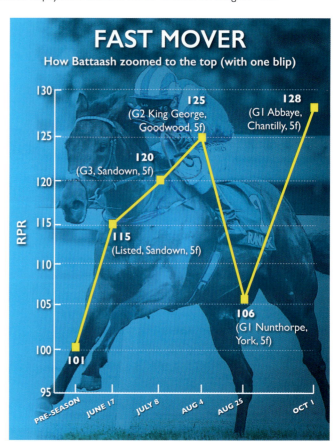

FAST MOVER
How Battaash zoomed to the top (with one blip)

101 (PRE-SEASON)
115 (Listed, Sandown, 5f)
120 (G3, Sandown, 5f)
125 (G2 King George, Goodwood, 5f)
106 (G1 Nunthorpe, York, 5f)
128 (G1 Abbaye, Chantilly, 5f)

RPR axis: 95, 100, 105, 110, 115, 120, 125, 130
Time axis: PRE-SEASON, JUNE 17, JULY 8, AUG 4, AUG 25, OCT 1

HORSE OF FORTUNE (SAF)
Multiple Stakes Winner in HK with earnings
of HK$10 380 475
(courtesy of HK Jockey Club)

SOUTH AFRICA - bringing you great fortune!

2018 MAJOR RACES

L'Ormarins Queens Plate
Kenilworth Racecourse   6 January   Cape Town

Sun Met
Kenilworth Racecourse   27 January   Cape Town

SA Derby
Turffontein Racecourse   5 May   Johannesburg

Vodacom Durban July
Greyville Racecourse   7 July   Durban

Sansui Summer Cup
Turffontein Racecourse   24 November   Johannesburg

2018 PREMIER YEARLING SALES

Cape Thoroughbred Sales
Cape Premier Yearling Sale   20 - 21 January   Cape Town
For the full sales calendar and latest news:
www.capethoroughbredsales.com

Bloodstock South Africa
National Yearling Sale   24 - 26 April   Johannesburg
For the full sales calendar and latest news:
www.bsa.co.za

Racing South Africa in conjunction with the Thoroughbred Breeders' Association of SA

THE THOROUGHBRED BREEDERS'
ASSOCIATION OF SOUTH AFRICA

Tel: +27 (0)31 769 2961/63 • Email: info@racingsouthafrica.co.za
www.racingsouthafrica.co.za

Tel: +27 (0)83 640 1155 • Email: catherine@tba.co.za
www.tba.co.za

XPRESSIONS ADV & DESIGN

his field in devastating style, recording an RPR of 125, 5lb in advance of anything he had shown before.

He was an improving sprinter with a formidable natural armoury, but he still wasn't bombproof, as his next run in the Nunthorpe at York was to show. Unwilling to be loaded into the gates, he used too much of his zest too soon and faded into fourth place, beaten not so much by the rise into Group 1 company as by the effects of a hard schedule on his bubbling psyche.

"You know he's good but he's still got a bit of a temperament issue," Hills says. "He's got a bit of a short fuse and when he loses it, he loses it properly, which is what happened at York. He boiled over, but although it's a very good racecourse, some horses can get worked up there, and I think the occasion, the bump he got coming out of the stalls that lit him up a bit and the fact that it was his fourth run in six weeks just got the better of him.

"Everybody says he's a difficult horse but this season he's run five races and won four of them, so he's not that bad. Let's just say I'd like a few more difficult ones like him."

Battaash went into York at his lightest racing weight of the season, but with time to freshen up and put back a few pounds of muscle, he headed for his season's finale at Chantilly in the pink of condition, pleasing the trainer with his appearance and demeanour. The ground was soft and the opposition hot in the Prix de l'Abbaye, but the 9-4 favourite – who had been weak in the late market moves at York – burst out of stall two and made practically all the running before treating the chasing pack to a distant view of his powerful backside. He won by four lengths from Marsha, comprehensively turning the tables on the Nunthorpe winner.

It was the crowning glory of a season that confirmed him as a top-rank sprinter. It also dispelled the final doubts about his temperament for the task of galloping flat out yet in harmony with his rider.

▶▶ Continues page 24

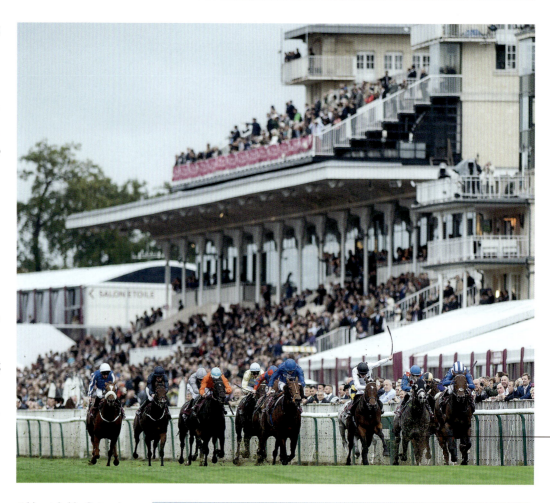

▶▶Uncatchable: Battaash (right) blasts home in the Prix de l'Abbaye at Chantilly, securing his first Group 1 victory for Charlie Hills (below)

HIGH SPEED

When Muhaarar became champion sprinter in 2015, Charlie Hills would surely have found it hard to believe that he would have an even better speedster only two years later.

Hills started 2017 with high hopes of making an impact on the sprint scene with Magical Memory and Cotai Glory (respectively 118 and 117 on Racing Post Ratings), both of whom had been Group 1-placed in previous seasons.

Hills's impact on a high-class sprint season was indeed dramatic but it came with Battaash, who had an RPR of 101 as a juvenile but zoomed past the stable's established sprinters – and all the rest bar Harry Angel in a strong division. He ended the year on 128 and that also took him ahead of Muhaarar, who had an RPR of 127 after his four Group 1 wins in 2015.

Battaash raced exclusively at five furlongs, while the Clive Cox-trained Harry Angel did likewise over six furlongs, and they shared top billing in the division. It is a mark of their quality that since 2000 they have been bettered by only three other European-trained sprinters – Mozart (2001), Oasis Dream (2003) and Dream Ahead (2011) all had an RPR of 129.

Caravaggio, Lady Aurelia and Marsha also took starring roles in a strong division and, with both Battaash and Harry Angel staying in training, 2018 promises to be just as exciting.

Best sprint RPRs in Europe in 2017

Battaash 128
Harry Angel 128
Caravaggio 124
Lady Aurelia 124
Signs Of Blessing 123
Marsha 122
Librisa Breeze 121
Blue Point 120
Brando 120
The Tin Man 120
(below)

LANE'S END

THIS IS WHAT
WE STAND FOR

From standing all-time greats like A.P. Indy, Kingmambo and Smart Strike, to current leading sires like Candy Ride (ARG), Quality Road and Union Rags, Lane's End has helped shape the sport through one proven stallion-making formula. Our team of trusted horsemen and women are committed to building success both on the racetrack and in the sales ring.

CANDY RIDE (ARG) | CONNECT | HONOR CODE | LANGFUHR | LEMON DROP KID | LIAM'S MAP | MINESHAFT | MORNING LINE
MR SPEAKER | NOBLE MISSION (GB) | QUALITY ROAD | THE FACTOR | TONALIST | TWIRLING CANDY | UNIFIED | UNION RAGS

"He flew over to France and as soon as he got on the aeroplane he was relaxed and never got worked up about a thing," Hills says. "The only foot he put wrong was getting a little bit anxious for a slight moment when he got loaded, but Gary and Craig Witheford [the equine behaviour experts] had done some work at the stalls with him after York and it was nothing really. As soon as he broke there was nothing that could go with him.

"I was watching it from the furlong marker and when he came past a length and a half clear I thought 'we've won this', but I never imagined he'd win as far as he did. He just kicked away from them in unbelievable style and hit the line very hard in a pretty quick time considering the ground."

There will be few rivals anywhere in the world keen to cross swords with this swashbuckling sprinter when he resumes next year. Even Harry Angel, with whom he shared a field at Ballyphilip Stud in his formative days, will have his work cut to keep pace with him in their hopefully inevitable clash.

"There's no rush to sort out next year just yet and we'll sit down and talk to Sheikh Hamdan's team," Hills says. "He'll go back to Shadwell, where they did such a fantastic job with him last year, until Christmas and then come back in and we'll start making plans, but I'd say the King's Stand looks the most sensible early route for him – and then who knows. The only way he can improve is through his temperament, just getting him to race different ways so he's not too one-dimensional in the way he runs, but he doesn't have to improve much, does he?

"His perfect race? Any Group 1, I'd say, but I'm sure he'd be better on fast ground. I'm not trying to sound clever and we don't want to get too greedy, but those are his targets now. It looks like being a thrilling year for everybody. The sprinters stood out this season and it's good that Harry Angel will be kept in training as well, so somewhere down the line they'll have to meet."

Racing fans everywhere must be nodding in agreement.

CROWLEY SHINES ON BIG STAGE

It may seem odd to say it of a man who rode Battaash and Ulysses, the two best horses of his career, to success in a string of races at the top level in 2017, but the transition from champion Flat jockey to accepted Group 1 rider was every bit as demanding for Jim Crowley as the switch from jump racing to the Flat.

Crowley was unfortunate to land his 2016 title in an era where the championship has lost so much of its lustre that its winners tend to be dismissed as journeymen, only on top of the heap because the real top jockeys have decided to disassociate themselves from the daily grind in favour of pot-hunting in more lucrative territories.

The 39-year-old, in accepting the job as number one to Sheikh Hamdan Al Maktoum this season, was himself following Paul Hanagan, a two-time title winner who nonetheless struggled to persuade his critics that he was more than just a rider whose dominance was numerical and earned by the number of miles travelled on the motorways of Britain, rather than characterised by success in the upper echelons.

In his championship year, Crowley rode a pair of Group 3 winners and six in Listed grade; his other 181 winners from his other 1,009 rides came in lesser contests. When he assumed responsibility in the blue and white of the Sheikh, he knew he would be playing a different game, travelling where he was required rather than where he might find the fullest book; saving himself for the big days; eschewing another shot at the title. His number of rides inevitably slipped and his strike-rate stayed largely the same, but the figure that tells the most pertinent tale is on the right-hand side of the ledger, the column that says he won more than £5m in prize-money in 2018 rather than somewhere south of £2m in his year as champ.

That kind of figure comes from delivering the goods on the big occasion and, although it makes not a jot of difference to the championship rankings, it reflects a season lit up not only by the Prix de l'Abbaye winner Battaash in the Hamdan silks – important as it was to land his first Group 1 for the boss – but also by a string of victories that came the way of a jockey now seen as the go-to fellow when a spare ride comes up in the biggest races.

When he lost the ride on Eminent in the Eclipse, he was snapped up by Sir Michael Stoute for the winning ride on Ulysses. Stoute is not a man given to handing out such mounts on a whim, so to put up a new jockey in a race that might have made or broken the colt's reputation was the most telling of vindications.

Andrew Balding needed no second bidding to reunite Crowley and Here Comes When for the first time in a year for their shock success in the Sussex Stakes and Stoute saw no reason to change his mind when Ulysses went to York to land his second Group 1 of the campaign.

Rather than remaining the numerical champion who never quite won over the critics, Crowley honed his big-race instincts, showed nerve and verve in equal measure and convinced the professionals who really matter. In 2017 he went from being champion to being a bona fide big-race draw.

GO RACING IN IRELAND 2018

Wherever you are in Ireland, you're never far from a race meeting and if you want to understand one of our country's great passions, choose from over 300 race meetings at any of the 26 racecourses around the country. Play the odds, raise a glass and enjoy good times with friends – you'll have a day out you'll always remember. So what are you waiting for?

It's time to go racing... because nothing else feels like this.

2018 RACING FESTIVALS

LEOPARDSTOWN
Dublin Racing Festival
3rd – 4th February

CORK
Easter Festival
31st March – 2nd April

FAIRYHOUSE
Easter Festival
1st – 3rd April

PUNCHESTOWN
National Hunt Festival
24th – 28th April

KILLARNEY
Spring Festival
13th – 15th May

CURRAGH
Guineas Festival
26th – 27th May

DOWN ROYAL
Ulster Derby
22nd – 23rd June

CURRAGH
Irish Derby Festival
29th June – 1st July

BELLEWSTOWN
Summer Festival
4th – 7th July
(now 4 days)

KILLARNEY
July Festival
15th – 19th July
(now 5 days)

CURRAGH
Irish Oaks Weekend
21st – 22nd July

GALWAY
Summer Festival
30th July – 5th August

TRAMORE
August Festival
16th – 19th August

KILLARNEY
August Festival
22nd – 25th August

LAYTOWN
Beach Racing Festival
6th September

LISTOWEL
Harvest Festival
9th – 15th September

LEOPARDSTOWN & CURRAGH
Longines Irish Champions Weekend
15th – 16th September

GALWAY
October Festival
27th – 29th October
(now 3 days)

DOWN ROYAL
Festival of Racing
2nd – 3rd November

PUNCHESTOWN
November Winter Racing
17th – 18th November

FAIRYHOUSE
Winter Festival
1st – 2nd December

LEOPARDSTOWN
Christmas Festival
26th – 29th December

LIMERICK
Christmas Festival
26th – 29th December

HORSE RACING
IRELAND

To plan your day at the races or for a FREE racing information pack, please call the Marketing Team on **+353 45 455 455** or visit **www.goracing.ie**
facebook.com/goracing   twitter.com/@goracing   @horse_racing_ireland

ANGEL
WINGS

Harry Angel shared top billing with Battaash
among the sprinters after blistering Group 1
successes at Newmarket and Haydock

By David Carr

THE renowned British summer weather came mighty close to costing us one of the most spectacular displays of the year. Perhaps it was down to global warming or perhaps it was because God is a jumps fan but there was plenty of rain around during the latest Flat season. Which meant that many a big race was preceded by a 'will he? won't he?' hokey cokey over whether a fancied runner would take part.

Welfare issues, not to mention potential thousands in prize-money and millions in stud fees, mean that decisions about taking a chance on rain-softened ground are a serious matter. Racegoers, the ordinary men and women who pay to go through the gate, are part of the equation too and the ones who went to Haydock on the second Saturday in a soggy September would have missed out on something special had Clive Cox made a different decision about Harry Angel's participation after he walked the track before racing.

In the end, supported by an enthusiastic Godolphin team, Cox gave the go-ahead for his stable star to line up as 2-1 favourite for the Haydock Sprint Cup. The three-year-old had announced his presence on the Group 1 stage with second place in the Commonwealth Cup and victory in the July Cup, both on good to firm ground, and seemed to be improving as fast as his legs could carry him – which was very fast. The question was whether the heavy ground at Haydock would blunt his speed and suffocate his progress.

Nothing of the sort. Having won the July Cup from Limato eight weeks earlier with a Racing Post Rating of 122, Harry Angel

accelerated to a different level with a runaway four-length win at Haydock that took him to an RPR of 128 and a share of champion sprinter honours with five-furlong flyer Battaash. It was the biggest winning margin in the race since Habibti bolted up by seven lengths in 1983 and his RPR was the highest achieved in the contest since Dayjur in 1990.

"He's so potent. He's awesome," Cox said in the Haydock winner's enclosure. "It's hard to change gear on ground like that but he just lengthened away from them and to beat them by four lengths is wonderful."

****

IF THE outcome of the Sprint Cup was cut and dried, the decision to run had been much less so. Overnight rain had turned the ground heavy and it is long odds-on that, but for the recent four-year programme of redevelopment and drainage work at Haydock, the Sprint Cup would have been called off. That is something to be borne in mind by those still decrying the collateral damage of the loss of the old chase track with its drop fences – one of the venues where Cox plied his trade as a willing jump jockey in the 1980s.

Cox knows the track well and he had been stung there before when he ran his 2013 July Cup winner Lethal Force in the Sprint Cup on officially good to soft ground. The grey finished a dismal ninth.

"All the way there it was pouring down and the wipers were on as fast as they could be," said the trainer, recalling the mounting worries over Harry Angel's particpation. On arrival, Cox walked the track, probing with his stick all the while, and anxiously discussed the situation on the phone with the Godolphin team.

"The concern was that he'd broken the track record so impressively in the Sandy Lane [in May] on very fast ground. Having ridden on it as a jockey many years ago I know that heavy ground at Haydock is a different kind of heavy. We just wanted to avoid the deja vu when Lethal Force ran in this. It was beautifully prepared ground but it was very deep and extremely testing. But, as it turned out, Harry Angel was amazing."

Amazing indeed. Adam Kirby rode him as though the ground was not an issue, having him in front from the off, and his mount proved the most willing of partners, never looking in danger and pulling almost effortlessly clear.

"It would have been easier to take him out, because you want to look after the horse," Cox said. "But credit to the team at Godolphin, they let him take that jump into the unknown and he's repaid it."

****

A MISHAP 15 miles away at Aintree is the lingering memory of Cox's career in the saddle. On yet another wet day in the north-west in 1988, mudlark Sacred Path was backed in to 17-2 favourite for the Grand National only to get rid of Cox after crumpling on landing over the first fence.

It is greatly to his credit that Cox, who took his career tally to nearly 100 winners before hanging up his boots a couple of years later, always manages to smile rather than frown when that misfortune is brought up, seemingly every April since. Then again, he is a decidedly affable character and he has had an awful lot to smile about since swapping a riding helmet for a trainer's flat cap.

His Lambourn yard is now one of the most powerful operations in

the country and, since making his breakthrough when Gilt Edge Girl took the Prix de l'Abbaye in 2010, he has become a Group 1 regular thanks to Reckless Abandon, Lethal Force, Profitable, My Dream Boat and now Harry Angel.

All bar My Dream Boat did their winning at sprint trips and Cox was quick to recognise the speed that Harry Angel possessed. "He was always extremely talented and we knew we were dealing with a high-class individual from the beginning," said the trainer, who bought the son of Dark Angel for just £44,000 at Doncaster as a yearling.

Cox was also shrewd enough to know what he had. Many a trainer with a colt good enough to have landed the Mill Reef Stakes as a maiden second time out at two would spend the spring thinking of nothing but the 2,000 Guineas. "He was very precocious mentally and physically and to break his maiden in a Group 2 on his second start was quite special," he said.

"He had a Guineas entry because he'd won over six furlongs and he always galloped out well after his work. And I trained his brother by Nayef to win over a mile and a quarter, so it wasn't impossible. But as soon as we started working him in the spring it was clearly visible that he was an out-and-out sprinter. He had so much speed that we had to harness that."

That decision paid its first healthy dividend when Harry Angel bolted up in the Group 2 Sandy Lane Stakes on quick ground at Haydock in May, showing fine speed to lead all the way under Kirby and win by four and a half lengths. "Awesome, wasn't he?" Cox said in the winner's enclosure, and he wasn't the only one to get excited about a sprinter having just his fourth run.

➤➤ Continues page 28

Within a week Harry Angel had been bought privately by Godolphin, hailed by their then chief executive John Ferguson as "one of the most brilliant young horses in training". Crucially, the new owners left him with Cox – a sure sign of the trainer's hard-won standing in the sport.

Godolphin's purchase rather suggested they fancied Harry Angel more than Blue Point, who had beaten him when getting weight at Ascot in the spring, for the Commonwealth Cup at Royal Ascot. And they were proved right when their new recruit got the better of his old rival by half a length in their rematch. But that reckoned without Aidan O'Brien, a dangerous thing to do in a Group 1 race in 2017, and his Caravaggio beat them both with a powerful display of sprinting.

Yet far from putting him in his place, that defeat was an important stepping stone to the top in the mind of his trainer. "I think he really grew up on that day," Cox reflected. "From that day forward it's been clear to see his progress and Adam was convinced Caravaggio wouldn't beat him next time. It was a very solid performance but he ran extremely fresh and was still quite green, it was only the fifth race of his career. But he came back from there with a deal more confidence."

Harry Angel proved Kirby right with a swaggering dismissal of Caravaggio when the pair met again in the July Cup at Newmarket. While his old rival could manage no better than fourth that day, runner-up Limato and third-placed Brando each advertised the value of the form subsequently and it took an undeniably top-drawer effort for Harry Angel to score by a length and a quarter, having looked the obvious winner some way from home.

It was the Haydock victory that confirmed him as the best six-furlong sprinter around, even if there was disappointment that Harry Angel could not come anywhere near the same level of performance in the British Champions Sprint in October when fourth to Librisa Breeze on ground that Cox reckoned was even more testing than Haydock.

Harry Angel will have the opportunity to prove the Haydock run was no flash in the plan as he stays in training in 2018, along with several of the other top sprinters.

Cox will be confident when his latest sprint star takes them on again. "We've had some really top-notch horses," he says, "and Lethal Force holds the course record in the July Cup – that's pretty spectacular when you think of all the horses who have been down that track – but there's no doubt Harry Angel is pretty special."

▶ First flush: Caravaggio beats Harry Angel in the Group 1 Commonwealth Cup but it was the runner-up who went on to take the highest rank; (below) Clive Cox tests the ground at Haydock before giving the go-ahead for Harry Angel

CARAVAGGIO FADES AWAY

Started well, soon made a name for himself but ended under something of a cloud – Caravaggio's career path has closely matched that of the artist after whom he was named.

Michelangelo Merisi da Caravaggio, to give him his full name, was a hugely influential Italian painter but life did not always go smoothly for him – he dodged one death penalty but died at the age of 38 amid suggestions he was murdered.

Things did not turn out quite that grimly for his equine namesake in 2017 but he certainly ended the year at a lower point in the pecking order than might have been expected.

Few would have begun the season with more expected of him. He had been unbeaten in four runs at two, culminating in success in the Group 1 Phoenix Stakes, and was the main rival to stablemate Churchill in betting on the 2,000 Guineas.

Anyone who had backed him for the Classic did their money but there was no arguing with the early results of Aidan O'Brien's decision to stick to sprinting with "one of the fastest horses I've ever seen". After an easy Group 3 win at Naas, he returned to Royal Ascot a year after his impressive Coventry Stakes success and did something similar to Group 1 rivals in the Commonwealth Cup.

Having lost ground when rearing slightly just before the off, he had to come from off the pace yet was still able to reel in those who had taken first run on him to score with an authority that made him look the obvious sprint champion. Yet that was as good as it got. In every run afterwards, he was at least 8lb below his Commonwealth RPR of 124.

Caravaggio could manage only fourth behind Ascot runner-up Harry Angel in the July Cup at Newmarket and was then sixth to Brando in the Prix Maurice de Gheest at Deauville, where O'Brien blamed himself for fitting shoes that apparently gave the colt no traction. While he made it 2-1 in his personal rivalry with Harry Angel in the British Champions Sprint at Ascot, having warmed up with Group 2 success at the Curragh, the pair were only third and fourth behind Librisa Breeze.

Still, Caravaggio is a Group 1 winner at two and three and has a pedigree that will be invaluable to Coolmore broodmares, providing an outcross to the predominant Danehill/Sadler's Wells sire line. The overall picture, then, is far from negative, but perhaps not as good as it could have been.

A TALE OF TWO FILLIES

Lady Aurelia and Marsha each landed a Group 1 sprint victory in breathtaking style

By Alastair Down

WITH no separate top-level programme for fillies in the sprint division, the best of both sexes are thrown together in a melting pot of speed and fury. Bubbling to the surface in such a competitive division is a huge challenge for a sprinter of any age or sex but the opportunity is there for all and one of the joys down the years has been to see the emergence of a series of top sprint fillies with speed to burn and the competitive fire to match.

In 2017, having just said goodbye to dual Nunthorpe heroine Mecca's Angel, sprint fans had the excitement of watching two more brilliant fillies mixing it in a high-class division alongside male flyers Battaash and Harry Angel. What's more, in securing a Group 1 victory apiece, Lady Aurelia and Marsha were chief protagonists in two of the races of the season.

Their first clash came at Royal Ascot in the King's Stand Stakes, where the four-year-old Marsha was 11-4 favourite following her reappearance success in the Palace House Stakes at Newmarket. The year-younger Lady Aurelia, the American speedster who had stormed home by seven lengths in the previous year's Queen Mary Stakes, was 7-2 second favourite. She had also started her season with a victory, back in her homeland at Keeneland.

There was a hitch for Lady Aurelia on raceday, however, when her intended rider Frankie Dettori – who had suffered an arm injury in a paddock fall at Yarmouth the previous week – was forced to admit defeat in his battle to be fit for the meeting. Fortunately for her trainer Wesley Ward, John Velazquez – the winning rider at Keeneland – was flying in for two booked mounts on the Ascot card. Urgently, Ward rang to tell the jockey he was on Lady Aurelia too.

▸ Continues page 32

"I got off the plane and was in customs. The phone was ringing and ringing but I couldn't answer it," Velazquez said later. "But as soon as I was through I picked up the phone and that's when I found out I was riding her."

The stage was set for a mighty battle between the two fillies, but the race became all about Lady Aurelia as she scorched the Royal Ascot turf for the second year running. She led a furlong out, palpably quickened and screamed home by three lengths in a searing 57.45sec, just 0.01sec outside the course record. Her dam is called D'Wildcat Speed and that is exactly what she showed in one of the performances of the season.

This was an eighth Royal Ascot success for Ward, but notably it was the first time he had managed to bring one of his flying two-year-olds back to win again at the meeting. "That was awesome. Lady Aurelia is a very special filly," he said. "This is a Group 1 with some of the fastest horses in the world, and to duplicate what she did last year she's a once-in-a-lifetime horse."

Velazquez was wowed by Lady Aurelia's power. "What a feeling, when you ask a horse to run and they respond like that. She settled in the first part of the race and when I asked her she responded right away with a great turn of foot – very quick. To come back here for a second time and do what she did today, she's got to be a special horse." He spared a thought for Dettori – "He's a good friend of mine and I feel really bad for him" – while treasuring his good fortune at picking up the best of spare rides. "For me this is a blessing," he said.

The rest never had a prayer with the fast conditions playing to the American filly's strengths. Marsha was a fraction disappointing in being beaten three and a quarter lengths into third, with the previous year's King's Stand winner Profitable sandwiched between the two fillies. But Marsha's trainer Sir Mark Prescott was philosophical, saying: "We know how fast Marsha is – she can tank – but she was off the bridle all the way. It just shows what a great race it was."

▸▸ Winning and losing: Lady Aurelia goes close to the track record as she powers to victory in the King's Stand before suffering agonising defeat against Royal Ascot third Marsha (white) in the Nunthorpe at York (previous page)

'WE'RE SO LUCKY'

Marsha has around 10,000 owners who pay £199 a year to join the Elite Racing Club, one of the longest-running and most successful syndicates in British racing. Each of the 10,000 owns an infinitesmally small part of the Sir Mark Prescott-trained filly – they can't say they have a leg in a racehorse; what they have is barely a hair of the mane each – but they all feel like Sheikh Mohammed when she wins a race as big as the Nunthorpe.

For the lucky few who won tickets for York in the members' ballot, the feeling was extra special. One of them was Gordon Birkett, who treated himself to a subscription to Elite when he retired 15 years ago after serving the NHS faithfully in the field of mental health.

"It's the ideal opportunity for someone of my ilk to get involved," he said at York. "I can't spend thousands on a horse, so membership of Elite gives me the chance to see how the other half live. This is the high point, the best day."

David Harris, a retired accountant, agreed. "It's a fantastic day, I've never known anything like it," he said. "There's nothing more special than winning a Group 1, and especially here at York."

Elite member Marsha Holliman won a competition to name the filly and chose her own. "Her mother is called Marlinka, so I thought, 'Why not Marsha?'" she explained. "I always send Sir Mark Prescott a big bunch of flowers when she runs. He calls me 'the namesake'. It's all so much fun.

"I'm not a special person, but this is special. Years ago I went to see a fortune teller and he told me one day my name would be known everywhere. And it's true now, isn't it? I love her immensely. We're so lucky to have her."

****

ROUND one to Lady Aurelia, then, and with some knockout punch. Ward immediately set his sights on the Nunthorpe Stakes at York in August as her next bout and Marsha would meet her there for a rematch, though only after suffering a pair of defeats at Group 2 level, the second of them behind the up-and-coming Battaash in the King George Stakes at Glorious Goodwood.

At York it was Lady Aurelia, with Dettori back on board, who was favourite at 10-11 and Battaash was seen as the main threat at 11-4. Marsha, whose star had waned, was 8-1 alongside Profitable.

The Lady Aurelia camp were distinctly upbeat even with the ground slower than it had been at Ascot and Dettori, having worked his old ally on the Knavesmire the Friday before the meeting, was positively brimming. "It's a long time since I rode her but she hasn't lost her speed. She's ultra quick," he said.

▸▸ *Continues page 34*

GAINESWAY

TAPIT

Dream Dancing
marks Tapit's 4th
G1 winner on turf.

Ponied to the start as always, Lady Aurelia broke smartly and soon led. When she produced her customary extra kick entering the final furlong, she looked home for all money.

But it was not to be. With a strong pace to aim at, Luke Morris sat off the leaders in the knowledge that Marsha would finish strongest of all. Despite being a fraction short of room just over a furlong out, she began to bear down on Lady Aurelia with Morris asking for every last ounce. And she didn't half respond. Unflinchingly, she fairly ate up the ground and flashed past the post in unison with Lady Aurelia, although at first sight the American filly on the far side looked as if she might have just held on. The two fillies had been wide apart across the track a furlong out and, although that distance had reduced by the line, it was still difficult to tell who had prevailed.

Dettori had no doubt, standing up in the stirrups to punch the air and put his finger to his lips in the now customary gesture of a winning rider. But it was the Italian's celebrations that were about to be silenced and ITV commentator Richard Hoiles, in one of the greatest split-second calls, said: "Frankie punches the air! He's sure, I'm not."

The photo proved Morris had got Marsha home by a nose. Dettori, having been on cloud nine, came down to earth with an almighty bump but took it well. Walking back to weigh in, he said: "Ow! I thought I'd won a neck. You've seen it on TV. I'm shocked."

Prescott, winning his second Nunthorpe following Pivotal in 1996, was not at York, having had a long-standing commitment to view Kirsten Rausing's yearlings in Ireland. He took time out to watch the race, of course, and said: "I thought Frankie was spot on when he felt he'd won but when I saw the slow-motion replay I became more hopeful. We got lucky."

Ward felt the rough end of the stick. "It's tough," said the trainer, also second in the Nunthorpe two years earlier with Acapulco. "One of these days I'll have to win it, hopefully next year. She likes the track and has run well on the soft, so I can't make any excuses. It looks like she was just a

▶Shellshocked: Frankie Dettori can't believe his eyes as he realises his celebrations on Lady Aurelia at York (below) were premature

EPIC FAILS

Frankie Dettori's premature celebration on Lady Aurelia at York was not the first high-profile example of jumping the gun

Richard Hills, Maraahel *(below, right) 2006 Juddmonte International*
Dettori was not even the first to make the mistake in a York Group 1, with Richard Hills having celebrated prematurely on Maraahel. Hills waved his whip in delight but had not bargained with an up-and-coming rider called Ryan Moore, who nabbed him on the line with Notnowcato.

Greg Hall, Doriemus *1997 Melbourne Cup*
One of the greats in Australia, Greg Hall was all out to reel in Might And Power at Flemington aboard Doriemus, and as the pair flashed past the post together 'The G' thought he had won his second Melbourne Cup. He saluted the huge crowd while standing up in the irons but unfortunately for him it was Might And Power and 'The Pumper' Jim Cassidy who had landed the spoils.

Kevin Shea, Lizard's Desire *2010 Dubai World Cup*
Joy turned to despair for Kevin Shea after he thought he had stolen what was then the world's richest race in the shadow of the post aboard the Mike de Kock-trained Lizard's Desire. Shea's emotional celebrations were triggered when the rider of close third Allybar, Ahmed Ajtebi, offered out a hand in congratulations. But Ajtebi had it wrong. The judge took so long to determine this one that Channel 4 Racing had gone off air by the time it was announced Gloria De Campeao had won.

millimetre away from victory. Even when Frankie stood up and thought he'd won I knew it was going to be close, and I knew it favours the horse nearer the stands in a photo. What are you going to do? It's in the books."

For Morris, a supremely hard-working jockey with as many as 1,500 rides a year, what was in the books was a first domestic Group 1 success. "That was superb," he said. "It was one of the races of the week, so to come home in front on Marsha was fantastic." Not just one of the races of the week. This was one of the races of the season, featuring two of its shining stars.

Only one of them would make another appearance on Europe's sprint stage, when Marsha went to Chantilly in October in an attempt to win the Prix de l'Abbaye for the second year running. This time she ran into Battaash on top form again and was firmly beaten four lengths into second, beating old male rival Profitable by a neck but proving no match for the brilliant winner.

Battaash was the champion on that performance but Marsha had done her thousands of owners proud by playing a big part in an outstanding sprint year. Without the fillies, it would have been a whole lot less entertaining.
Additional reporting by Nick Pulford

Unique honour for McCoy with statue at Cheltenham

CHELTENHAM marked the opening day of the 2017 festival with the unveiling of a lifesize bronze statue of Sir Anthony McCoy, who became the first person to be honoured in this way at Britain's premier jumps course. McCoy's statue stands near the paddock and joins sculptures of four Cheltenham Gold Cup-winning greats – Golden Miller, Arkle, Dawn Run and Best Mate.

"Unfortunately it looks like me," quipped the 20-time champion jump jockey after unveiling the statue, which had been draped in the green and gold colours of leading owner JP McManus, for whom McCoy rode in the second half of his illustrious career.

"I want to say a huge thank you to Cheltenham," McCoy added. "When I started coming here I would never have thought there would be a statue of me. I'm very proud and very honoured."

McCoy, who retired in 2015, won 31 races at the festival including two Gold Cups (on Mr Mulligan and Synchronised), three Champion Hurdles (Make A Stand, Brave Inca and Binocular) and a Queen Mother Champion Chase on Edredon Bleu.

McManus was present for the occasion and said: "It's a wonderful job and it's marvellous that he's honoured here with the great horses. It's very special."

The statue was created by Dublin sculptor Paul Ferriter, who is no stranger to famous subjects. He has also sculpted Barack Obama, golfers Nick Faldo, Jack Nicklaus and Seve Ballesteros, and Gaelic Athletic Association founder Michael Cusack. He was also commissioned by Michael O'Leary to create statues of the owner's two Gold Cup winners, War Of Attrition and Don Cossack.

Ferriter took six months to complete the statue, which involved first making a two-foot version that was then enlarged to lifesize. Having made a clay model, he sought McCoy's approval before casting in bronze.

"AP was very easy to work with and very likeable," Ferriter said. "For me, as a sculptor, he was a brilliant subject. He has a really great face with incredible cheekbones, a great jaw and chin.

"One challenge I had was the fact AP has changed a lot since he stopped riding. So I had to go over old photos – I really wanted to get the look he had when he was a jockey and at his racing weight. What I really wanted to try and capture was the kind of intensity he had, his total dedication. I basically produced the classic AP pose – standing with his arms folded and the whip under his arm, with an intense look on his face."

McCoy said: "Paul's dedication to getting it right was really outstanding and it was very enjoyable working with him." But he couldn't resist another quip: "A lot of my friends would say the statue has more personality than I do."

Picture:
EDWARD WHITAKER
(RACINGPOST.COM/
PHOTOS)

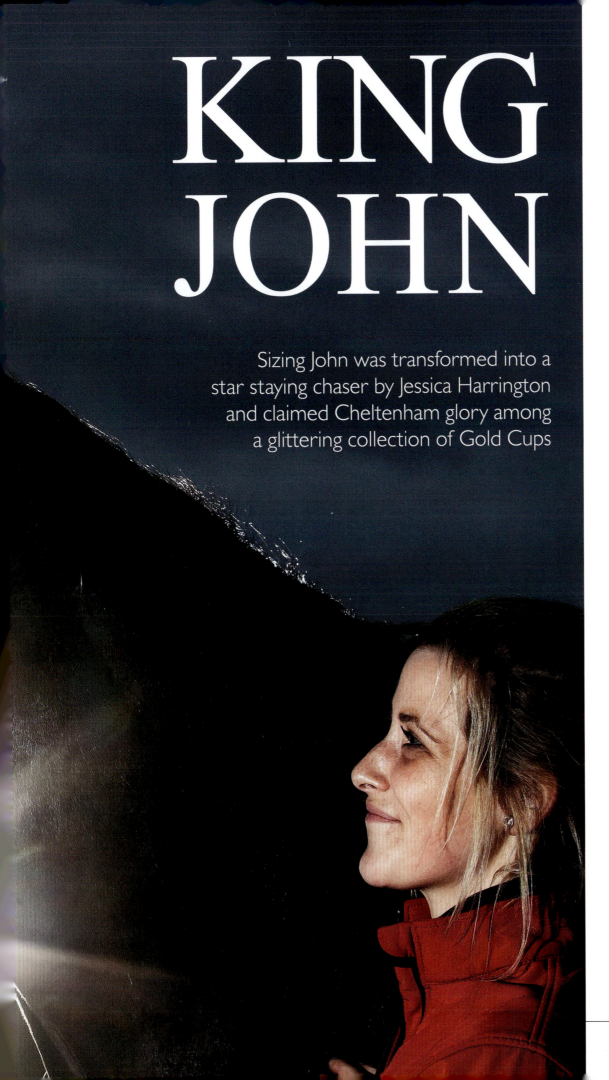

KING JOHN

Sizing John was transformed into a star staying chaser by Jessica Harrington and claimed Cheltenham glory among a glittering collection of Gold Cups

By Richard Forristal

AS this book reaches breakfast and coffee tables, still not a year will have passed since Sizing John made his debut for Jessica Harrington. Indeed, we will be into the second half of January before the anniversary of his first triumph for the esteemed County Kildare trainer comes around. He really did squeeze a lot in, and few could have envisaged the manner in which it all transpired. Fire up the DeLorean for a moment.

Before September dawned in 2016, Sizing John was a two-mile chaser seemingly destined to be remembered as Douvan's sacrificial punchbag. He was trained by Henry de Bromhead and Johnny Burke was the retained rider for his owners Alan and Ann Potts.

Nearly a year had already passed since his latest success. A Grade 1 winner two years earlier, he was a talented competitor but was treading water, his fate apparently sealed on May 13, 2010 when he was born four days after Douvan, doomed to live in the shadow of an immortal.

Now let's go back to the future. By the end of last season, Sizing John had become only the third horse to follow victory in the Stan James Irish Gold Cup with glory in the Timico-sponsored blue riband event at Cheltenham. More than that, he seized his own little piece of history by becoming the first to complete a Gold Cup treble when adding the Punchestown version. Three Gold Cups in three months, all at trips beyond three miles – a distance he had not attempted until the start of that golden run.

Trained by Harrington and ridden by Robbie Power, an axis that absolutely owned the second half of the jumps season, he was a bona fide star of the staying chasing ranks. Freed from the shackles of Douvan, the interminable nemesis to whom he had finished second in four Grade 1s and third in two others, his whirlwind transformation was complete.

▸ Continues page 40

Of course, the temptation is to conclude that the change of stable was the catalyst for his meteoric evolution, and that stepping up in trip was an associated epiphany. It might fit the romantic narrative, but it would also be grossly disingenuous.

De Bromhead isn't in the habit of banging his head against a brick wall for any longer than necessary and he had earmarked Down Royal's two-and-a-half-mile Grade 2 for second-season chasers in November as Sizing John's first proper venture over a longer trip.

When the Pottses opted to terminate their partnership with De Bromhead, which had yielded ten Grade 1s, including an Irish Champion Hurdle and a Champion Chase, the experiment was actually delayed rather than accelerated. Harrington took time to get to know the rising seven-year-old who was transferred to her yard in Moone and she sent him to Leopardstown after Christmas for another stab at Douvan over two miles.

For her, it was an exploratory venture, even if it did merely serve to confirm what everyone already knew. After Sizing John had scaled the highest of peaks at Cheltenham in March, Harrington even sought to deflect praise for the change of tack by crediting Power instead.

"It's thanks to Robert," she said. "He said at Christmas, 'he will stay'. Sizing John has gone from two miles at Christmas to winning over three miles and two furlongs here."

Power, for his part, also tried to downplay his input. "It was just a suggestion from me," he countered. "It's Jessie who does the training. She's a genius."

Neither protagonist seemed too keen to accept the plaudits for a development that changed the trajectory of both their lives. Deep down, certainly on Harrington's part, maybe that had something to do with the overall context.

"I do feel very sorry for Henry with this horse and Supasundae," she admitted at Cheltenham, Supasundae being another Potts-owned horse she received from De Bromhead who won the Coral Cup for her and Power on the Wednesday of the festival.

"I only inherited them in September and it's been a learning curve for me because I had to get to know them. Henry did all the hard work – he'd bought them and done all the work

▶▶ Golden triumphs: (from left) Sizing John leads home Empire Of Dirt and Don Poli in the Irish Gold Cup at Leopardstown; Robbie Power is congratulated by Bryan Cooper on his Cheltenham Gold Cup victory; Sizing John jumps the final fence in a thrilling Punchestown Gold Cup battle with Coneygree (left) and Djakadam; (previous page) Sizing John with groom Ashley Hussey

on them when they were young. If you think about it, if Douvan hadn't been around, we'd have stayed at two miles with Sizing John. The fact that Douvan is there forced us to step up."

It was a magnanimous concession that illustrated the solidarity that exists between jumps trainers. In a season shaped in many ways by owner-orchestrated equine musical chairs, De Bromhead gained as well as lost, a theme explored in detail elsewhere in these pages.

Both trainers are among the winter pursuit's finest practitioners, and Harrington's stock soared higher than ever after her bold campaigning of Sizing John. Having already plundered two Champion Chases with Moscow Flyer and a Champion Hurdle with Jezki, her legacy was already assured. Nonetheless, her Gold Cup coup saw her join an elite group, which now numbers just six, to have won the triple crown of the three traditional championship races at Cheltenham, and the way in which she grabbed her latest opportunity was invigorating.

Remember, while we can reflect with the benefit of hindsight on the conviction with which Sizing John

went about his business, things were far more equivocal before the event.

When he tackled the Kinloch Brae Chase on January 19, he was sent off at odds of 3-1 to beat Sub Lieutenant and Black Hercules. After a polished display, the Ryanair Chase, rather than the Gold Cup, was being spoken of as his chief target.

It was only the day after his superlative Irish Gold Cup success on his first stab at three miles that Harrington finally confirmed they would go for broke at Cheltenham. Returned an easy-to-back 100-30 to defeat more exposed staying rivals at Leopardstown, Sizing John put in a convincing performance that was a harbinger of things to come.

Having been runner-up to Douvan in the 2016 Arkle Chase, he arrived back at Cheltenham underestimated in a market dominated by established bruisers like Djakadam, Native River and Cue Card.

Sizing John, though, stamped his authority all over the race, travelling with sublime ease and fencing with aplomb en route to a straightforward near three-length verdict from the relentless Minella Rocco.

A star had been born. While the romantics had their hearts set on Cue Card or Native River doing it for the Tizzards or Djakadam getting over the line for perennial Gold Cup runner-up Willie Mullins, the hard reality was that Sizing John was simply the best horse in the race, an emerging force who had been underestimated amid the clamour for a tearjerker.

Besides, for all that De Bromhead's loss was unfortunate, this was still a happy ending. Harrington's Coral Cup success with Supasundae had already earned her the accolade of being the most successful female trainer in Cheltenham Festival history, and she would finish the week with a career tally of 11 wins there after

▶ *Continues page 42*

SUMMER HOLIDAY

In late summer Jessica Harrington gave Racing Post readers an update on Sizing John after his months of rest and recuperation from last season's exertions

Where did he spend his holidays? He's our Gold Cup hero, so we didn't let him go anywhere. He stayed here in Moone with me and I kept a close eye on him. He seemed to love every second of the sun and seeing him enjoying himself out in the field was always a lovely sight.

How did he summer? Fantastically. We were thinking of sending him to Weight Watchers as he looked as though he'd enjoyed his summer a bit too much, but he deserved that. He had a terrific spring for us and no horse deserved a bit of summer fun more than him. He's back to work now, though, as it's all systems go for the season ahead.

What is his long-term objective? The Cheltenham Gold Cup in March. He developed into a top-class stayer last spring and produced his best performance at Cheltenham. It would be great to get back there and defend his crown. It's the pinnacle for every staying chaser and he's the champion staying chaser at the moment.

What excites you most about him? He's still only seven and to win the Gold Cup at such a young age was a remarkable achievement. He's had only three runs over three miles or further and has won them all. I can never remember being so excited ahead of a season. We have two horses – Our Duke is the other – in the top four of the betting for the Gold Cup, and that's very unusual for me.

Power and Rock The World completed a Gold Cup day brace in the Grand Annual.

Before Sizing John went on to add the Gold Cup at Punchestown, Our Duke crowned Harrington's season with a dominant victory in the Boylesports Irish Grand National. "These are all firsts for me – it's not bad for a 70-year-old," said Harrington, whose triumph in the most valuable jumps race ever staged in Ireland meant she had secured her highest-earning season in both Britain and Ireland.

Almost out of nowhere, Harrington had claimed the season as her own with a pair of exciting young chasers and it constituted a personal triumph, having lost her husband Johnny in the weeks following Jezki's 2014 Champion Hurdle victory. He was one of the most popular and respected bloodstock men on either side of the Irish Sea and his death left the trainer without her "rudder".

At the time, she had contemplated quitting, a prospect that seemed faintly absurd when she stood radiant on the hallowed turf of the Cheltenham Gold Cup winner's enclosure.

"He'd be proud of me, wouldn't he?" Harrington mused quietly of her late husband in the heady moments after her finest hour. "I can't believe it," she later added. "It's absolutely fantastic."

Alan Potts, whose wife Ann sadly died in August, was no less overwhelmed. "It's unreal, it's my dream and it has come true," he gushed. "I can't believe it."

Incredibly, things got better still. Come Punchestown, Sizing John stepped into the ring once more in an attempt to reaffirm his new-found superiority and add the 'undisputed' tag to his title. He duly did, but not before we were treated to an epic steeplechasing bout.

With Coneygree pouring it on in front, Djakadam and Sizing John had to knuckle down early. When they finally conquered the 2015 Gold Cup hero, they persisted to slug it out between themselves in an enthralling heavyweight battle to the line. If Cheltenham had been the platform on which Sizing John announced his true talent, at Punchestown he proved he had the tenacity to match. His valiant short-head triumph was the mark of a true champion.

"There was no hiding place out there," Power said. "He had to dig deep and I was all out, but he's a very good horse." Harrington was equally in awe of a chaser she was still learning about. "He showed some guts," she said. "Everything was going against him – he also pulled off a front shoe – but he put his head down and battled."

That he did. The former punchbag was now the one indisputably landing the knockout blows.

▸▸ Dream come true: owners Alan and Ann Potts (immediately to the left of Sizing John) in the winner's enclosure at Cheltenham; (right) Jessica Harrington and Robbie Power with the Gold Cup

GOLDEN GENIUS

"It must be beginner's luck," said Jessica Harrington after winning the Cheltenham Gold Cup with her very first runner but Sizing John's rider Robbie Power had a more convincing explanation. "Jessica Harrington is a genius," he declared, and nobody was inclined to disagree.

Gold Cup victory took Harrington into a select group of trainers who have won the three monuments of the Cheltenham Festival, adding to her victories in the Queen Mother Champion Chase with Moscow Flyer (2003 and 2005) and the Champion Hurdle with Jezki (2014). She is the only woman to achieve that feat and just the third to send out a Gold Cup winner, following on from Jenny Pitman (with Burrough Hill Lad in 1984 and Garrison Savannah in 1991) and Henrietta Knight (Best Mate in 2002-2004).

Harrington is now the most successful female trainer of all time at the festival. She started the 2017 meeting level on eight winners with Pitman but her total grew to 11 over the four days, with Sizing John's golden success supplemented by Supasundae in the Coral Cup and Rock The World in the Grand Annual Chase.

The Gold Cup, of course, took pride of place. "To have a winner at Cheltenham is amazing, but this is the jewel in the crown," she said after welcoming Sizing John to the hallowed winner's enclosure. "As long as I've been watching racing it's a race I'd dreamed of winning, so to do it is special."

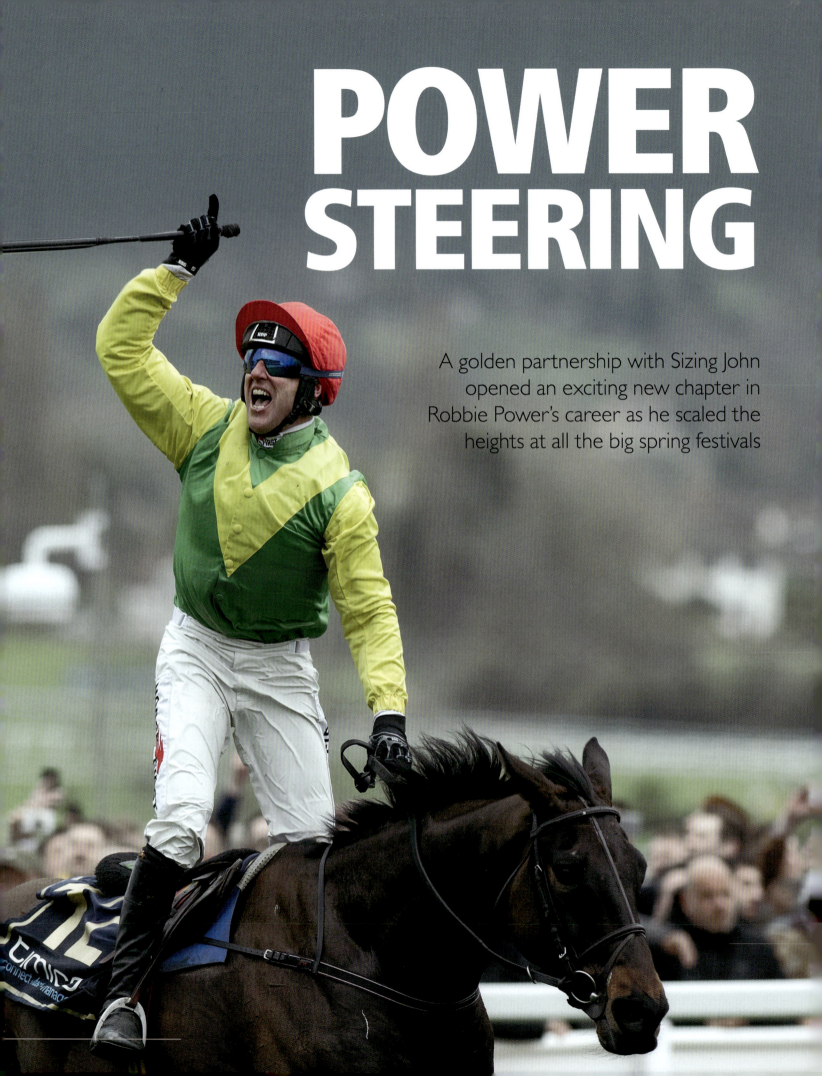

POWER STEERING

A golden partnership with Sizing John opened an exciting new chapter in Robbie Power's career as he scaled the heights at all the big spring festivals

By Richard Forristal

IT MIGHT be a crude prism through which to view a rider's career, but consider for a moment the breakdown of Robbie Power's Grade 1 roll of honour.

Up to the fifteenth anniversary of his first winner just before Christmas 2016, Power had accumulated eight Grade 1 wins. His first came in the weeks that followed his heady 2007 Grand National success aboard Silver Birch when Silent Oscar won Punchestown's Champion Hurdle for his great ally Jessica Harrington and he went on to record seven more in a timespan of just over five years.

After he landed the 2012 Future Champions Novice Hurdle at Leopardstown on Jezki, he endured a four-year barren spell at the highest level. Then Our Duke ended the drought when he ground it out in the staying novice chase at the 2016 Leopardstown Christmas festival, and the floodgates opened.

In a four-month flurry, Power plundered eight Grade 1s, doubling his career tally in the blink of an eye. The real beauty is in the breakdown, but the nuts and bolts of those figures illustrate his sudden and steep change in trajectory. At the age of 35, Power became an overnight sensation.

"When I was 25 and I won the Grand National, I thought it was easy and that everything was just going to fall into place," Power said at the height of his dizzy second half of the 2016-17 campaign. "Then a couple of years later, you realise you have to stay working at this – that you don't have a given right to win everything. Jessie has had the best quality of horse she's had since the Moscow Flyer days, so that helps, but it's maturity. There's no point getting older if you don't get wiser and learn from your mistakes."

Notwithstanding his Aintree heroics, Power has been a slow-burner whose talent as a horseman was always obvious but who was never precocious. While he endured his share of brickbats along the way, he worked hard and never stopped believing or improving.

Then fate finally shone favourably on him. Granted, he had already carved out a decent career for himself and earned a reputation as being a

▸▸ Continues page 46

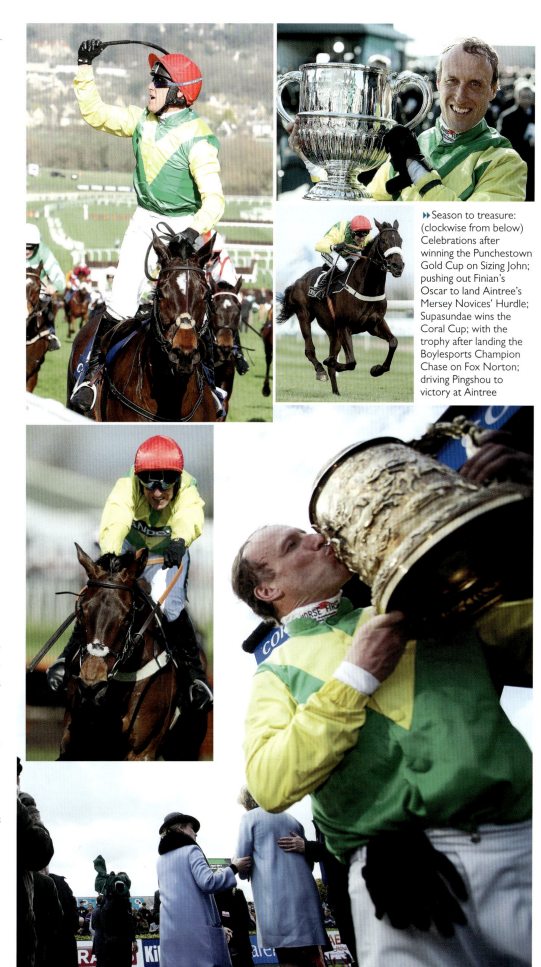

▸▸ Season to treasure: (clockwise from below) Celebrations after winning the Punchestown Gold Cup on Sizing John; pushing out Finian's Oscar to land Aintree's Mersey Novices' Hurdle; Supasundae wins the Coral Cup; with the trophy after landing the Boylesports Champion Chase on Fox Norton; driving Pingshou to victory at Aintree

dependable rider, but at times you need something unscripted to happen to shake things up. In Power's case, there were two specific and related plot twists that put the cat among the pigeons.

Firstly, Alan and Ann Potts removed their horses from Henry de Bromhead's care. Harrington was one of the beneficiaries, with Sizing John and Supasundae among those to end up with her following the dispersal.

Then the Potts's retained Irish-based jockey Johnny Burke, whose delegation had been decimated by the decision to send the majority of the string to England, decided to vacate the post. Few would have predicted it at the time, but all of a sudden Harrington and Power had been privy to life-changing opportunities. And how they seized them.

Courtesy of a characteristically composed Power steer that illustrated every facet of the refined rider he had become, Sizing John's beautifully fluent Timico Cheltenham Gold Cup success saw the new triumvirate reach a glorious crescendo in the Cotswolds.

"It couldn't have gone much smoother," Power said of his first ride in the sport's showpiece event.

Supasundae had already got the partnership off to a flying start in Wednesday's Coral Cup and then the trainer and jockey went on to complete a festival treble with Rock The World in the Grand Annual finale. Remember, Power had previously ridden only one festival winner, all of six years earlier.

"Supasundae winning on the Wednesday meant we could relax a bit, and I'd say Rock The World won with a stone and a half on his back, because I was floating above him by the time the Grand Annual came around," Power reflected. "I ended up a long way back, but when your confidence is that high these things just work out."

The week was a snapshot of an incredible second half of the campaign for Power that still seems barely plausible. After Our Duke's Christmas coup, he secured a Kinloch Brae triumph on Sizing John en route to the handsome seven-year-old coming of age in the Irish Gold Cup.

▶▶ Another one in the bag: a big smile as Robbie Power wins the Irish Grand National with Our Duke

Still high on the fumes of his incredible week at Cheltenham in March, he farmed four more wins at Aintree to be crowned leading rider there, with Fox Norton's emphatic Melling Chase victory sandwiched between other Grade 1s aboard Pingshou and Finian's Oscar.

By then, the Pottses had come to a formal arrangement with Power for him to ride all their horses on either side of the water for the rest of the season, an acknowledgement of his new-found status as a marquee jockey.

Far from being a final destination, though, Power's appointment was just another stop on his merry way. The County Meath native enjoyed local glory when Our Duke confirmed himself a chaser of enormous potential with a superlative turn in the Boylesports Irish Grand National.

Then Punchestown rolled around and the Power juggernaut kept on pulverising everything in its path. Reunited with Fox Norton back over the minimum distance, he conspired to inflict a first defeat on Irish soil (in completed starts) upon the recently crowned Ryanair Chase hero, Un De Sceaux.

If that wasn't a suitably epic climax to the campaign, he executed the very same trick aboard Sizing John 24 hours later in a pulsating dust-up with Djakadam and Coneygree. Five wins in as many days saw him depart with another leading rider
▶▶ Continues page 48

CLEAR ANSWER

A few months before his golden run of 2017, Robbie Power's riding career appeared to hang in the balance after he suffered fractures to his left eye socket and cheekbone in a fall at Galway, leaving him with double vision when perched in his riding position.

"The eye problem was quite frightening," he admitted. "It only arose when I was riding and initially I thought it was just a lack of fitness, but I went to Gowran Park one day to ride Bobabout and I couldn't see a stride at all going to the last hurdle. He stepped at it and fired me out over his head. I was lying on the ground thinking, 'This is madness,' and when I got back into the weigh room Ruby [Walsh] had my phone in his hand, about to ring my wife Hannah to tell me to stop riding, but I'd already made up my own mind."

Power sought medical help and now wears a prism attached to the inside of his goggles to correct the issue. "I went to see Mr Flitcroft, an ophthalmologist in Dublin, and he knew what the problem was straight away, as he'd seen it before with snooker players, swimmers and basketball players, because they also have to look out of the top of their eyes. Surgery is an option but that would keep me out for a year, so he started fitting prisms and found one that worked. I haven't had a problem since and it doesn't bother me in day-to-day life."

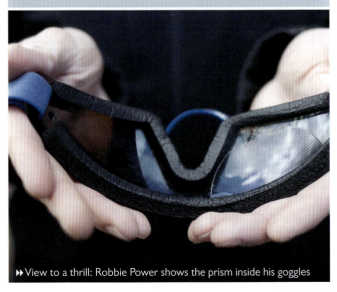

▶▶ View to a thrill: Robbie Power shows the prism inside his goggles

award, having seemingly foiled the maestro Ruby Walsh at every turn.

"He's a great person to have on your team," Harrington said of her ally in the spring. "He's a hard worker and I'm over the moon he has got all the breaks over the last few months. He has been around the block long enough to know that you're only as good as your last ride, so he'll always have his feet firmly on the ground."

All this, and in a way it is only half the story, for Power had to show real resilience to reap the rewards he did. Bouncing back from injury might be a basic requirement for a jump jockey, but some of the physical torment Power endured last season would make you wince.

He suffered fractures to his left eye socket and cheekbone in a fall at Galway last summer and, although he returned to the saddle briefly after six weeks, the injury would eventually sideline him until the end of October.

He was left with double vision when perched in his riding position, an issue that was remedied only when ophthalmologist Dr Ian Flitcroft fitted a prism to the inside of his goggles.

Power also then ruptured a disc in his back mid-race just over two weeks before the Irish Gold Cup. "I nearly cried coming out of Beacon Hospital that day," he said of the diagnosis, which was initially meant to keep him out for between four and six weeks.

With the mount on Sizing John looming at Leopardstown, Power kept going back to his specialist Jabir Nagaria. "He asked what the big deal was, and I told him the Irish Gold Cup was on Sunday week," said the rider. "Six days later he gave me two injections into the disc and one into the sacroiliac joint. Honest to God, I walked out of there that day 100 per cent."

Seventeen days after Power had suffered the injury, Sizing John announced his status as a rising star of the chasing ranks with that emphatic Irish Gold Cup success under Power at Leopardstown. The rest is history.

GOLDEN RUN

How the big winners stacked up for Robbie Power during the second half of the 2016-17 season

29 Dec 2016 **Our Duke**
Neville Hotels Novice Chase (G1), Leopardstown
Trainer: Jessica Harrington
Prize-money: £37,500

19 Jan 2017 **Sizing John**
Kinloch Brae Chase (G3), Thurles
Jessica Harrington £23,077

12 Feb 2017 **Sizing John**
Irish Gold Cup (G1), Leopardstown
Jessica Harrington £73,718

15 Mar 2017 **Supasundae**
Coral Cup (G3), Cheltenham
Jessica Harrington £54,103

17 Mar 2017 **Sizing John**
Cheltenham Gold Cup (G1), Cheltenham
Jessica Harrington £327,463

17 Mar 2017 **Rock The World**
Grand Annual Hcap Chase (G3), Cheltenham
Jessica Harrington £59,798

7 Apr 2017 **Pingshou**
Top Novices' Hurdle (G1), Aintree
Colin Tizzard £56,130

7 Apr 2017 **Fox Norton**
Melling Chase (G1), Aintree
Colin Tizzard £112,310

8 Apr 2017 **Finian's Oscar**
Mersey Novices' Hurdle (G1), Aintree
Colin Tizzard £56,168

17 Apr 2017 **Our Duke**
Irish Grand National, Fairyhouse
Jessica Harrington £235,043

25 Apr 2017 **Fox Norton**
Champion Chase (G1), Punchestown
Colin Tizzard £128,205

26 Apr 2017 **Sizing John**
Punchestown Gold Cup (G1), Punchestown
Jessica Harrington £128,205

DURALOCK
PERFORMANCE FENCING

Racerail • Post & Rail • Crowd Barriers • Jump Wings

+44 (0)1608 678238   sales@duralock.com   www.duralock.com

MADE IN BRITAIN

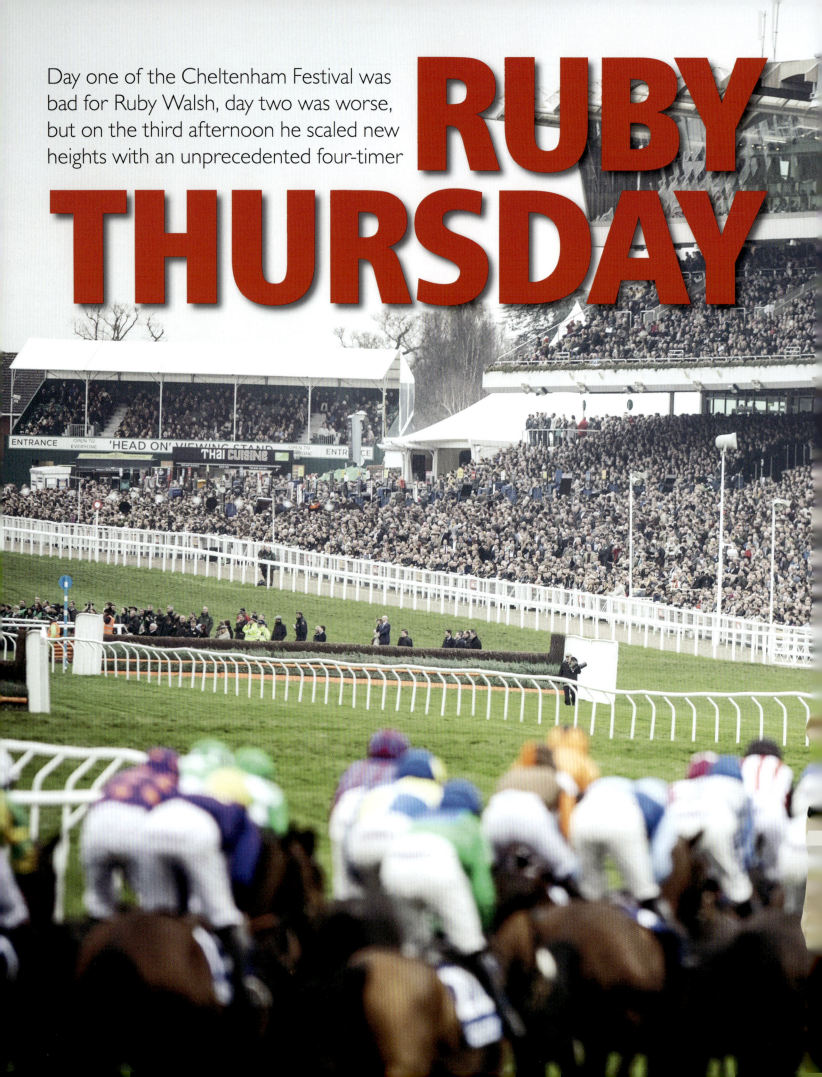

Day one of the Cheltenham Festival was bad for Ruby Walsh, day two was worse, but on the third afternoon he scaled new heights with an unprecedented four-timer

RUBY THURSDAY

By Alastair Down

FOR the first two days of the Cheltenham Festival the giants were not so much slumbering as out for the count. Willie Mullins and Ruby Walsh, usually to the forefront on any given festival day, went winnerless through Tuesday and Wednesday – a 14-race losing streak for the perennial leaders of the pack that included three beaten favourites, most shockingly Douvan at 2-9 in the Queen Mother Champion Chase.

Day three would turn out very different; not so much a case of normal service resumed as a new kind of service altogether with Mullins providing the ammunition for Walsh to become the first jockey in festival history to record a four-timer. The winners flowed thick and fast as the festival's most successful pairing took the day's three Grade 1 prizes with Yorkhill in the JLT Novices' Chase, Un De Sceaux in the Ryanair Chase and Nichols Canyon in the Sun Bets Stayers' Hurdle, then just for good measure added the Grade 2 Trull House Stud Mares' Novices' Hurdle with Let's Dance.

After Nichols Canyon had taken the day's feature race to complete a Grade 1 treble for trainer and jockey, Mullins summed up his feelings: "The first win was relief. The second was grand but the third was pure joy because I didn't expect it." Later, after three became four, he paid tribute to his stable jockey. "He gave those horses some rides to win from the positions they did, because in the previous two days horses weren't winning from there. Four winners shows how good he is – we've been lucky in our time to witness Sir AP McCoy and Ruby Walsh, two fabulous jockeys with different styles, but at the top of their profession."

The trainer was right: this was a feat for the ages. But it took great strength of mind as well as tremendous ability for

▶ Continues page 52

FAB FOUR How Walsh's historic feat unfolded

1.30 Walsh breaks his 2017 festival duck as 6-4 favourite Yorkhill lands the Grade 1 JLT Novices' Chase by a length from Top Notch

2.10 No threat in the Pertemps Final as 14-1 shot Isleofhopendreams finishes 14th

Walsh to write another chapter in the festival history books after the travails of the first two days.

****

ON the opening afternoon Walsh had a beaten favourite in the Supreme Novices' Hurdle when he was second on favourite Melon and later in the afternoon another market leader, Limini, was only third behind Apple's Jade and stablemate Vroum Vroum Mag in the Mares' Hurdle. It was the first time in nine years Walsh left Cheltenham without a winner at the end of day one but, although it was frustrating, the losses did not amount to evidence that Mullins' horses, who can turn up at the meeting looking everything from magnificent to moderate in the paddock, were out of form.

Wednesday, though, was worse. The day started badly when 4-1 chance Bacardys was badly hampered in the Neptune and Walsh pulled him up – next time out he won a Grade 1 at

'He wrote the textbook on the black look partly because he is frighteningly competitive but also because as he returns to unsaddle he is already conducting a personal post-mortem'

Punchestown. Three races later it was the Champion Chase and the expected coronation of Douvan.

But the axe fell with a shocking thud. Never jumping with anything resembling fluency and having made three palpable mistakes, Douvan finished lame, something the public almost wanted to hear as confirmation that the world was still spinning on its axis.

Throughout these purgatorial 48 hours Mullins wandered round beaming as ever with not a bother on him, as the Irish say. He subsequently confessed that plenty of doubt and dark thoughts assailed him on

Wednesday night, although the outside world would not have known it.

As Walsh says: "Willie is Willie and doesn't change. He's no more jovial when he's winning than when he's losing. He's in the same humour and sticks to the same approach."

Mullins' stable jockey is a different character. Walsh does not do unflappable geniality when things go wrong. He wrote the textbook on the black look partly because, like all top jockeys, he is frighteningly competitive but also because as he returns to unsaddle he is already conducting a personal post-mortem and savaging himself that he might have done something wrong. By the end of day two, the outlook had rarely been darker at the festival.

When it is put to Walsh that he can look like he's about to kill someone, he laughs: "My face might portray that but I promise it's not going to happen."

Looking back at the festival

2.50 Another winning favourite in Grade 1 company as Un De Sceaux takes the Ryanair Chase at 7-4 with Sub Lieutenant a length and a half behind in second

3.30 Odds-on favourite Unowhatimeanharry is only third as Walsh claims the Grade 1 Sun Bets Stayers' Hurdle on 10-1 shot Nichols Canyon, holding off Lil Rockerfeller by three-quarters of a length

4.50 Festival history is made as Walsh has his fourth winner from five rides on the day, swooping late on 11-8 favourite Let's Dance in the Trull House Stud Mares' Novices' Hurdle to score by two and three-quarter lengths from Barra

setbacks, he adds: "Douvan was lame but the others had run well, though the disappointment at the time made that less easy to see. And we were convinced that Yorkhill on the Thursday was possibly our strongest chance of the week."

On the Wednesday night, instead of retiring for wound-licking purposes to his base near the course, Walsh went out for a meal with the usual crowd. Hope and expectation still accompanied the Mullins battalions, with such strength in depth and so many big names yet to come. Even so, with Walsh still winnerless, the woman who sat next to him at the table recalls with a laugh: "I drew Ruby because there wasn't a queue for the job."

****

THE Mullins team knew the best shot of beginning the rally on Thursday was Yorkhill in the opening JLT Novices' Chase. Walsh would have gone to post steaming with determination and he recalls: "I had

to get him to settle and he travelled really well, but I got in a bit of a pocket coming down the hill to the second last. But then Daryl [Jacob] and Top Notch drifted out a bit and, while you would rather have made your move at the last, the opportunity was only going to appear once. When he won the year before I took the gaps as they came – at the festival more than anywhere that's what you have to do."

One of the reasons Walsh is a master round Cheltenham is that he knows how momentary the openings can be in the frantic hurly-burly. He plays the assassin to perfection in the knowledge that there will be only a fleeting moment to squeeze off the

▶▶ Four-midable: (above, from left) jubilant scenes after the festival victories of Yorkhill, Un De Sceaux, Nichols Canyon and Let's Dance, all trained by Ireland's champion Willie Mullins (below)

shot before the target is covered up and the bad guys are all over him.

Yorkhill fluffed the last but was still more than good enough. The hole in the Closutton dyke had been plugged and the stands rang once more to the chant of Ruby, Ruby, Ruby, Ruby, though it was but a throat clearing for the banshee chorus that would mount through the afternoon.

"He's a very difficult horse to ride, Ruby was very good," Mullins said, although nobody was in any doubt about Yorkhill's quality. "People criticise his jumping but he has a huge kink in him," Walsh said after the race. "People never realised the job Paul Nicholls did with Denman because he was the same. He had a kink too and they are two chestnut Presentings. I do think he's a Gold Cup horse. He gives you the exciting feel Kauto Star and Denman had."

Two races later Walsh was on another red-hot

▶▶ *Continues page 54*

favourite with Un De Sceaux in the Ryanair Chase. This time bravery, that stock-in trade of the jump jockey, and sheer derring-do were required as Un De Sceaux jumped boldly and barrelled his way to the front by the fifth fence. "He has always been a horse with his heart on his sleeve and every day gives all he has," Walsh says. "He was a total thrill to ride that day. I tried to settle him early on but as he passed the two-mile start he latched on and from that moment onwards he was never inside a wing again.

"It was seat-of-the-pants stuff and you're dealing in very small margins but he was a real joy to ride. It was live by the sword, die by the sword and I was throwing everything at him. Two out and again at the last if he hadn't done what I asked it wouldn't have been pretty."

By now the cacophony was building after two backable winning favourites for the Mullins-Walsh alliance and every chance of another to come in the shape of Let's Dance later in the day.

But there was no ebb in the Walsh tide, which was by now running like a rip. His next ride was Nichols Canyon in the Stayers' Hurdle and there was more hope than expectation with this one, although as Walsh pointed out: "Whatever way you looked at it, this fella had won seven Grade 1s, albeit at shorter distances."

Racing over three miles for only the second time, Nichols Canyon would have to be held up and Walsh said later he formulated a simple plan. Looking up at the big screen, he was reminded that Unowhatimeanharry was odds-on and decided to follow him, reasoning that the favourite would be in the right place at some time.

"He was up against a pile of confirmed stayers but he's always had plenty of class about him and is the only horse to have beaten Faugheen," Walsh says. "I knew I had to sit on him and take the one shot at them and when you're on a 10-1 chance you can take more chances than you can on an even-money shot."

Nichols Canyon suddenly appeared in the race two out and led on the run-in, Walsh's grabbing of the rail proving a big help in holding off the

admirable Lil Rockerfeller. A lovely leap at the last was a great help too, as winning owner Graham Wylie observed: "Once Nichols Canyon locks on to a hurdle it's done and dusted, because he's going to get half a length at it, and then he'll battle. He was made for Ruby – they both love having to get a jump and a battle."

With three Grade 1 races snugly in the poacher's pocket, the Ruby tumult was running riot. He had taken races by the scruff of the neck on Yorkhill and Un De Sceaux, daring the others to catch him, and employed classic hold-up tactics on Nichols Canyon. Now, with confidence coursing through his veins, he gave a final masterclass on Let's Dance, judging the pace to perfection and delivering a rapier thrust at the end.

The 11-8 favourite appeared to have been given plenty to do by Walsh, but they picked their way through the field and arrived at the last to pull away from Barra and Dusky Legend. "I enjoyed that one, and the ride Ruby gave her," Mullins said. "To be able to ride

▶ Continues page 56

▶ Electrifying: Un De Sceaux soars to a second victory of the day for Ruby Walsh; (below) Clondaw Warrior after winning the Galway Hurdle – the rider's most valuable victory in Ireland in the 2016-17 season

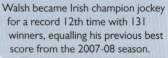

FRONT RUNNER

Ruby Walsh gave his rival jockeys a head start at Cheltenham 2017 but his Thursday four-timer ensured he ended the week as leading rider for the fifth year in a row and the 11th in all. Now on a remarkable 56 winners, he increased his lead as the winningmost rider at the festival to 22 ahead of Barry Geraghty, who missed the 2017 meeting due to injury.

Walsh became Irish champion jockey for a record 12th time with 131 winners, equalling his previous best score from the 2007-08 season. The runner-up was teenage sensation Jack Kennedy, albeit a long way back on 68 winners.

Walsh's most valuable success in the Irish season came in the Galway Hurdle with Clondaw Warrior, part-owned by his wife Gillian, and he had 13 Grade 1 winners in Britain and Ireland. His biggest prizes in Britain were the Stayers' Hurdle and Ryanair Chase on Ruby Thursday at the festival.

Osarus

LA TESTE 2018 SALES DATES*

Breeze-Up sale : 25th April 2018

Yearling sale : 4th & 5th September 2018

*All dates subject to change

SANDS OF MALI
Gimcrack Stakes **Gr.2** at York
2016 La Teste September Yearling sale
Sold €20,000 by Haras des Faunes to Con Marnane

©Racingfotos

infos@osarus.com

www.osarus.com

with that sort of confidence and have the balls to be able to sit there and wait for the race to open up around her.

"To have Ruby on our side is worth so much, because he can change his mind two or three times in races when things aren't going to plan – he can read races and do what needs to be done and take a chance. He's a huge asset."

****

TWO years earlier Walsh had been on the verge of a festival four-timer on the Tuesday until Annie Power's final-flight fall in the Mares' Hurdle and now he had set the record straight. Little is lost on Walsh and his live mind did not need time or perspective to let the four-timer sink in. "I was immediately aware of the enormity of it," he says. "Nobody had ever ridden four Cheltenham Festival winners in a day and I had missed the opportunity once. I appreciated it all the more because after Annie I never thought it would happen."

Looking back, Walsh admits Let's Dance flirted with the same disaster that befell Annie Power. "In a way she was a little bit lucky. Three strides from the last she was fine but she got a squeeze in the second stride and you can see her prick her ears. For a hundredth of a second she wasn't concentrating and she barely got there."

For those in the stands and riveted to their televisions across the islands, Walsh's feat was undoubtedly rendered all the more extraordinary because the glut had followed the famine of the opening 48 hours. It was a joyous day, with Mullins his usual source of bonhomie and Ruby smiling so widely that his ears nearly fell off. There was, too, a feeling of the normal order being restored.

In a letter written in 1944 the great scholar and writer JRR Tolkien coined the word "eucatastrophe" – think euphoria bolted on to the front of something that has been all bad. Tolkien defined it as: "The sudden happy turn in a story which pierces you with a joy that brings tears. A happy ending."

And who doesn't enjoy one of those?

THE LONG GAME

Nichols Canyon was bought with the Stayers' Hurdle in mind but he took quite a circuitous road to festival glory in the Graham Wylie colours that became synonymous with the race through three-time winner Inglis Drever.

"It's the race that brought me into the sport in the first place," said Wylie, also owner with his wife Andrea of Yorkhill, another star of Ruby Thursday. "Very early doors in my time as an owner I was lucky enough to own

some very special horses, including Inglis Drever. Nichols Canyon reminds me of him – he's not big, but he's like a terrier. Willie rang me one day to say he had a horse for me and he could be the next Inglis Drever, and he was proved right."

Nichols Canyon, though, did not race over three miles until the end of his second season with Mullins and ten of his 16 jumps outings before the Stayers' Hurdle had been over two miles. "I got a bit caught trying to win two-mile races and Champion Hurdles with him, but at least he's

back now at the right trip," the trainer said at Cheltenham. "It's taken a long time to settle him, and Ruby used to ride him differently by jumping out and saying go, because he's such a good jumper and a good battler. [In the Stayers'] he changed tactics, dropped him in, got him settled."

Having beaten Unowhatimeanharry into third at Cheltenham, Nichols Canyon was favourite to confirm the form in the Champion Stayers Hurdle at Punchestown but he was beaten a head into second in a thrilling battle. "A fantastic race," said Harry Fry, Unowhatimeanharry's trainer. "There was 18 lengths back to the third [Footpad] and that says plenty about the first two."

Unowhatimeanharry's only defeat of the season was at Cheltenham and he ended the campaign level with Nichols Canyon on a Racing Post Rating of 168. Between them, they won all the Grade 1 hurdles over 3m-plus in Britain and Ireland which one or both of them contested.

Now that Nichols Canyon has proved himself a high-class three-miler, the pair look set for more mighty tussles in what could be another exciting era for staying hurdlers.

▶▶ Smiles better: Ruby Walsh with Graham Wylie following Yorkhill's victory and (above) with owner Susannah Ricci after making history with Let's Dance

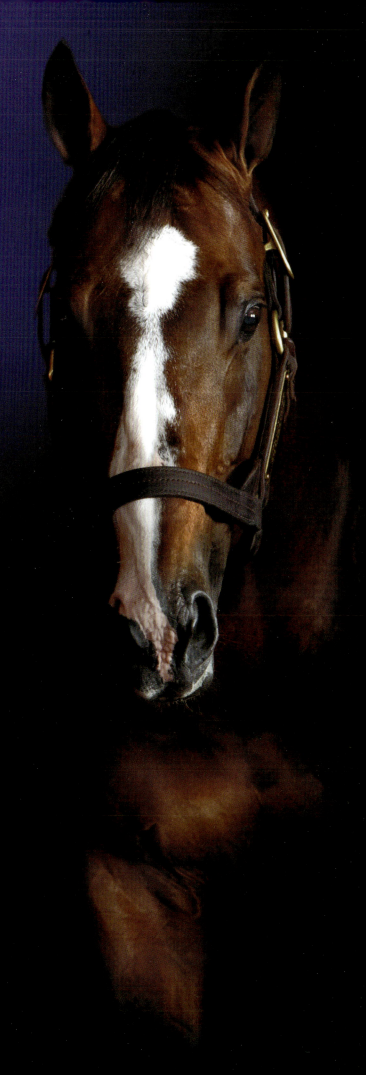

WINNING HAND

Buveur D'Air and Altior took big pots as Nicky Henderson shuffled his pack and came up trumps with a string of major successes and the British jumps trainers' title

By Lee Mottershead

NICKY HENDERSON talks about horses as if they were people. Sometimes you might swear they speak the same language. Seldom can there have been a trainer whose intuitive connection with what he apparently perceives to be equine humans is so strong. There is a bond between Henderson and his horses. In the 2016-17 jumps season that bond once again helped him become the sport's champion trainer.

This was a campaign that highlighted the gulf in quality between the athletes housed in the yards of Henderson and his nearest

▶ *Continues page 60*

rival, Paul Nicholls, whose title he stole, just as he had from the same man four years earlier. Henderson had a trio – Buveur D'Air, Altior and My Tent Or Yours – who earned more than £200,000 each and three (this time take out My Tent Or Yours and insert Might Bite) in the 170s on Racing Post Ratings. Nicholls had none in either category.

In the circumstances Nicholls deserves credit for having finished only just over £300,000 adrift of Henderson, as in terms of high-end firepower he well and truly lagged behind. It was, though, testament to Henderson's tremendous ability to reinvigorate and replenish that it was he who on a Sandown Saturday in April regained the crown, having earned £2,846,487 and won eight Grade 1 races, three of them at the Cheltenham Festival.

The first transfer of that crown to Henderson's head had come 31 years earlier. His maiden championship, which came one year after mentor Fred Winter's last, was secured before any of those won by Martin Pipe. Lambourn's chief flagbearer is in his fourth decade as an elite jumps trainer and his powers are arguably stronger now than they have ever been.

RECORD WINNERS

Buveur D'Air was the sixth Champion Hurdle winner for Nicky Henderson, taking him past the legendary Peter Easterby to sole ownership of the record for the race. His previous five wins came with See You Then (1985, 1986, 1987), Punjabi (2009) and Binocular (2010) *(below left is Punjabi, centre, winning his title from Celestial Halo, right, and Binocular)*.

Henderson also notched a record sixth triumph in the Arkle with Altior. His previous five winners were Remittance Man (1991, *bottom right*), Travado (1993, *top right*), Tiutchev (2000), Sprinter Sacre (2012) and Simonsig (2013).

Along with the Triumph Hurdle, those are Henderson's most successful races at the Cheltenham Festival among a total of 58 winners. He leads Willie Mullins by four in the all-time trainer standings at the festival.

Henderson ended the season with two official champions: Buveur D'Air (top hurdler at both 2m and 2m3f+) and Altior (top 2m novice chaser, and joint top overall with Thistlecrack among the novices).

With Might Bite, L'Ami Serge and Top Notch also Grade 1-winning youngsters for the stable last season, the future looks bright indeed.

It was in the opening month of the new jumps season that Henderson got back into the habit of tasting big-race success, although he did it in a Flat race. No Heretic's annexing of the Chester Cup came at a time when many of the Seven Barrows boxes were empty, their normal residents having headed off on summer holidays. Soon enough they started mopping up contests even bigger than the Roodee marathon.

Sprinter Sacre, the greatest horse Henderson has trained, and perhaps the greatest trained in British jump racing history, was one of those who came back to work. He also went back to many of the racecourses he had graced in an extraordinary career but he did so without actually racing.

On an enormously emotional afternoon at Cheltenham in November – of which more later – he was retired. There was inevitably talk that the man who had nurtured him so brilliantly had lost the ace in the pack. We need not have worried. It soon became clear the pack was full to the brim with quality.

Moreover, that talent for constant renewal was highlighted by the fact that Henderson's first Grade 1 of 2016-17 was won by a young jumper

whose mission is to become the next Sprinter Sacre. Altior, so devastating when winning the 2016 Supreme Novices' Hurdle, got off the mark over fences at Kempton and shortly afterwards stepped up to the top level to land the Racing Post Henry VIII Novices' Chase, with the manner in which he devoured the hill only serving to enhance the impression he truly was the heir apparent.

As the Cheltenham build-up gathered pace, Henderson continued to send a steady stream of exciting novice chasers to Britain's racecourses. There were two Doncaster wins for Might Bite that sandwiched a shocking final-fence fall in Kempton's Kauto Star Novices' Chase. But for crashing out he would have scored by around 20 lengths. Whisper, later a familiar rival for Might Bite, became the first winner of ITV's new racing era in the Dipper Chase on Cheltenham's New Year's Day card, while the following month Top Notch struck in Grade 1 company, landing Sandown's Scilly Isles Novices' Chase seven days before Altior did another impression of Sprinter Sacre when laughing at senior stars in Newbury's Game Spirit Chase.

****

AN operation that in some recent seasons had been rather lacking in young chasing talent now had it in abundance. For some months, that accomplished group also contained Buveur D'Air.

At the 2016 Cheltenham Festival the French import had posted a fine third to Altior before notching a narrow Aintree success. Thereafter JP McManus bought him to join his team and surely that was with fences in mind. Buveur D'Air had managed smart form in novice hurdles but he had not necessarily come across as a likely future Champion Hurdle hero. He therefore went over fences and immediately made the decision to send him down that path look sensible, winning at Haydock and Warwick, the latter success coming on the final day of the year. As the new year developed, so did a new thought in Henderson's head. He became fixed on the notion of sending Buveur D'Air back over hurdles.

On January 25, the previous season's Champion Hurdle winner

▸▸ Stars new and old: Nicky Henderson with Champion Hurdle winner Buveur D'Air (left) and swamped by fans of the retired Sprinter Sacre at the Lambourn Open Day; (below) with the champion trainer trophy on the final day of the 2016-17 season at Sandown

Annie Power was ruled out of the 2017 race by Willie Mullins and six days later Henderson announced Buveur D'Air would seek to become her successor. Another six days later Mullins revealed 2015 Champion Hurdle winner Faugheen had also been pulled out of Cheltenham.

It is true the sport's premier hurdle race suddenly looked there for the taking, but it is also true McManus already had the horse widely deemed best placed to take it. Yanworth, fresh from trial wins at Ascot, Kempton and Wincanton, was sent off 2-1 favourite on the day of judgement and he carried McManus's first colours, with Buveur D'Air and My Tent Or Yours, twice before a Champion Hurdle runner-up for Henderson, further down the order both in terms of the betting and the distribution of riding caps.

The supposed supporting players took the main roles, however, as Yanworth toiled in seventh place – and was later disqualified for testing positive for an anti-inflammatory drug – while

▸▸ *Continues page 62*

Festival stars: Altior and Nico de Boinville after winning the Arkle; (below) Might Bite heads to victory in a dramatic RSA Chase

Buveur D'Air and My Tent Or Yours led the way home. The unfortunate My Tent Or Yours once again found one too good – far too good, in fact – with his younger stablemate travelling like a dream before storming to a four-and-a-half-length victory under 41-year-old weighing-room veteran Noel Fehily.

"I was always happy this was the right thing to do and it has worked on the day," said Henderson in jump racing's most hallowed winner's enclosure. "He was going to be a good chaser but he had only had four hurdles races in his life. After Altior went chasing Buveur D'Air followed him down that road, but then I thought, 'hang on, we've got to be doing this wrong somewhere'.

"I felt there was room to come and do this. The decision was right, but all I've done is stopped My Tent winning a Champion Hurdle, which he so deserves to do."

Explaining how Henderson had broached the change of plan, McManus recalled: "I can't remember what Nicky said but he said it more than once. He was pretty insistent we should go back over hurdles. In the end I let him have his way. He's a top man. You have to go along with what he says."

Buveur D'Air would go on to win again at Aintree. So, too, would Might Bite, who had landed the most dramatic race of the season when almost surrendering a clear lead in the RSA Chase by pulling himself up after the final fence only to kick on again

when stablemate Whisper galloped past. Another to complete a massive spring double was Altior, whose mirroring of Sprinter Sacre was maintained when he put his own name against the Racing Post Arkle Trophy and Sandown's Celebration Chase.

****

FOR Henderson there was much to celebrate at Sandown. Over the final weeks of the season he had turned the title race around. At the start of the Cheltenham Festival he sat in third position, almost £500,000 behind Nicholls. Once the festival was over it was he who had the lead, to the tune of almost £150,000. Nicholls tried to chip away at the deficit, and was helped when Vicente made it back-to-back Scottish Nationals, but he did not have the same earning power. Henderson was champion again.

The master of Seven Barrows, now 66 but as driven as ever, then started the 2017-18 season as favourite to retain that championship with an array of stars, including strong fancies for the Gold Cup (Might Bite), Champion Chase (Altior) and Champion Hurdle (Buveur D'Air). Highlighting his strength relative to Nicholls was the fact that whereas Henderson had saddled 15 horses in the Grade 1
▶ Continues page 64

MIGHT – AND PROBABLY WILL

Might Bite might crash through the final fence, might veer across the track, might pull himself up, might then get going again and might very well give connections and backers severe palpitations.

Those were the lessons to be learned from the novice chasing campaign of an exciting jumper who might also be a Cheltenham Gold Cup winner in waiting.

Not once but twice was the Nicky Henderson-trained youngster the major character in one of the 2016-17 jumps season's most dramatic finishes.

At Kempton on Boxing Day he held a near 20-length lead approaching the final fence of the Kauto Star Novices' Chase. Then, quite appropriately in a race named after a superstar who in his early days often waited until a race's final jumping test before making an appalling error, Might Bite rooted the birch, taking a horrific-looking fall and handing victory to Royal Vacation.

On that occasion it was Daryl Jacob's misfortune to be sent flying through the Surrey air. Come the RSA Chase regular aide Nico de Boinville was back in the saddle and he experienced something of a rollercoaster ride.

Approaching the last fence Might Bite was once again clear. Another serious argument with the fence on this occasion failed to divide the human-equine partnership. Much, however, was still to happen.

As the run to the line began Might Bite veered dramatically right towards the gate from where horses enter and exit the track. Having then applied the brakes, he was headed by charging stable companion Whisper 130 yards from home. Seeing that happen, Might Bite consented to gallop again and regained the lead in the very last stride.

"Might Bite could well have snatched defeat, then victory, from the jaws of both," said ITV commentator Richard Hoiles. That is exactly what Might Bite did in a finish that will live long in the memory.

"He's such a talented horse," observed De Boinville. "He's very special but we just have to deal with the fact he's a bit of a thinker sometimes."

A thinker, yes, but an extremely talented one.

FOUR ACES IN THE SEVEN BARROWS PACK

ALTIOR

The heir apparent to Sprinter Sacre metamorphosed from superb novice hurdler into brilliant novice chaser with unbeaten campaigns in both spheres. He claimed the Arkle but was much more impressive against senior opponents either side of those wins, particularly when thumping Special Tiara at Sandown

Grade I wins Supreme Novices' Hurdle, Henry VIII Novices' Chase, Arkle Chase, Celebration Chase

RPR 177

What they said "We know where we've got to go next year and Altior is following in Sprinter's shoes" *Nicky Henderson*

What the future holds Connections will be hoping for further flattering comparisons with Sprinter Sacre in a season that will be dominated by a tilt at the Queen Mother Champion Chase

MIGHT BITE

His chasing career was put on hold after a disappointing debut at Cheltenham in November 2015 but he came back with a vengeance last season, albeit with some big quirks attached. He fell when clear in a Grade I at Kempton's Christmas meeting but put that behind him to take major prizes at Cheltenham, despite almost throwing away the race again, and Aintree

Grade I wins RSA Chase, Mildmay Novices' Chase

RPR 170

What they said "He has his quirks, but he's so quick through the air and travels so well. He has tremendous talent" *Nico de Boinville*

What the future holds "The future is obviously enormous," according to Nicky Henderson, whose focus has long been on the King George VI Chase

BUVEUR D'AIR

Third to Altior in the 2016 Supreme Novices' Hurdle, he was sent chasing last season before being switched back to hurdles with devastating effect. Quickly back into his stride in his Sandown prep, he took the Champion Hurdle in impressive style from stablemate My Tent Or Yours and stepped up to 2m4f to beat him again, by a little further, at Aintree

Grade I wins Champion Hurdle, Aintree Hurdle

RPR 171

What they said "I knew we were going down the wrong road and he needed to revert back to hurdles as we had unfinished business. He's a genuine Champion Hurdler" *Nicky Henderson*

What the future holds All roads lead back to the Champion Hurdle – with no unusual detours this time

L'AMI SERGE

Not yet in the class of the others, but he's a second Champion Hurdle winner in the yard after taking the French version in June. Funnily enough, like Buveur D'Air, he went chasing before reverting to hurdles on the first day of 2017. He took time to win but a step up in trip and the fitting of a hood and a different bit helped him to a new level

Grade I wins Grande Course de Haies d'Auteuil

RPR 156

What they said "When you think he was beaten a neck in the County Hurdle under a big weight over two miles, to then go and do that [in France] is quite extraordinary" *Nicky Henderson*

What the future holds French Champion Hurdle victory over 3m1½f opens a wealth of options at staying trips

---

novice events at the Cheltenham Festival, Nicholls had fielded only a single representative. The disparity between the two great opponents, also great friends, was considerable.

Yet Henderson – who in June also took the French Champion Hurdle with the enigmatic L'Ami Serge – knows full well how fortunes can flip. He saw it at Cheltenham on the final day of the 2016 November meeting.

A press briefing had been called prior to racing and word got out Henderson was to announce the retirement of Sprinter Sacre. Henderson has often been seen to shed tears on a racecourse and he

duly shed some more as he confirmed the mighty one was signing off.

Worse was to come once racing started. At the third fence of the Shloer Chase, the race that had heralded Sprinter Sacre's renaissance 12 months earlier, Simonsig, who at one point looked to have the world at his feet, suffered an injury that cost him his place in the world. Even though a race was being run, Cheltenham fell all but silent.

"I'm so gutted for Nicky," said his former stable jockey Mick Fitzgerald. "People have no idea how much he loves his horses."

A few minutes later, anyone who

> 'Henderson understands and adores his horses. As we saw during a remarkable campaign, he also trains them magnificently'

did not know about that love had it laid bare in front of them when Henderson spoke of one of his horses as though he was a friend – a human friend. "Triolo D'Alene will be in bits tonight," he said. "They literally live together. I hadn't thought about Triolo. What's he going to say? They're like two little mates. They live in a box together and go out in a field together every day. Triolo's going to cry tonight. So am I."

You just know he will have done. Henderson understands and adores his horses. As we saw during a remarkable campaign, he also trains them magnificently.

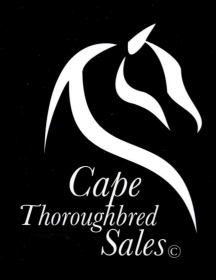

CAPE PREMIER YEARLING SALE
20 - 21 JANUARY 2018

SOUTH AFRICA'S LEADING YEARLING SALE

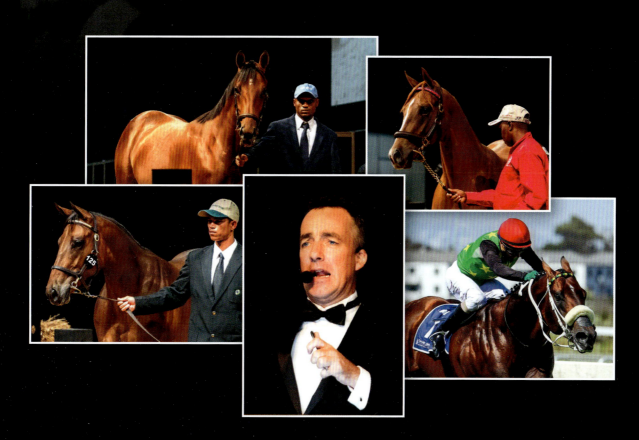

It's A Lifestyle

Contact **Kerry Jack** (Bloodstock Manager) **E:** kerry@cthbs.com **M:** +27 (0) 82 782 7297
European Representative: **Mick Flanagan** **E:** mick@townleyhallbloodstock.com **M:** +353 86 609 8119
W: www.capethoroughbredsales.com

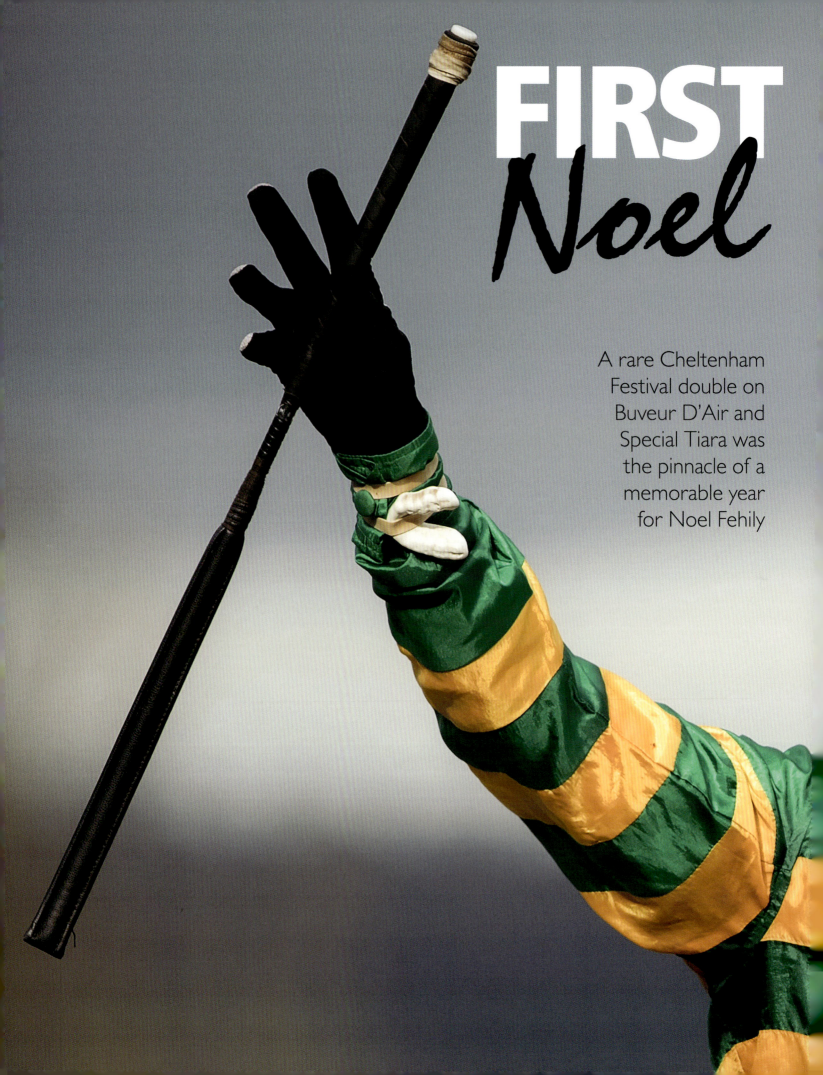

FIRST
Noel

A rare Cheltenham
Festival double on
Buveur D'Air and
Special Tiara was
the pinnacle of a
memorable year
for Noel Fehily

By Nick Pulford

NIAMH FEHILY had one simple question for her father after the prize giving for the Queen Mother Champion Chase at the Cheltenham Festival. "Daddy, why do you always get to kiss the trophy?" she asked with wide-eyed innocence.

The four-year-old's enquiry was understandable, considering she had seen dad Noel do exactly the same the previous day at the Champion Hurdle presentation and knew no different, but those with longer memories realised this was something out of the ordinary.

In fact, it would take racegoers of a certain vintage to recall the only other jockey who had won both the Champion Hurdle and the Champion Chase in the same year, turning their minds all the way back to 1971 when Paul Kelleway rode two of the greats, Bula and Crisp, to victory in those monuments of the festival.

Noel Fehily's wins on Buveur D'Air and Special Tiara took him into that rarefied company and he went on to complete the feat of a first-three placing in each of the festival's major races, finishing third on Unowhatimeanharry in the Stayers' Hurdle and runner-up in the Gold Cup on Minella Rocco. That was some week and, even if time erodes young Niamh's recollection of events, it will live long in the rider's memory.

Buveur D'Air started the roll in the opening-day feature when Fehily drove him up the hill for a clear-cut victory over My Tent Or Yours. The questions that had swirled around the Champion Hurdle and Buveur D'Air for weeks finally had a most emphatic answer.

It was only six weeks since the Nicky Henderson-trained six-year-old had returned to hurdling from novice chasing and, while Fehily always had a chance of riding him after their successful partnership the previous season, confirmation did not come until after Barry Geraghty was ruled out of the festival by injury. As JP McManus's retained rider, Geraghty would have had first pick of Champion Hurdle favourite Yanworth, Buveur D'Air and My Tent Or Yours.

Fehily's chance of picking up a top-quality spare had increased with Buveur D'Air's return to hurdling but still he had to wait for the call-up, even with the path cleared by Geraghty's unfortunate injury. "He'd won his two chases and hadn't done a lot wrong, but as soon as Nicky Henderson wanted him back over hurdles I thought it'd be very interesting to see what he could do," Fehily says. "He was such a good hurdler as a novice and when he won for me at Aintree, I thought he could be a genuine Champion Hurdle contender.

"I only knew I was going to be back on him for sure close to the festival. I schooled him the week before Cheltenham and he jumped brilliant. You couldn't tell he'd
▸ *Continues page 68*

been over fences, he was electric straight away."

Buveur D'Air went off 5-1 second favourite for the Champion Hurdle – Yanworth, ridden by McManus's Irish jockey Mark Walsh, headed the market at 2-1 – and Fehily was pleased to find his mount could still produce fast, fluent hurdling at race speed. "He'd always been a brilliant jumper of a hurdle, even in his novice days. He's not the type to stand off, he gets in tight and gets from A to B very fast, up and down quickly. He's not spectacular, he's just very fast. He reminds me a lot of Rock On Ruby in that way.

"You worry after chasing that they might jump a bit big and slow for a Champion Hurdle, but he jumped great and after the first two hurdles I was very happy with where I was sat. It was the plan to be just behind the leaders and everything went very smoothly. He was bang there coming down the hill and the way he picked up off the bend I knew he'd be hard to pass. I knew he'd stay well."

There was never any danger of being caught and Fehily had his second Champion Hurdle winner, five years after Rock On Ruby. "The first time you're almost in shock and it kind of passes you by a little bit, but I think it means more the second time around because you take it in more. You appreciate it more because you know how hard it is to do."

One aspect that added to the pleasure was that this time he could share the winning moment with his children, Niamh and Michael, 2, as well as wife Natasha. Niamh was not born until a few months after Rock On Ruby's Champion Hurdle. Like many sportsmen, Fehily will tell you having children brings a fresh sense of perspective at the low times that inevitably come along, but this was at the other end of the scale and having Niamh and Michael on course with Natasha made it even more special.

****

DAY two was to bring another celebration with the family on the winner's rostrum, and this time victory came from an unexpected quarter. Fehily arrived at the course with high hopes of more success with

Harry Fry's Neon Wolf, 2-1 favourite for the Neptune Novices' Hurdle, but they were dashed in a head defeat by 14-1 shot Willoughby Court. Two hours later, in the Queen Mother Champion Chase, it was Fehily's turn to bring a favourite crashing down.

Not just any favourite either. This was Douvan, at 2-9 the biggest banker of the festival, who arrived unbeaten in nine starts over hurdles and fences for Willie Mullins and with combined winning distances of nearly 140 lengths.

Fehily was on his old friend Special Tiara, twice third in the Champion Chase but surely no match for the mighty Douvan. "I was very relaxed really because Douvan was such a short-priced favourite but I thought we had a great chance to finish second or third," he says. "There's only one way to ride Special Tiara, everyone knows what he's about, he jumps, he gallops, and there was no point me going out to ride him any different to pick up place money. The best way to ride him was to let him roll and jump, so I just got on with what suits him. He got into such a good rhythm that day, it's probably the best he's ever jumped, especially down the

▸▸ Floating on air: Noel Fehily and Buveur D'Air pull away from the pack (top) for Champion Hurdle victory (below), five years after the rider won with Rock On Ruby (centre)

back, and I thought it was a really good performance."

Douvan on top form almost certainly would have picked off the front-runner but the longer the race went on, the more Fehily began to wonder where the favourite had got to. "I hadn't a clue really. Between the last two I was thinking he'd be coming soon but by the time I got to the last fence I thought he'd be upsides me by now if he was going well. I was waiting for his head to loom up at my girths, but when he didn't appear I thought there must be something wrong. I wasn't hanging around waiting for him, I was just kicking for home."

The challenger turned out to be Fox Norton, but perhaps this was where Fehily reaped the benefit of taking no notice of where Douvan was in the race. He had ridden his
▸▸ *Continues page 70*

2018 Racing Dates

McCARTHY INSURANCE GROUP RACEDAY
Saturday 6th January (NH)

CORK'S REDFM STUDENT RACE DAY
Thursday 22nd March (NH)

RACING HOME FOR EASTER FESTIVAL
Saturday 31st March (F)
Sunday 1st April (NH)
Monday 2nd April (NH)

Sunday 15th April (F)

START OF SUMMER 2 DAY MEETING
Friday 4th May (E)(NH)(BBQ)
Saturday 5th May (F)

Friday 18th May (E)(F)(BBQ)

FATHERS DAY MEETING
Sunday 17th June (F)

MALLOW TOWN SUMMER RACE EVENING
Friday 13th July (E)(NH)(BBQ)

2 DAY BANK HOLIDAY FAMILY MEETING
Monday 6th August (BH)(NH)

Saturday 11th August (F)
Wednesday 3rd October (F)
Wednesday 10th October (F)
Sunday 21st October (NH)

THE PADDYPOWER CORK NATIONAL
Sunday 4th November (NH)

Sunday 18th November (NH)

THE KERRY GROUP HILLY WAY CHASE
Sunday 9th December (NH)

Get your heart racing...

- **Premium Level Restaurant Package**
- **Premium Level Barbeque Package**
- **Social Package**
- **Premium Level Admission**
- **General Admission**
- **Children go FREE**

Book your tickets today

BUY NOW ONLINE

corkracecourse.ie
t: +353 22 50207

Cork Racecourse MALLOW

twitter
@corkracecourse

facebook
Cork Racecourse Mallow

corkracecourse

own race in front and judged the pace to perfection, holding just enough back for the final heave up the hill. "He'd galloped all the way up the hill the year before when he was just done on the line for second by Un De Sceaux, so I knew he wouldn't stop. I kept kicking and he kept going to the line." The winning distance was a head and, even if Douvan's dumbfounding seventh laid the form open to question, it looked a much better performance by the end of the season after Fox Norton's Grade 1 triumphs at Aintree and Punchestown.

For Fehily, there was a particular sense of satisfaction. "I remember watching horses like Viking Flagship when I was growing up and it's a race I really wanted to win. It's great to have done it. I think if you asked any jockey they'd probably say that's the race that gives you the biggest buzz. There's no room for error – it's a test of speed, they have to stay, they have to jump. It's a great race to watch and it's a great race to ride in."

Above all, a great race to win.

****

ALL of a sudden Fehily went into day three with a great chance of an incredible big-race hat-trick, having had the plum ride of Unowhatimeanharry in the Stayers' Hurdle thrown back to him after Geraghty's injury. Fehily had been the regular rider during Unowhatimeanharry's remarkable rise for the Harry Fry Racing Club, which led to festival success in the Albert Bartlett Novices' Hurdle, but the mount had then passed to Geraghty when McManus became the owner.

Unowhatimeanharry arrived back in Fehily's hands as 5-6 favourite for the Stayers' with a winning run for Fry that now stood at eight, but this was the one that got away. The favourite did not run badly but he wasn't at his sharpest and could not get to grips with Nichols Canyon and Lil Rockerfeller.

"I suppose I was a little bit unlucky that he didn't quite fire on the day," Fehily says. "If that had come off as well, that would have turned a great festival into an unbelievable festival. It had never been done to win the three, it would have been nice to do that."

The form book for the final day shows Fehily went even closer to Gold Cup glory – two and three-quarter lengths – after a stirring finish on Minella Rocco, although realistically there never seemed much hope of catching the impressive Sizing John.

"I was in a good position at the top of the hill but then they quickened a little bit and that just tapped him for toe, but once we got to the bend he was staying on again," Fehily recalls. "I thought off the bend I had a great chance of finishing in the first four, then by the time I got to the last I thought I might nick third, and he galloped up the hill so strongly that we got second. To finish second was fantastic."

****

WITH Robbie Power winning the Gold Cup at the age of 35 and Ruby Walsh, at 37, victorious in the Stayers' on Nichols Canyon and the

▶ Special occasion: Noel Fehily arrives in the winner's enclosure (below) after landing the Queen Mother Champion Chase with Special Tiara (above)

Ryanair Chase on Un De Sceaux, Fehily was the oldest member of the senior contingent who dominated Cheltenham's big prizes. When he moved to Britain 19 years ago, still an amateur, the prospect of being in the weighing room at the age of 41 – let alone competing for the biggest races – would have seemed remote.

Two decades ago, 35 was the retirement age for most jump jockeys but advances in care and fitness have opened the door to a longer career and few have grasped that opportunity as eagerly as Fehily. If he had retired on his 35th birthday, he would have departed with a solid enough record but just two Grade 1 wins and a solitary festival success. Now, after a golden autumn to his career, he has won two Champion Hurdles, a Champion Chase, two King Georges on Silviniaco Conti and a host of other big races. His Grade 1 tally stands at 22 and he has ridden five festival winners.

"A lot of people say it's come around late, but it's so hard finding
▶ *Continues page 72*

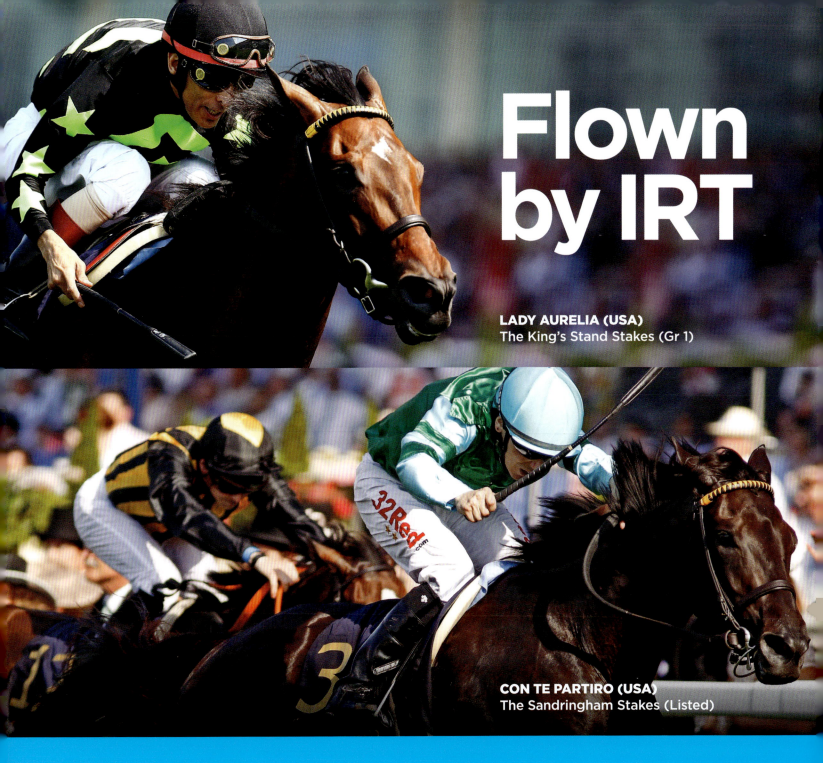

good horses," he reflects. "I'm in the lucky position that I've come across good horses to ride and I have lots of good people to ride for. Things have changed. When I started, very few jockeys got past 34 or 35. Jockeys are fitter now, every racecourse has a physio, jockeys are looked after better and we probably look after ourselves better too."

Fehily's fitness regime revolves around the spin bike and rowing machine, but above all the late blossoming of his career owes much to his riding experience and expertise, which has earned him a reputation as a professionals' professional. That explains why trainers such as Henderson, Fry, Paul Nicholls and Nigel Twiston-Davies will entrust him with their best horses, with his list of mounts last season including Altior, Fox Norton, Grand National favourite Blaklion, Aintree Grade 1 novice chase winner Flying Angel, My Tent Or Yours and Vaniteux, in addition to his top festival rides.

Riding Altior in his first three chases, including the Grade 1 Henry VIII Novices' Chase, was a special privilege. "He's an unbelievable

racehorse. He's the best I've ridden, he's exceptional. When I rode against him on Special Tiara at Sandown, he came by me like I was stood still. His jumping is so good and he'll be difficult to beat because if you go slow he'll beat you for toe, and if you go fast he stays really well too. He'd have no problem getting two and a half miles. If he comes up against Douvan this season, that'll be some race."

The 2016-17 season still had one more thrill left for Fehily in the Stayers' rematch between Unowhatimeanharry, Nichols Canyon and Lil Rockerfeller at Punchestown. The three finished in a different order this time, with Fehily prevailing over Walsh on Nichols Canyon in a ding-dong battle where he led all the way up the straight and fought off every renewed effort from his dogged challenger.

"He

▶▶In the spotlight: Fehily poses for the cameras after winning the Champion Stayers Hurdle at the Punchestown festival on Unowhatimeanharry in a ding-dong battle with Nichols Canyon (below)

showed at Punchestown how good he is and what a tough nut he is," Fehily says. "What a battler he was that day. Any time you come up against Ruby you've got to have a willing partner with you. He was brave at the last when I needed him and he kept his head down the whole way. He wanted it as badly as I did. Buveur D'Air, Special Tiara, Unowhatimeanharry, they're all very willing partners, that's why they're Grade 1 horses. They all have a great attitude to racing."

So does Fehily himself. While he has horses of such quality to ride and more big-race thrills to experience, retirement is not an option.

Stone Farm Bred & Raised

ASCEND
2017 WOODFORD RESERVE
MANHATTAN S.-G1

MASTERY
2016 CASHCALL FUTURITY-G1,
2017 SAN FELIPE S.-G2, ETC.

AIR FORCE BLUE
3-TIME G1 SW
2015 CHAMPION 2YO COLT

Three *MORE* Gr. 1 Winners

Stone Farm-Raised horses include: 4 ECLIPSE CHAMPIONS, 3 KENTUCKY DERBY winners,
2 EUROPEAN CHAMPION 2YOs, 2 BREEDERS' CUP CLASSIC winners,
2 PREAKNESS winners, and 1 BELMONT winner

"We're trying to raise you a good horse."

For inquiries, please contact Arthur Hancock at (859) 987-3737
200 Stoney Point Road, Paris, KY 40361   E-mail: stonefarm@stonefarm.com   www.stonefarm.com

SPECIAL DELIVERY

Henry de Bromhead lost Sizing John but still had old favourite Special Tiara to lead the way for him

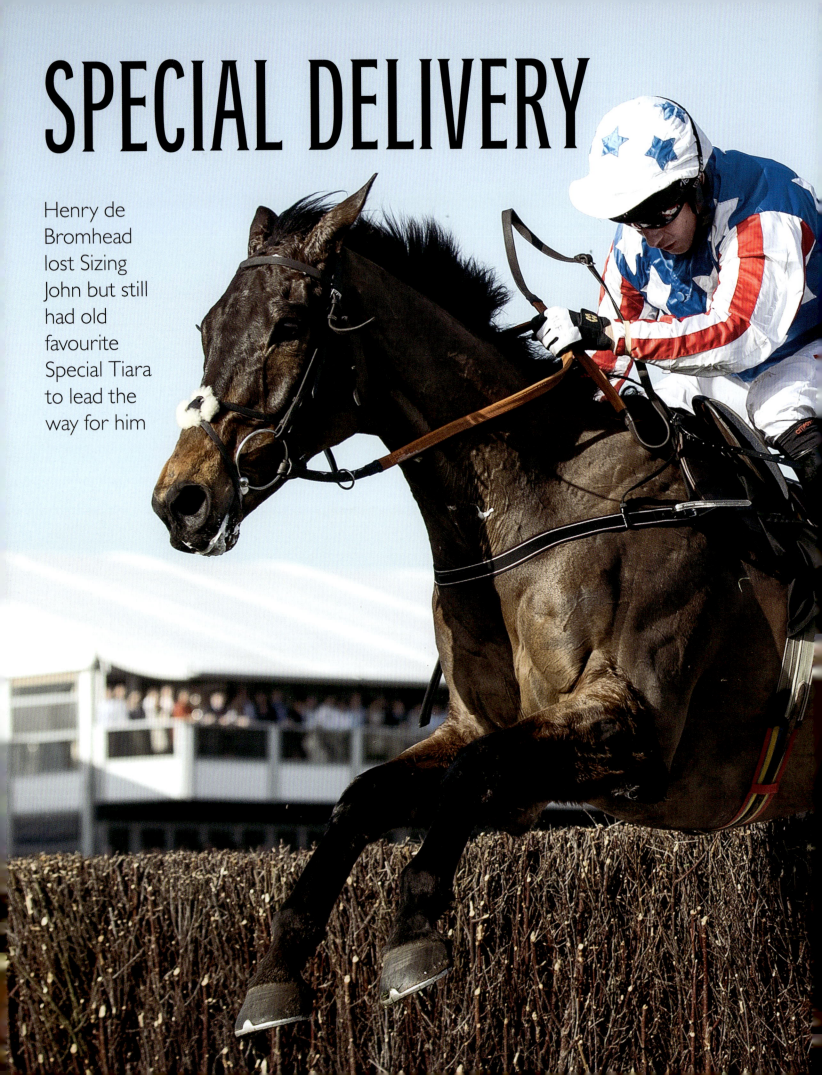

By Alan Sweetman

THE imagery of the fairground was in vogue during the 2016-17 Irish jumps season. A merry-go-round of changed allegiances by leading owners, a rollercoaster for several top trainers, and ultimately a swings-and-roundabouts outcome for some, including Henry de Bromhead.

The County Waterford trainer ended up having his career-best season, taking third place in the Irish championship with 68 wins. He also saddled three winners in Britain, where Special Tiara captured the Queen Mother Champion Chase.

The ten-year-old made virtually all under a brilliant ride from Noel Fehily, who gave him a vital breather on the downhill run to three out and kept enough in reserve to hold off Fox Norton in a dramatic race that featured the shock eclipse of 2-9 favourite Douvan.

Summer 2016 was merging into autumn when influential owners Alan and Ann Potts severed their link with De Bromhead. The trainer, who succeeded his father Harry in 1999, announced his arrival at the top table when the Potts-owned Sizing Europe won the Irish Champion Hurdle in 2008. By the time the 2011 Champion Chase winner retired in 2015, winner of 22 of his 45 races, the trainer had given his main patrons another Grade 1 winner, Sizing John, in a novice hurdle at Leopardstown's Christmas meeting in 2014.

Sizing John, soon to be the Cheltenham Gold Cup winner for Jessica Harrington, was among the Potts horses who left, but De Bromhead took the setback with dignity. It is not that he lacks ambition or drive. Far from it, but there is a laid-back sense of equanimity at the heart of his character.

"Of course it was a blow, but I enjoyed great times with Alan and Ann," he says. "We still had plenty of nice horses to work with, especially Special Tiara. You can look back and say we lost a Gold Cup winner, but then we were lucky enough to get to train some very good horses other people had put a lot of work into. I couldn't possibly have any complaints looking on back on how things worked out."

If the stable needed a morale boost after the split, it was not long before the likes of Valseur Lido and Petit Mouchoir arrived in the wake of another dramatic owner-trainer rift, between Willie Mullins and Gigginstown House Stud, with whom De Bromhead had already shared Grade 1 success with Identity Thief.

"It was a big boost to get more horses from Gigginstown. Valseur Lido got off to a great start when winning the Grade 1 [Champion Chase] at Down Royal and Sub Lieutenant won the Grade 2 on the same day. Petit Mouchoir is a star. Then we were fortunate Roger Brookhouse sent us Champagne West, who won the Thyestes."

De Bromhead is enthusiastic about all his horses. Yet one senses a special affection for Special Tiara, whose progress he followed from birth.

"He was bred by my uncle David Young in Dorset and I saw him there when he was a baby. He was still a baby when I ran him at four in a point-to-point at Boulta. He was second then, and I managed to get him beaten in a couple of maiden hurdles before he won at Kilbeggan,

"We always felt he was a chaser in the making and sent him straight over fences. He went to Ballinrobe and made a bad mistake early in the race but Philip Enright sat tight and he beat Plan A, a decent horse of Gordon Elliott's who had run well in several of the big handicap hurdles."

Special Tiara's career profile is unusual, a British-bred Irish chasing star whose only domestic wins have come in humble surroundings. Good ground and front-running tactics have been key to the son of Kayf Tara and he emerged as a leading light in the two-mile division when winning the Desert Orchid Chase at Kempton in December 2014. In the spring of that season he built on a fine third behind Dodging Bullets in the Champion Chase by defeating Sprinter Sacre in the Celebration Chase at Sandown.

"Irish racegoers haven't seen him often and certainly they haven't seen the best of him," says De Bromhead. That is an understatement. Special Tiara has run only twice on home territory since 2014 and they were undistinguished efforts, a remote last of four finishers in Navan's Fortria Chase in November 2015 and again in rear in the 2016 BoyleSports Champion Chase at Punchestown.

After another Champion Chase third in 2016, last season involved more visits to Britain. It was soft when he kicked off with a tame third at Cheltenham in November. The ground was also against him when he struggled in the Clarence House in January. In between he ended a 20-month drought by winning the Desert Orchid for the second time.

In March De Bromhead and owner Sally Rowley-Williams approached the Champion Chase with hopes of a place again, any more substantial ambition tempered by the overarching reputation of the brilliant Douvan, who had trounced Sizing John in the previous year's Arkle and on many other occasions.

"We thought we were playing for minor money but I knew he was in great form," the trainer says. "The ground was right and he has always had a big heart. Sometimes he has jumped a bit high but he was really slick and Noel was absolutely terrific on him. It was hard to believe, but it was amazing."

Two days later De Bromhead offered unfeigned congratulations to the Pottses and Harrington after their Gold Cup victory with Sizing John. Swings and roundabouts.

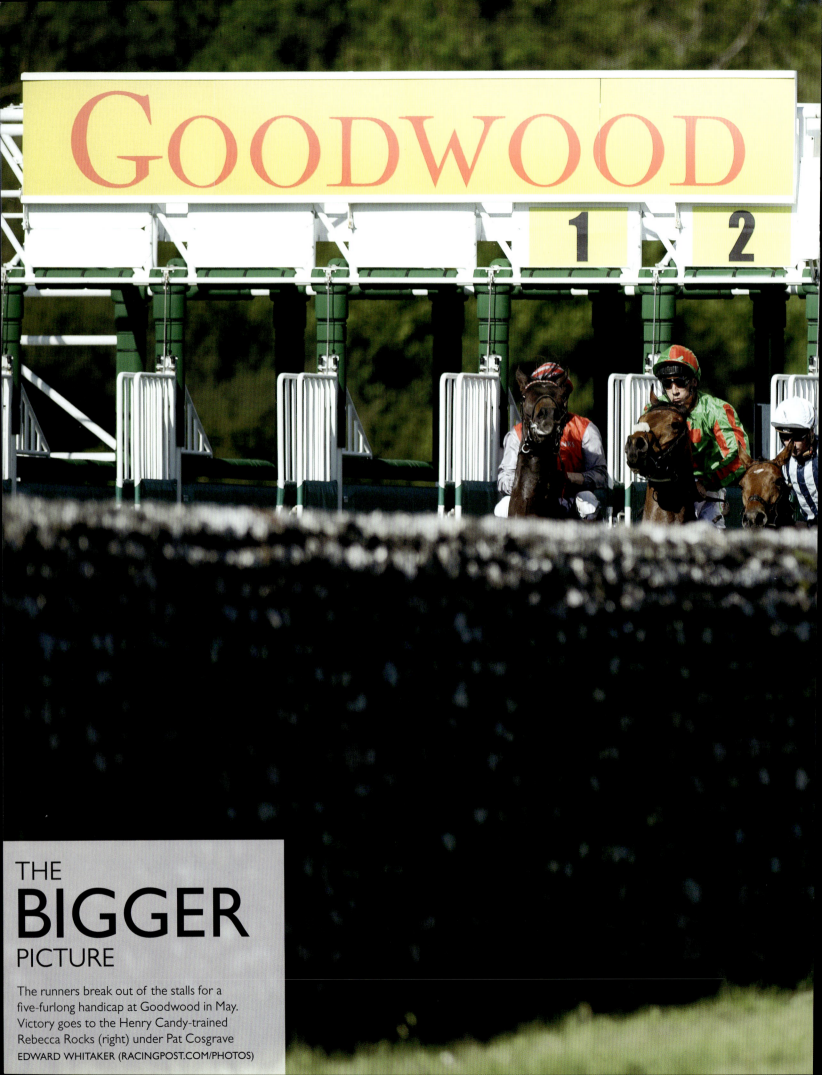

GOODWOOD

1 2

THE
BIGGER
PICTURE

The runners break out of the stalls for a
five-furlong handicap at Goodwood in May.
Victory goes to the Henry Candy-trained
Rebecca Rocks (right) under Pat Cosgrave
EDWARD WHITAKER (RACINGPOST.COM/PHOTOS)

Padraig Beggy took his big chance on his first Derby ride with a sensational triumph on 40-1 outsider Wings Of Eagles

'THERE'S ONLY ONE DERBY A YEAR AND I WON IT'

By Alan Sweetman

SAM ARNULL is the first name on the list. The Derby roll of honour started in 1780 and after 238 runnings the names bear testament to one of the world's great races, an iconic event in British sport, a focus of ultimate ambition. Fred Archer, Steve Donoghue and Lester Piggott are just some of the greats who cemented their legendary status with Derby success. Gordon Richards needed 28 attempts to join them, and Frankie Dettori 15, but they got there in the end.

Padraig Beggy is on the Derby-winning list now, along with all the famous names, and he joined the club on his first ride in the race. That was his day of days, but pretty soon he went back into the shadows, out of the spotlight, while his mount, the 40-1 chance Wings Of Eagles, disappeared from the scene after only one more race.

It is tempting to regard the 2017 Derby result as an aberration. It was certainly a tale of the unexpected from the perspective of the

▸▸ Continues page 80

punter, the form analyst, and indeed the winning trainer. When Wings Of Eagles swept past much-fancied stablemate Cliffs Of Moher in the closing stages, the television cameras turned on Aidan O'Brien. As he prepared to greet his sixth Derby winner, puzzlement was etched on his face and he admitted afterwards: "You never really know going into this race. They're all bred for it and until you test them on this course over a mile and a half you don't know how they will do – anything can happen."

What most people expected to happen was for O'Brien to win with 5-1 shot Cliffs Of Moher or one of his other fancied runners from a team of six, Capri perhaps, or for John Gosden to thwart him with 7-2 favourite Cracksman. Or maybe Eminent, also 5-1, could step up from a mile to give Martyn Meade the biggest success of his training career. It didn't look an especially watertight Derby form-wise, but even so Wings Of Eagles was difficult to consider as a live outsider.

"Lacks Classic class," said one newspaper guide on the day. He had won just one of his five career starts and had only two below him in the betting list – that pair would go on to occupy the last two places in the 18-runner race. His 31-year-old jockey had ridden just three winners since returning from a spell in Australia, his career in disarray following a positive test for cocaine that had resulted in a lengthy ban, and his number of rides in 2017 was not yet into double figures.

Yet this odd couple were about to turn the race upside down. Ryan Moore, riding Cliffs Of Moher, and Dettori on Cracksman would have to settle for minor placings behind the Derby newcomer.

****

WINGS OF EAGLES was bred in France by Aliette and Gilles Forien by 2011 Derby winner Pour Moi out of Ysoldina, a Group-placed mile winner by Kendor. At the time he was sent to the Arqana Sales in August 2015 he was a half-brother to two winning fillies by Oasis Dream. A couple of months after his purchase by MV Magnier for €220,000, another half-sister, by Sea The Stars, won a two-year-old race at Chantilly.

The colt was registered to the Derrick Smith/Michael Tabor/Sue Magnier partnership four days before his debut at the 2016 Galway festival.

▸▸Off and running: Wings Of Eagles registers the first victory of his career when scoring under Emmet McNamara at Killarney in August 2016; (previous page) in the winner's enclosure at Epsom ten months later

Sent off 7-1 joint third favourite, he was hooded to load into the stalls and failed to make any significant impression, other than betray inexperience, in finishing seventh of 11 runners.

Nonetheless, Racing Post correspondent Justin O'Hanlon wrote: "It would be a big surprise if he didn't improve significantly."

Three weeks later he reappeared in a six-runner contest at Killarney, the mount entrusted to Emmet McNamara, a former star apprentice whose career has stalled in recent seasons. Despite running very green, hanging left and right at various stages and demonstrating an awkward head carriage, Wings Of Eagles asserted well in the last 50 yards or so to become one of only two 2016 winners for his jockey from 98 rides. Perhaps, in hindsight, we can see the faint outline of a pattern.

He had two more runs as a juvenile. He still looked raw and met trouble in running when fourth of 12 behind Coronet in the Zetland Stakes over a mile and a quarter at Newmarket. The form turned out to be influential. The winner and third-placed Permian both gained Royal Ascot honours at three

▸▸ *Continues page 82*

in the Ribblesdale and King Edward VII Stakes respectively, while runner-up Cunco started his three-year-old campaign brightly with victory in the bet365 Classic Trial at Sandown.

All that was in the future. For now, Wings Of Eagles was struggling to make his presence felt as O'Brien continued to sort out potential Classic hopefuls for 2017.

For his final start at two he was the outsider of the stable's four runners in the Group 1 Criterium de Saint-Cloud. Capri, Douglas Macarthur and Taj Mahal finished in close proximity, third, fourth and fifth respectively behind Waldgeist. Wings Of Eagles ended up ninth.

When Wings Of Eagles reappeared in the spring there was no suggestion he was any closer to the front rank at Ballydoyle. He was dispatched in a four-strong contingent, comprising half of the field, as O'Brien attempted to win the Chester Vase for the eighth time in 11 years. Previous winners included subsequent Irish Derby scorers Soldier Of Fortune and Treasure Beach, as well as the 2013 Epsom hero Ruler Of The World.

This time the team was spearheaded by Venice Beach, winner of a Tipperary maiden on his third start and the choice as Moore's mount. His status as a half-brother to King George and Arc winner Danedream entitled him to consideration as a

▶▶ Trial run: Wings Of Eagles (8) finishes runner-up to stablemate Venice Beach under Seamie Heffernan in the Chester Vase on his first start of 2017

Derby candidate and he duly justified 5-2 favouritism, but without showing any real authority.

It looked an ordinary edition of the race, dominated by O'Brien, who also supplied the second and third. Scant attention was paid to the placed horses, though Racing Post analyst Mark Brown noted runner-up Wings Of Eagles "finishing well despite not looking entirely at home on the track". He finished a nose in front of The Anvil, a Dundalk maiden winner.

O'Brien declared all three horses as part of a six-pronged Derby challenge led by the Dee Stakes winner Cliffs Of Moher and backed up by two of the horses who had finished in front of Wings Of Eagles at Saint-Cloud the previous November, Capri and Douglas Macarthur.

****

BEGGY, a trusted work rider but a long way down the list of race jockeys available to O'Brien, hoped
▶▶ *Continues page 84*

APPRENTICE RULED OUT

While Padraig Beggy won the Derby, a jockey with four times as many rides as him in 2017 was barred from the race on grounds of inexperience.

This was the controversial case of Gina Mangan (below), 25, an apprentice with John Jenkins who was lined up to ride the stable's 1,000-1 shot Diore Lia in Britain's premier Classic despite having had only 69 career rides and one winner. The BHA initially suggested there was nothing in the rules to stop the 7lb claimer from taking the ride, but three days before the Derby it invoked little-known rule 83, which gives discretion to refuse the declaration of a rider, to prevent Mangan's participation.

The BHA's intervention sparked outrage from Diore Lia's owner-breeder Richard Aylward, who was running the filly to raise money for Great Ormond Street Hospital. "We're in the Derby to have a go at it, and the BHA have been got to. They've changed their mind," he said.

BHA chief regulatory officer Jamie Stier said in a statement: "Miss Mangan has never ridden at Epsom and certainly never ridden in a race on the scale and stage of the Derby, with all the unique challenges it presents. Should the BHA have not acted and an incident have occurred, then the disappointment of one rider could have been placed in stark contrast with the potential consequences."

The BHA said the twice-raced maiden filly with a Racing Post Rating of 52 could take part with a more experienced rider and Diore Lia was declared with Paddy Pilley, a 19-year-old apprentice, but in the end she was withdrawn on the day with a pulled muscle.

In a strange twist the Derby was then won by Beggy. Like Mangan, he had never competed at Epsom before his ride on Wings Of Eagles and came in to the race with just eight rides in 2017 – compared with 34 for Mangan.

Beggy was, of course, vastly more experienced than Mangan both as a race jockey and a work rider – "world class," Aidan O'Brien called him – but the irony was noted in many quarters nonetheless.

Win more with Plus 10

+ **More than £11.3 million** paid out to date, rewarding 550 different owners

+ **£6.3 million** worth of bonus prize money on offer in 2018

+ **Increased opportunities for 3YOs** in race programme from 2018 onwards

+ **Breeders win up to £2,000** if their horse wins a Plus 10 race

Foal Registration:	Yearling Registration:	Owner Registration:
31 August in foal year	**30 June** in yearling year	**28 February** in 2YO year

For more information visit **www.plus10bonus.com** or contact **+44 (0)20 7152 0026**

for a bit part in one of the most important weeks of any year for Ballydoyle.

"A week or so before [the Derby] Aidan's plans were falling into place and it was beginning to look as if he would have five or six runners," he said, reflecting later in the summer on those life-changing days. "At that stage I began to be hopeful I'd be in line to ride one of them. I'd ridden Hydrangea to win a Group 3 at Leopardstown in April and Aidan and the owners had been very good to me. They let me keep the ride in the two Guineas and I was placed on her behind Winter and Roly Poly at the Curragh. We had four in the race that day, so I was thinking I might get the call for Epsom."

Beggy had ridden Wings Of Eagles in a few pieces of work in the spring. "I liked him. He was physically strong. He was still very raw but you could tell he had the makings of a very good colt. Seamie [Heffernan] rode him when he was second in the Chester Vase and thought he would come on a lot. Seamie and Donnacha [O'Brien] rode him in the weeks before the Derby and they were happy with his work. When Aidan told me I was going to ride him at Epsom I was more than happy."

He firmly rejects the notion that Wings Of Eagles was there simply to make up the numbers. "Definitely not. We all talked about the race and

reckoned there was very little between them. Yes, we thought Cliffs Of Moher was the best of them, but it was only a matter of a couple of pounds here and there with all of them. You didn't know which ones would handle the track best, or who would get the run of the race, but when it's Aidan O'Brien and the Derby you know this is the day they've been trained for. You wouldn't want to write off any of them."

Beggy was determined to enjoy his day in the sun. "We all walked the course with Aidan and he gave us our instructions. We talked among ourselves about how the race might pan out. The draw made things easy for me in a sense. I was drawn beside Ryan on Cliffs Of Moher. We knew a couple of ours were going to be prominent, but Cliffs Of Moher was going to be held up, and the obvious thing was to try to follow him."

As race time approached, Beggy admits he was struck by the sense of occasion. "You're a professional jockey, so you want to treat it as just another race, but I got a real buzz when I walked into the parade ring. 'This is the Derby,' I was thinking, 'one of the great races, and I'm riding in it. How many very

▶ Flying high: (above from left) Wings Of Eagles charges down the outside to snatch Derby victory under Padraig Beggy; the 40-1 shot is led to the winner's enclosure; Beggy and winning trainer Aidan O'Brien; (below) the next day's Racing Post front page; (bottom) owners Derrick Smith (left) and Michael Tabor (centre) with O'Brien

good jockeys never get this chance?' It was a special moment, no doubt."

He was more than hopeful of a good showing. "He gave me a great feel going down, he probably pulled a little hard. I was on a good horse and he looked a million dollars – a lot of the jockeys down at the start said I was on the paddock pick."

****

BREAKING from stall 14, Beggy was two minutes and 33 seconds from history. A few days later, speaking to the Racing Post, he relived how he had brought Wings Of Eagles on a weaving run, an erratic but irresistible charge, extracting the colt from potential trouble before pushing him out with hands and heels to edge ahead of Cliffs Of Moher. The dramatic late thrust was reminiscent of Pour Moi, the colt's sire, on the same stage six years earlier.

"My lad got into a big rhythm from the word go and had a free run round until we found trouble two out. Oh, I cruised into the race, going as well as anything. Then, when Ryan switched out [on Cliffs Of Moher], a gap opened and my lad went in there quicker than I thought he would and we ended up

on the heels of the one in front. I had to sit and suffer for a second and catch hold of him again. I switched him right but Ryan had flown, gone four or five lengths. So then I thought we'd run on for a place, and I'd be very happy.

"He picked up when I pulled my stick through, I got him balanced, got him rolling, and had him in top gear a furlong and a half out. He didn't just pick up, he found another gear. I took hold of him again and gave him a few reminders. The others were in fifth gear, I was in sixth gear from the furlong pole to the line. He got me out of trouble really.

"I put the stick down 100 yards out because he was flying for me, I vaguely remember saying to myself, 'put your stick down, keep him straight and balanced, and he'll win the Derby'. I thought I'd win. I had them all covered. Four strides from the line I passed Ryan and I knew there wasn't anything coming from behind me. And I won the Derby."

****

BEGGY and Wings Of Eagles were gone from the limelight almost as quickly as they arrived. The jockey gained notoriety more than fame a week later with an ill-judged ride on Ballydoyle pacemaker Taj Mahal in the Eclipse, and there was no place for him on the roster of jockeys in the Irish Derby. As summer turned to autumn, Beggy still had only two

winners in 2017 – albeit both of them Group victories, with Wings Of Eagles and Hydrangea.

Wings Of Eagles did take part in the Irish Derby and this time he was favourite, with Moore on board, but he suffered a career-ending injury to his near-fore sesamoid in finishing third behind two of his Epsom victims, Capri and Cracksman. "It was a really brave effort in the circumstances as the injury obviously happened at some stage of the race," O'Brien said. "Not being able to race him again is a big loss."

The Derby form kept developing, however, and did not look half bad later in the season, with Cracksman winning the British Champion Stakes, Capri adding the St Leger to his tally, and two Royal Ascot winners among the Epsom also-rans, as well as several other Group-race winners.

The easy narrative that Wings Of Eagles had produced a shock result in an unremarkable year no longer carried great weight. In any case, it is his name in the record books next to Aidan O'Brien's and Padraig Beggy's.

"As people have reminded me since," Beggy said, "there's only one Derby a year. I won it. There's only a hundred of them in a century. No-one can ever take it away from me. It's history."

Two hundred and thirty-eight years of history now, from Sam Arnull to Padraig Beggy.

CLASSICS MASTERS

Wings Of Eagles was the sixth Derby winner for Aidan O'Brien, putting the current master of Ballydoyle alongside Vincent O'Brien – the man who built the County Tipperary training empire – as joint-holder of the post-war record.

The second O'Brien had his first Derby triumph with Galileo in 2001 and has followed with High Chaparral (2002), Camelot (2012), Ruler Of The World (2013), Australia (2014) and now Wings Of Eagles. Those six winners in 17 runnings make him quicker than his namesake (but no relation), whose sextet came between 1962 and 1982.

The only trainers ahead of the Ballydoyle giants, with seven, are Robert Robson (whose wins came between 1793 and 1823), John Porter (1868-1899) and Fred Darling (1922-1941).

O'Brien's total of British Classics now stands at 29 after he took four out of the five in 2017 with Churchill (2,000 Guineas), Winter (1,000 Guineas), Wings Of Eagles and Capri (St Leger).

He also won four of the five Irish Classics with Churchill (2,000 Guineas), Winter (1,000 Guineas), Capri (Derby) and Order Of St George (St Leger). His total is now 39 – as a comparison, Vincent O'Brien won 16 Classics in Britain and 27 in Ireland.

An O'Brien Classics clean sweep in both countries in 2017 was prevented by Enable, winner of the Oaks and Irish Oaks. In both races O'Brien had the runner-up (Rhododendron at Epsom and Rain Goddess at the Curragh).

O'BRIEN'S SIX DERBY WINNERS

Year	Winner	Best RPR
2001	Galileo	132
2002	High Chaparral	130
2012	Camelot (right)	126
2013	Ruler Of The World	125
2014	Australia	129
2017	Wings Of Eagles	121

THE MASTER

Aidan O'Brien was the star turn at Ballydoyle as he sent out a record number of Group 1 winners despite lacking an outstanding champion

By Alan Sweetman

AIDAN O'BRIEN'S bid to reach Bobby Frankel's world record of 25 top-level wins in a calendar year supplied one of the main narratives to the closing months of the 2017 Flat season in Britain and Ireland. Although ambition in that direction was underplayed by the trainer, momentum built steadily through the late summer and the autumn, as the target increasingly began to look attainable, and he finally scaled the peak on British Champions Day.

In a fitting link to the early stages of a memorable campaign, Hydrangea, who delivered the stable's first Pattern success of the season in a 1,000 Guineas trial at Leopardstown, brought O'Brien level with the American maestro by winning the Group 1 Fillies & Mares Stakes at Ascot.

The big day at Ascot underlined the magnitude of O'Brien's feat in more ways than one, for the results highlighted some of the adversities experienced by the trainer in his pursuit of the record. In finishing third in the Queen Elizabeth II Stakes and the British Champions Sprint respectively, Churchill and Caravaggio, a pair for whom it had seemed a case of 'the sky's the limit' early in the season, were exposed as horses who had not lived up to their billing. This may seem a harsh assessment of high-class Group 1 performers, but Coolmore and O'Brien are looking for superstars and champions. The second half of the season showed neither horse falls into this category.

▶ *Continues page 88*

▶▶ Winning machine: (clockwise from above left) Aidan O'Brien with his trophy after saddling the first four home in the Group 1 Dewhurst Stakes; thumbs-up at Newmarket during the Dubai Future Champions festival; congratulations for the trainer on British Champions Day at Ascot after equalling the record for 25 Group 1 winners in a season

Champions Day opened with a Group 2 victory for Order St George, who contributed an Irish St Leger to a tally of eight British and Irish Classic wins for O'Brien. However, he too might have been expected to add more to the Group 1 count, losing out instead by a short head to Big Orange when odds-on to win a second Ascot Gold Cup.

Also in action at Ascot in October was Highland Reel, third to the brilliant Cracksman in the Champion Stakes. He made a notable contribution in winning the Coronation Cup and the Prince of Wales's Stakes but then lost out to Enable in the King George and Cracksman, further evidence that the champions lay elsewhere.

But while he lacked a superstar to measure up to the many he has produced in the past, this will be remembered as a banner year for O'Brien that demonstrated his mastery of his profession in the superb handling of the strength in depth available to him at Ballydoyle.

****

IN THE race won by Hydrangea at Leopardstown back in April, O'Brien also supplied runner-up Winter, a Dundalk juvenile maiden winner added to the team following the retirement of David Wachman. This

was an early hint of the strength in depth among the three-year-old fillies that would prove crucial to the record chase. The occasion also marked a first Pattern win for jockey Padraig Beggy, of whom more would be heard.

At the beginning of May, as O'Brien was finalising plans for the Guineas meeting at Newmarket, the brilliant Minding made her seasonal debut in the Group 2 Mooresbridge Stakes at Naas. The Galileo filly sauntered home in what looked like an ideal stepping stone to a campaign in which she seemed a near certainty to add further lustre to a career record featuring seven Group 1 victories. It was not to be, however, as she suffered a subsequent pastern injury and was retired in July.

O'Brien took the first steps on the record-breaking trail with a Newmarket Classic double, shared between Ryan Moore, who partnered the National Stakes and Dewhurst winner Churchill to justify 6-4 favouritism in a ten-strong field for the Qipco 2,000 Guineas, and Wayne Lordan, who guided Winter to defeat the Moore-ridden Rhododendron in the Qipco 1,000 Guineas.

Churchill, a son of Galileo out of a five-furlong Listed winner by Storm Cat, started the season as Coolmore's prime stallion prospect among the

▶▶ Moments to savour: (from left) Highland Reel wins the Coronation Cup at Epsom; Ryan Moore with Churchill after landing the 2,000 Guineas; Winter streaks home in the 1,000 Guineas; Roly Poly wins the Falmouth Stakes

Classic crop. The manner of his Newmarket victory was professional without being extravagant, achieved with the help of intelligent tactical support from Donnacha O'Brien on fourth-placed Lancaster Bomber, and naturally his performance stimulated debate about his prospects of getting the Derby trip. However, pedigree concerns persuaded the Coolmore strategists to keep him at a mile to contest the Irish 2,000 Guineas and the St James's Palace Stakes. Sent off at 4-9 at the Curragh, Churchill again left an impression of efficiency rather than brilliance in claiming a second Classic.

O'Brien's team of fillies consolidated

'THE GOLD STANDARD'

John Gosden had the Flat superstars of 2017 with Cracksman and Enable, but he left no doubt of his admiration for Aidan O'Brien's training skills and what it takes to beat the master of Ballydoyle.

"I have enormous respect for the quality of the horses and the superb training of them. Any time you compete against him you know you're absolutely taking on the pinnacle and I find the challenge fascinating. I just spend all my time trying to work his tactics out. It's like a Rubik's cube but I really enjoy the challenge of it," Gosden said in October.

"He is completely and absolutely absorbed in what he's doing, every moment and every horse. My son and I spent Sunday morning with him after the Irish Derby this year and I was fascinated to watch the incredible attention to detail, everything was immaculate. It's the gold standard, it really is."

its grasp on the evolving season when Winter swept to a convincing victory over stablemates Roly Poly and Hydrangea in the Irish 1,000 Guineas.

The influence of Galileo on Ballydoyle's record-breaking season was quite phenomenal. Of the six fillies who contributed 12 Group 1 victories between them, five are daughters of Coolmore's flagship sire and the other, War Front filly Roly Poly, is out of the Galileo mare Misty For Me, who grew immensely in stature as Roly Poly's brother US Navy Flag came out of the Ballydoyle pack to establish himself as a top juvenile.

Winter went from strength to the strength through the summer and next she led home the same one-two-three from the Irish Guineas in the Coronation Stakes at Royal Ascot. O'Brien then decided to let her skip the Falmouth Stakes, instead dispatching Roly Poly, who took the opportunity by scoring at the main expense of Godolphin's 2016 Prix Marcel Boussac winner Wuheida.

By the time Winter was given the go-ahead to resume her campaign over 1m2f in the Nassau Stakes, Roly Poly had added a second Group 1 to her record in the Prix Rothschild at Deauville. At Goodwood, Winter extended her Group 1 sequence to four with a comfortable success,

beating the Andrew Balding-trained outsider Blond Me, who later gained top honours in the EP Taylor Stakes at Woodbine.

Despite an interrupted preparation Winter was sent off even-money favourite in the Matron Stakes at Leopardstown in September. Moore sent her into a narrow lead approaching the final furlong but could not fend off the rallying effort of stablemate Hydrangea, who had tracked the pace-setting Roly Poly for much of the way.

****

WHILE the fillies carried all before them, marked by further success for Roly Poly in the Sun Chariot and Rhododendron in the Prix de l'Opera, it was a mixed bag with the colts.

In the build-up to the Derby, Douglas Macarthur, Venice Beach and Cliffs Of Moher won key trials without creating major ripples. On the big day Wings Of Eagles swept to an improbable victory under Beggy, but it was sixth-placed Capri who became the team's principal standard-bearer among the three-year-old colts.

In beating Cracksman in the Irish Derby and confirming his stamina with victory in the St Leger, he proved progressive in a fashion that contrasted with Churchill, who went to Royal Ascot as hot favourite for the

▶▶ Headline news: Racing Post front pages following Churchill's 2,000 Guineas victory, Winter's win in the 1,000 Guineas and Capri's St Leger success

St James's Palace but could finish only a tame fourth as Richard Hannon's Guineas runner-up Barney Roy beat Lancaster Bomber.

Withdrawn from the Sussex Stakes, Churchill could not cope with Ulysses when going up to 1m2f in the Juddmonte International and failed to rehabilitate himself when unplaced behind Decorated Knight in the Irish Champion Stakes. He failed again at Ascot, finishing third behind Persuasive, whose victory shed further reflected glory on her Leopardstown conquerors Hydrangea and Winter.

It was a similar story for Caravaggio. The 2016 Coventry and Phoenix Stakes winner stretched his unbeaten record to six when beating Harry Angel in the Commonwealth Cup before losing his aura of invincibility in the July Cup and then finishing out of the money in the Prix Maurice de Gheest. There was no great redemption in a Group 2 win at the Curragh in September, nor in his Ascot third.

****

A SOFTLY-SOFTLY approach by O'Brien with his juvenile runners was one of the main features of the domestic season, with first-time-out winners increasingly rare. Several of the stable's top two-year-olds were
▶▶ *Continues page 90*

allowed to develop at their own pace, a strategy that brought the best out of US Navy Flag.

The War Front colt had run four times, including an undistinguished display in the Coventry Stakes, before winning a Curragh maiden. Despite taking second in the July Stakes and fourth in the Phoenix Stakes, he appeared to be a little short of top class until stepping up from an emphatic Group 3 win at the Curragh to capture the Middle Park and the Dewhurst.

Churchill's sister Clemmie was third in a Curragh maiden and seventh in the Albany Stakes at Royal Ascot before she too set out on an upward curve with a Group 3 Curragh win. She took the Group 2 Duchess of Cambridge Stakes in July and returned to Newmarket in late September to exact revenge over the French-trained Albany winner Different League in the Group 1 Cheveley Park.

Sioux Nation went to Royal Ascot with a record of three defeats and a virtually meaningless maiden win in a five-runner contest at Cork. He beat 16 rivals in the Norfolk Stakes and gained Group 1 honours in the Phoenix Stakes.

In contrast to those three, September, a daughter of Deep Impact, won her first two starts, including the Chesham. She then seemed to fall behind a couple of her stablemates in the pecking order before reasserting her Classic claims when going desperately close in the Fillies' Mile at Newmarket in October.

Happily, unplaced behind September on her debut in a maiden at Leopardstown, won four of her next five races, the exception being when she lost to stablemate Magical in the Group 2 Debutante Stakes at the Curragh in August. She recovered from that defeat to notch Group 1 wins in the Moyglare Stud Stakes, beating Magical and September, and against the colts in the Prix Jean-Luc Lagardere.

In a sense that last victory over the colts was a suitable reflection of a campaign in which the fillies provided the key to O'Brien's extraordinary success.

MOORE IN DRIVING SEAT WITH CAPRI

Capri arrived at Doncaster in September with plenty of mileage – like any remaining models of Ford's classic 1970s coupe bearing the same name – but in winning one of the stronger renewals of recent years Aidan O'Brien's grey colt carried Ryan Moore to a full set of British Classics, *writes Jon Lees.*

The Irish Derby winner was Moore's inevitable pick of the O'Brien quartet in the 11-runner Leger and went off 3-1 favourite but he was far from a certainty in a high-quality field. Moore was an admirer of Sir Michael Stoute's Crystal Ocean, having won the Gordon Stakes on him the previous month, and John Gosden saddled Goodwood Cup winner Stradivarius and the Ribblesdale-winning filly Coronet.

O'Brien's pacemaking plan failed hopelessly as The Anvil charged off far too quickly. He was already tailing off by the time Capri engaged with Stradivarius and Coronet from three furlongs out to set up one of the most absorbing finishes of the season. At first it looked to be a battle of the confirmed stayers but just as Coronet faded and Capri appeared to be mastering Stradivarius, the held-up Crystal Ocean arrived with a strong challenge. Moore and his willing mount found

more, however, to hold off Crystal Ocean by half a length with Stradivarius a short head back in third.

For Moore, this was his tenth British Classic winner and ticked the last one off the list, adding to his three wins in the 1,000 Guineas and two apiece in the Derby, 2,000 Guineas and Oaks. The full set is a notable achievement – Frankie Dettori is the only other current jockey to have done it – even if it might not matter that much to Moore.

Speaking in 2010, the year he won his first Classics with Snow Fairy in the Oaks and Workforce in the Derby, Moore said: "There was only one Classic I ever had any interest in. I don't remember when I was a kid watching the Oaks or the Leger. I remember watching the Derby, Breeders' Cup and Arcs."

The Coolmore partnership place much greater emphasis on the Classics than their first jockey does and all eight of Moore's British Classic winners since Snow Fairy and Workforce have been for them. With O'Brien's Ballydoyle set-up being one of the St Leger's staunchest supporters, it was only a matter of time until Moore wore the traditional winner's cap at Doncaster.

▶▶ Classic combination: Capri on his way to victory at Doncaster and Ryan Moore with his Leger cap

FULL HOUSE
Ryan Moore's British Classics

2010 Snow Fairy **Oaks**

2010 Workforce **Derby**

2012 Homecoming Queen **1,000 Guineas**

2013 Ruler Of The World **Derby**

2015 Gleneagles **2,000 Guineas**

2015 Legatissimo **1,000 Guineas**

2016 Minding **1,000 Guineas**

2016 Minding **Oaks**

2017 Churchill **2,000 Guineas**

2017 Capri **St Leger**

By Richard Forristal

SUPER KEANE

Colin Keane shot into the top rank of Irish Flat jockeys with a brilliant breakthrough season

IT has been a long time since anybody made such an immediate and potentially lasting impact in the higher echelons of the Flat jockeys' championship in Ireland as Colin Keane has done.

In terms of a whirlwind ascent, Joseph O'Brien's fleeting brilliance en route to two titles is the only comparable breakthrough in recent times. However, given O'Brien's physique, his tenure as a jockey was never going to last. Keane is here to stay.

Long before the outcome of the 2017 Irish jockeys' championship was known, it was clear that this bright young talent had forced open the doors to the exclusive club of top-level jockeys where the kingmakers for so long have been Ballydoyle, Dermot Weld and Jim Bolger. This was Keane's year.

Seminal championship bouts that resonate with those looking in from outside racing's confines are rare. Trainers' dust-ups don't always capture the wider world's imagination but the intensity of a jockeys' head-to-head, like that served up by Keane and reigning champion Pat Smullen, is different.

Jockeys are out there in the thick of the action, consumed by the pursuit of glory and pitting their wits against each other in the white heat of battle. During an unrelenting joust for a title, every month, week, day, race and furlong comprises a multitude of infinitesimal decisions. Some will be more obviously significant than others, but the cumulative effect inevitably reveals the character of the protagonists.

In that respect, we can reflect on Keane's season and conclude that this is not just a jockey of exceptional talent, but one possessed of a single-minded sense of purpose whose focus never flinched. When Smullen, a giant of the weighing room who was riding winners before Keane was even born, trained his sights on the insouciant tyro, the response was emphatic. The 23-year-old didn't just not shrink when Smullen loomed large, he visibly grew to meet the challenge. It was a sight to behold.

Ten clear of Smullen in the middle of August, Keane refused to be intimidated into conceding that the natural order would inevitably restored. The wily 40-year-old bore down on him, with a Roscommon four-timer on the last Monday in August a real statement of intent.

At the end of September in Tipperary, with Dermot Weld's string beginning to shake the effects of a virus, Smullen drew level with the young pretender. The bookies went 1-4 about his retaining the title and the momentum seemed to be his. Undeterred, Keane went to Dundalk three days later and plundered an 84-1 treble. Thou shalt not pass!

"It has been a game of cat and mouse," Keane said. "I would ride a winner and be chuffed with myself. Then Pat comes out and rides a winner in the next race. I might ride a double and he goes one better and rides a treble. It has been some rollercoaster."

Maybe the most visually satisfying vignette of Keane's defiance came at Dundalk in early October. Four up going into the meeting, he might have been deflated after Smullen bagged four of the first five races. Not a bit of it. In the finale, our heroes served up a mesmerising encounter.

"They're level in the championship

and they're level with a furlong to go here," screamed Des Scahill as Smullen tried to coerce Bold Knight past Keane's Thunder Crash. He couldn't do it, and it felt like a microcosm of the season. Keane had led and Smullen got to within a flared nostril as the contest reached a crescendo, but overhauling such a determined individual is another thing. It was in those pivotal moments that we began to get a glimpse of Keane's steely resolve.

Quietly spoken and a man of relatively few words but with a sharp sense of humour, Keane has a conviction in the saddle that had long been evident. However, the mark of a true champion is to consistently display such authoritative self-belief. That's what Keane kept doing, and then came what felt like the coup de grace at Naas.

At Cork on October 14, he plundered two wins to go five clear. The following day at the Kildare venue, he drew first blood aboard Moonlight Bay in the Birdcatcher, before Smullen pulled one back in the next. Then Keane drove the dagger through the perennial champion's heart in two of the next three races, consigning his nemesis to the runner-up berth both times to stretch his lead to seven.

By now it was clear this was a fight Smullen might not win and, just as significantly in the long term, that Keane had all the nerve and verve required to be a champion, not merely a challenger.

A pony racing marvel, Keane had been crowned champion apprentice with 54 winners in 2014. He then finished second to Smullen in 2015 and 2016 with respective totals of 66 and 77. That is a rapid ascent by anyone's standards and his graph remains on a stratospheric trajectory.

A son of small-scale County Meath handler Ger Keane, he has long spoken openly of his desire to be champion. Arguably, the move that did most to set Keane on that path was his switch to Ger Lyons' increasingly prolific stable.

In June 2014, despite having first call on the holders of three champion apprentice titles in Gary Carroll and Emmet McNamara, Lyons nominated Keane – then a 19-year-old claimer – as his stable jockey. That illustrated not just the trainer's faith in the youngster, but also his vision, and in many ways Keane's story this season has been Lyons' too. An emerging force rather than one of the traditional powerhouses of Irish Flat racing, the trainer has repeatedly produced the goods for his stable jockey en route to a career-best campaign of his own.

Kindred spirits in the sense that they are grafters who set themselves ambitious goals and are meticulous in their pursuit of them, Lyons and Keane make for an irresistible combo, not least as Sheikh Fahad Al Thani's go-to men in Ireland.

"I wouldn't be in the position I am if it wasn't for Ger," Keane said. "His horses have improved every year that I've been there, so I'm very lucky."

To a certain extent, both of those clauses are true. However, neither refers to the jockey's own prowess, which is considerable. Keane has blown the riding scene on the Flat wide open in Ireland and he won't stop there. The world is his oyster.

▶▶ Running battle: Colin Keane (right) comes with a late surge on Elegant Pose (below, yellow cap) to catch title rival Pat Smullen on Making Light (red cap) at Naas in October

By Peter Thomas

IT'S official: Sir Michael Stoute is back. Which must come as a relief to the ten-time champion with 15 British Classic winners to his name, although it's equally possible that he never even noticed he'd been away.

The emergence of Ulysses in the upper echelons of European turf racing catapulted Stoute back into the spotlight in 2017, of that there is no doubt, yet for all his smiles after a Juddmonte International Stakes success that followed hard on the heels of victory in the Coral-Eclipse, there was a sense that for the 71-year-old master of Freemason Lodge this was very much business as usual, whatever you may have read to the contrary.

True enough, there have been times of late when Stoute's statistics have dipped some way below the high-water marks of a 45-year career, but suggestions that this has been caused by a sudden failure to recall the best means of getting the most out of a thoroughbred racehorse have never rung true.

Rumours of Stoute's professional decline may have gained traction among the mathematical community, but even the slide from almost £3.5 million in prize-money in the championship season of 2009 to barely £1 million in 2012 couldn't convince the racing aficionado that the man with more than 3,000 winners to his name was suddenly a spent force.

When the insinuations started, Stoute was unmoved. If you haven't got the horses, there's nothing you can do, he shrugged, and if there was a failing in his method it was simply that: he had temporarily failed to get horses good enough to sustain his reputation in a world that increasingly seeks to make sense of the nonsensical by the application of numerical values.

Stoute had lost many of his

▶▶ Continues page 96

CLASS ACT

Ulysses bloomed into a top ten-furlong performer with victories in the Eclipse and International, putting Sir Michael Stoute back in a central role on the grand stage

▶▶ Winning partnership: Jim Crowley celebrates a second Group 1 victory of the year with Ulysses in the Juddmonte International at York

reliable old owner-breeders, seen the Aga Khan depart the scene, been shorn of Arab patronage by the emergence of Godolphin and the death of Maktoum Al Maktoum; he had been undone by the turning of the wheel, but a 45-year survivor has seen it all before and is scared of none of it.

There had been many ups and downs between his first title in Shergar's year of 1981 and his latest in 2009, and the one consoling inevitability for a man of Stoute's talent is that class will out. Steadily the good horses came back to their rightful place on Newmarket's Bury Road, and if the yard had to wait until November to bag its first top-level triumph of 2016 – courtesy of Queen's Trust, owned by those enduring owner-breeders at Cheveley Park Stud, in a thrilling Breeders' Cup Filly and Mare Turf – the 2017 season yielded its bounties a little more readily.

****

AS Ulysses received the admiration of the York crowd after his win in August's Juddmonte International, Stoute was understandably a man in demand. His reluctance to enter into protracted post-race debate is the stuff of legend, but he remains a popular figure with media and public alike and they all wanted to know what it felt like to be back in the big time.

The famous Stoute sidestep couldn't save him this time, but he wasn't about to change the habit of a lifetime when cornered by the press in the immediate aftermath. Yes, it was a good performance, he agreed, but you didn't have to be a genius to spot that Ulysses was going to be a good horse, even a year ago. What's the plan now? We'll go home and have a good think, rather than conjecture pointlessly right now.

It was predictable, if not in keeping with modern methods. Stoute took no notice when he was being talked of as

yesterday's man, and he wasn't about to go overboard now that he was flavour of the month again. To him, this was simply a job well done, the same as the other five International winners, and a pleasure to be helping a good horse do itself justice.

Ulysses had first captured the imagination in May 2016, when his win in a Newbury maiden turned him into the year's Derby 'springer', despite Stoute's familiar refusal to engage in ante-post bluster. Epsom proved to be a damp squib for the son of Galileo, but he ended the campaign as the winner of the Group 3 Gordon Stakes and a creditable six-and-a-quarter-length fourth to Highland Reel in the Breeders' Cup Turf.

Starting the new campaign on the same upward trajectory, he landed the Group 3 Gordon Richards Stakes at Sandown before getting five lengths closer to Highland Reel when third in the Prince of Wales's Stakes at Royal Ascot. Where Ulysses' dam, the Oaks winner Light Shift, had sparked an Indian summer for Stoute's old compadre Sir Henry Cecil, here was

▶▶ *Continues page 98*

EPIC LANDMARKS

Homer's Odyssey describes the ten years' wanderings of Odysseus (or Ulysses, in the Latin) on his way home from the Trojan war and it was entirely fitting that the horse bearing the name of the heroic king should put Sir Michael Stoute back on the roll of honour of two of Europe's top middle-distance races after a decade away.

Ulysses' victories in the Eclipse and International took Stoute to a record six in both races, ending the long wait since Notnowcato gave him a fifth International in 2006 and then a fifth Eclipse in 2007. Stoute now has the most wins of any trainer in the International and shares the record in the Eclipse with early 20th century trainer Alec Taylor jnr. As a measure of Stoute's place in the Newmarket pantheon, Sir Henry Cecil had four winners of each race.

The Group 1 winners that flowed so freely for Stoute in the 1980s and 1990s have reduced to a trickle in this decade and Ulysses' wins ended a significant drought in Europe's flagship events. When Stoute's new middle-distance star took the Eclipse, he was the trainer's first male Group 1 winner in Europe since the great year of 2010 when Workforce landed the Derby and Arc and Harbinger took the King George VI and Queen Elizabeth Stakes.

STOUTE'S ECLIPSE WINNERS	STOUTE'S INTERNATIONAL WINNERS
1993 Opera House	1986 Shardari
1994 Ezzoud	1993 Ezzoud
1996 Pilsudski	1994 Ezzoud
2001 Medicean	1997 Singspiel
2007 Notnowcato (right)	2006 Notnowcato
2017 Ulysses	2017 Ulysses

Looking for
Classic winners...

BBAG graduate WINDSTOSS leads home
a remarkable 1-2-3-4 in the „148. IDEE
Deutsches Derby" (Gr. I)

BBAG-Kauf DSCHINGIS SECRET
winner of the „Grosser Preis von Berlin" (Gr.I)
winner of the „Grosser Hansa-Preis" (Gr. II),
„Gerling Preis" (Gr.II)
„Prix Foy" (Gr.II)

Spring Breeze Up Mixed Sale: 1st June 2018
Premier Yearling Sales: 31st August 2018
Sales & Racing Festival: 19th and 20th October 2018

BBAG   **www.bbag-sales.de**   **BBAG**

another top-class performer in the famous Niarchos colours set to rekindle memories of past glories.

The fruition began in the Eclipse. Although Ulysses was chilly at 7-1 in the betting, in the face of a strong three-year-old challenge from Cliffs Of Moher, Eminent and Barney Roy, the older horse sauntered through a leisurely opening mile under Jim Crowley. All around him, drama and consternation were unfolding, with Coolmore's pacemaker Taj Mahal tacking across to the inside rail after two and a half furlongs, stopping Decorated Knight in his tracks and, as the ripples of chaos spread outwards, almost bringing down his Ballydoyle stablemate Cliffs Of Moher.

Derby-winning jockey Padraig Beggy was handed an eight-day ban for the manoeuvre, but Crowley remained a casual bystander throughout, watching the fun from the rear of the field, perhaps catching a glimpse of Eminent – from whom he had been jocked off in favour of Silvestre de Sousa – attempting to bite a lump out of the luckless Decorated Knight, before easing Ulysses stylishly down the outside to take the lead a furlong out.

If his backers thought the race was over, however, they were mistaken, as James Doyle summoned one last lunge from the resolute Barney Roy that took him to within a whisker of success.

Crowley had learned at Royal Ascot that patience was the key to victory on the strong-travelling colt, and the lesson was reinforced at Sandown, even in victory. "I didn't want to hit the front too soon, and having ridden him at Ascot I knew I could afford to wait a bit," said the man who ultimately hung on to his fourth Group 1 winner by a mere nose, leaving Stoute to sweat on the photograph that confirmed he had equalled Alec Taylor jnr's record of six Eclipses.

After victory had been confirmed, Stoute talked uncharacteristically in terms of the Breeders' Cup, pointing out that Ulysses "has only ever had one blip and that was in the Derby, when he got knocked over twice". The trainer's faith remained intact; he had a proper horse on his hands and was adamant that a step back up to a mile

and a half for the King George was a sound next assignment.

Unfortunately for Stoute, the experiment was spoiled by a full-on deluge at Ascot that he would later describe as "a swamp" – and the not inconsiderable matter of the superstar filly Enable, who beat Ulysses soundly into second place.

The drop back to ten and a half furlongs for the International was less an admission of defeat and more a logical progression through the Pattern to a race Stoute had won five times before. He knew the demands of the York event better than anybody and Crowley, forewarned and forearmed by experience, once again held up his willing partner for a delayed challenge.

This time there was to be none of the kind of drama that had unfolded in the Eclipse, as Ulysses muscled up to the pace set by Cliffs Of Moher and motored past 2,000 Guineas winner and runner-up Churchill and Barney Roy, then stayed on strongly to put the Classic generation in their place once again.

Any lingering doubts about his status as a top-class Group 1 performer had been blasted out of the water. He may not have set the world alight as a three-year-old, but when the dust finally settled on the Knavesmire, even the level-headed

▶▶ Face in the crowd: Sir Michael Stoute at Sandown on Eclipse day when Ulysses gave him a record-breaking sixth victory in the big race; (below) how the Racing Post reacted to the Eclipse and International triumphs

Stoute, with a record sixth International in his pocket, was tempted into a little dreaming.

"I think today's performance would put him up there if not in front of them," he declared, when asked how Ulysses compared to his previous winners Shardari, Ezzoud (twice), Singspiel and Notnowcato. "It all just went so smoothly. There was never a blip, he's become a very professional athlete now and I still think he's as good at 12 furlongs."

Good, yes, but nowhere near as good as Enable, who put him in his place again in the Prix de l'Arc de Triomphe. Crowley sat on Enable's tail all the way into the straight but when the filly turned on the turbo she left him almost four lengths back in third.

"It's another very good, sound race," Stoute said at Chantilly. "I'd prefer Ulysses on a faster surface – you've just got to look at his action – but the filly is too good for him."

At Sandown and York, however, Stoute had shown his mastery once again in two of the signature races where he has enjoyed such success over the decades, and after Cracksman and Enable he had Europe's next-best middle-distance performer. Perhaps there was just a little bit of the great man that felt relieved to be back, even if the gift undoubtedly never left him.

Leading
the field in **concept, design and safety...**

Barriers International have been supplying specialist barrier systems to the sports industry worldwide for over 25 years

Our first clients are still operating with running rails they purchased over two decades ago! Designs are flexible and strong and the rails will withstand the full force of contact, absorb any impact, then return to their original shape. Our systems are installed on racecourses and training centres World-Wide including: Australia, France, India, USA, Germany, Italy, Spain, Japan and UAE.

Barriers International
SPORTS FENCING SPECIALIST

STORM FORCE

Ribchester was the dominant miler in Europe as he thundered to three Group 1 wins but on a couple of occasions he was blown off course

▸▸ Flying start: Ribchester opens his European campaign with Lockinge victory over Lightning Spear

By Mark Storey

WINNING the Lockinge, Queen Anne and Prix du Moulin made 2017 a very good year for Ribchester but it could easily have been a vintage one. Such distinctions often turn on small margins and in Ribchester's case it was a couple of severe storms that quite possibly denied him a perfect five Group 1 wins from five starts in Europe.

Goodwood had its foulest day in a generation when trainer Richard Fahey sent him out for the Sussex Stakes and then Storm Brian blew across Ascot on Champions Day. Both times there was a gale in Ribchester's face, testing ground underneath and a couple of mud-loving rivals waiting to pounce. It was a credit to his courage that he got beaten by just a neck in one race and a length in the other, fighting back after getting headed.

"I'm proud of him but disappointed," were Fahey's words after Ribchester's Queen Elizabeth II defeat to Persuasive on Champions Day, reflecting his admiration for the four-year-old and frustration at what might have been.

Fahey and owners Godolphin have much to be proud of in his latest campaign. In defeat it was his heart and in his three Group 1 wins it was his class, especially at Royal Ascot where he broke the track record in the Queen Anne on the only occasion he encountered quick ground all season.

Ribchester's four-year-old campaign began amid a mood of excitement around the Fahey yard about what the son of Iffraaj might achieve over a mile. Success in the Group 1 Prix Jacques le Marois had been the principal reward for a season of steady improvement in 2016 and further justification for Godolphin's decision to widen their network of trainers by leaving him in Fahey's capable hands after buying him as a juvenile.

Third place in the Dubai Turf over a furlong further than he likes was a respectable enough start in

March and teed him up nicely for the Lockinge Stakes at Newbury, where he was sent off the 7-4 favourite under William Buick.

Things did not immediately go to plan as pacemaker Toscanini missed the break, leaving Buick to take charge of affairs in front. But a field including old rival Galileo Gold, who had mastered Ribchester in the Guineas but not at Deauville the previous year, was blown away as Fahey's star made all to romp home by three and three-quarter lengths from Lightning Spear.

That merited a Racing Post Rating of 126, his best yet, and quotes of 2-1 for a date in the Queen Anne in June. The Newbury performance hardened Ribchester's reputation as a horse short-price punters could put their faith in, an easy-to-spot operator, brave and honest, out in front topped by blue silks. Banker material.

By off time at Royal Ascot he had tightened to 11-10, with Dubai Turf fifth Mutakayyef, reverting to a mile, considered the biggest threat. This time it all went perfectly. Toscanini bolted off in front, Ribchester sat prominently and, in what would become a familiar image as the season unfolded, took the lead two furlongs out. He edged left but it mattered little as he scorched away to win by a length and a quarter from Mutakayyef in course-record time.

The RPR was 125 and Ribchester had cemented his place as Europe's top miler, a status not lost on Fahey. "Ribchester has to be the best horse I've ever trained," he said. "He broke the track record and that's not being disrespectful to the others but he's just exceptional."

In the winner's enclosure there was excited chatter about the prospect of a showdown with dual Guineas hero Churchill in the Sussex Stakes, the first chance for the hottest three-year-old around, who had posted an RPR of 125 in his Irish 2,000 Guineas win at the Curragh, to take on his elders. But first, that same afternoon, Churchill had to take care of the St James's Palace Stakes.

Odds of 1-2 suggested it was a formality for the Aidan O'Brien-trained son of Galileo, But it proved not as he trailed in fourth to Guineas runner-up Barney Roy,

▸▸ *Continues page 102*

the middle leg of an opening-day treble for a Godolphin operation looking to make a statement following the recent departure of chief executive John Ferguson.

It was left to Ballydoyle stablemate Winter, winner of the 1,000 and Irish 1,000 Guineas, to emerge from Berkshire with her reputation enhanced following victory in the Coronation Stakes. But Churchill's Ascot performance, running flat before being eased, had the whiff of a one-off and confidence had grown again as Glorious Goodwood approached.

Godolphin teammate Barney Roy would not be standing in Ribchester's way there, as trainer Richard Hannon instead chose to campaign him over a mile and a quarter, and nor would Winter, who also went up in trip, a move rewarded by victory in the Nassau Stakes.

Goodwood describes itself as the world's most beautiful racecourse and no-one would argue when the sun is shining. But in poor weather it can be foul and Sussex Stakes day was just such an experience. Clerk of the course Seamus Buckley, who retired in October, described that August afternoon and its aftermath as the hardest of his 23 years at the course as 50mm of rain fell in 12 hours.

It was enough to persuade O'Brien to pull Churchill out of the Sussex an hour beforehand, the champion trainer describing the conditions as "extreme", and that left French raider Zelzal to provide the stiffest market opposition to 8-13 shot Ribchester.

The official going was soft but jockeys in earlier races had described it as heavy and that was how it looked as the seven runners slogged through the driving rain. Typically Ribchester led the way, and in scenes familiar to his followers was asked to quicken away and win the race two furlongs from home. But his acceleration was blunted by the ground, cries of "Go on Ribby, go on Ribby!" from his groom on the steps of the Richmond Stand unable to make a difference as the unconsidered seven-year-old Here Comes When swept by to claim a Group 1 win at 20-1 for Andrew Balding.

Ribchester, at one point looking

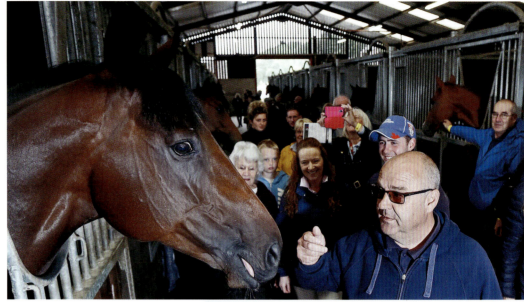

well beaten, rallied to go down by a neck and if there was further comfort for Fahey it came from the Racing Post analysis of the race, which read: "Ability to handle the ground was the only factor, and on the whole this is probably form to put in the bin."

The concern was whether the experience had left a mark and the plan was to wait for the QEII but Fahey felt his stable star was so well that he could tackle the Prix du Moulin first. The soft ground was not ideal but Ribchester toughed it out, racing prominently, taking the lead two furlongs out and doing enough to secure a fourth Group 1 of his career, this time under James Doyle.

The gap to Champions Day was six weeks but the bigger concern was how much the ground might have deteriorated by the third Saturday in October. Ascot's decision two days before not to use their unwatered inner course was followed by downpours that made the track testing as Storm Brian swept in.

This time Churchill did run. Again Ribchester was favourite, again he was up with the leaders and again he led two furlongs out. Here Comes When had nothing to offer this time but the John Gosden-trained filly Persuasive did, angled out for a run by Frankie Dettori and flying past to record a career-high RPR of 121 in victory. Ribchester was beaten but the final 100 yards said plenty about his character as he fought back to get

▶▶ Home and away: Ribchester is the centre of attention with Richard Fahey at the Malton open day in September (top) and in the Royal Ascot winner's enclosure after his Queen Anne triumph

within a length of the winner and finish second, one place ahead of Churchill.

It is logical to ponder whether Ribchester has been committed to the front too soon in his defeats but Fahey says the colt's character has a lot to do with that. "He's just an enthusiastic racehorse," he said after the QEII. "He goes from nought to 35 in four strides and he's the same at home. I've never known a horse like him. He has to go in front because he can't go slow. He's like a supercar, and when you touch the pedal he's gone.

"I think the lads are riding him really well. He just wants to get on with it, and it's not in a free sort of way. He just cannot go slow and we aren't going to change that now."

Given that only Enable and Winter won more Group 1s in Europe than Ribchester in 2017, not too much needs to change.

Be wahou,
be Barrière

B READY + BREAKFAST

Hôtels Barrière Deauville Normandy - France

UP TO -20%*

OFF YOUR ROOM AND BREAKFAST INCLUDED

Exclusively on www.resortbarriere-deauville.com
or +33 (0)2 31 14 39 50

RESORT
BARRIÈRE
DEAUVILLE

ORANGE & GOLD

James Doyle received the late call to ride Big Orange in the Gold Cup at Ascot and grabbed his chance in one of the year's best races

By Scott Burton

THE Gold Cup at Ascot has rediscovered a happy knack of producing sporting theatre of the highest order in recent years and the 2017 edition proved to be a vintage one. This may be one of the longest races in the Flat calendar, supposedly contested by slowboats who cannot hack the pace at middle distances, but it produced one of the most exciting finishes of the year – and one of the best winning rides.

Defending champion Order Of St George, burnished with class enough to have been placed in the 2016 Arc, was brought wide and late by a possessed Ryan Moore in a desperate attempt to run down the hugely popular Big Orange and late stand-in James Doyle. It is doubtful many stayers of the recent past could have resisted Order Of St George's thrust but, to the delight of the packed stands and the delirium of trainer Michael Bell and his team, the 'Big O' just kept finding more.

In the immediate aftermath Bell described the 2017 Gold Cup as "a proper horse race" and lauded his champion for possessing "a heart as big as himself". The trainer's association with the stable favourite is long and deep, as it is for the six-year-old's owner-breeder Bill Gredley, but for Doyle this was his first ride on the strapping gelding. And what a ride.

The call-up had come barely 48 hours earlier, when Frankie Dettori was forced to declare himself unfit for the meeting that means more to him than any other week of the year. Parachuted in on Tuesday morning, to ride what he described as "the people's horse", Doyle felt a huge sense of responsibility. Towards the end of the season, as he reflected on how he made light of that burden with an assured ride, he retained a unique clarity about the 48 hours before the race and, more pertinently still, the four minutes and 22 seconds that defined one of the great races of the year.

Let's go back and ride with him and Big Orange into Royal Ascot folklore . . .

THE CALL-UP For Michael Bell the morning of Tuesday, June 20 marks the moment where months of planning for his stable star, the dual Goodwood Cup winner Big Orange, hit a nasty and unwelcome bump in the road. With declarations for Thursday's Gold Cup looming, he suddenly finds himself without a jockey when Dettori fails to recover from an arm injury. And with a big field nearly guaranteed, the hunt for a top-class replacement will not be easy.

But as trainers can often find, when the race is big enough and the mount up for grabs is classy enough, fortune has a way of finding you. Doyle has already spotted the opportunity.

"I know Tim Gredley [Bill's son, and part-owner] and when I found out I sent him a message to say 'if you're looking for a jockey, I'm your man'," Doyle recalls. "Luckily enough Michael Bell rang me. I think it was between me and Pat Smullen and because I could go and sit on him on Wednesday morning I think that swayed the decision in their minds. I went in on Wednesday morning for a routine canter and it all went from there."

With such a high-profile ride – not to mention the daunting task of defeating Order Of St George, the odds-on favourite – Doyle is not about to rely solely on the pre-race chat before getting the leg-up from Bell on Thursday afternoon.

"I spoke not only to Frankie but to Jamie Spencer, who rode him quite a bit. They both told me not to interfere with him. They said he'd dictate what pace he wanted to go and warned me not to pull him around, to just leave it to him and naturally he would give himself a breather coming up the hill."

THE FIRST MEETING The serious miles on Newmarket Heath are safely logged in Big Orange's legs by the day before the race but for Doyle the chance to get acquainted, to feel the horse beneath him, proves an invaluable aid.

"It was nice just to get to feel his stride pattern and his mannerisms. He's quite a sweet horse with a huge, long stride and he has a way of carrying himself. He's really long – a proper old-fashioned racehorse – and he carries his head quite low and down. When I set off cantering I think I had him on too short a rein and he was tugging me a bit, so I gave him a bit more and he was comfortable. It definitely helped."

THE EARLY STAGES Part of Big Orange's public profile is down to his willingness to go out and do his own running, unencumbered by the actions of others around him. As the clock ticks down to race time, Bell assures the rider that he is under no obligation to

▶ *Continues page 106*

make the running. But the tactics of the Quest For More team mean that, within the first minute of the race, Doyle must make a decision that will have enormous implications when Big Orange goes into uncharted territory in the final half-mile.

"He handled the prelims well and we floated down to the start. We were really pleased that the ground was fast. I had heard Mr [Roger] Charlton might be planning to go forward with Quest For More and use his stride. I just thought we'd see how we were going. Michael told me to have the confidence, if he was happy, just to sit in and take a lead if they were going too fast."

Big Orange breaks well and looks relaxed as he leads the 14-runner field past the stands, Doyle keeping him off the rail for the moment. But decision time arrives soon enough after Jamie Spencer, who knows Big Orange so well, gives a long glance over his shoulder before angling Quest For More across to take the lead.

"As Jamie crossed me he put the brakes on. I tried to stay behind him but Big Orange tried to fight me a bit and the pace really did slacken. I knew I was doing the wrong thing by trying to fight him. When you turn past the stands to run down the hill, if the pace is steady and he's fighting I'm definitely going to be pulling all the way down the hill. I was interfering with him – exactly what I shouldn't be doing – so I elected to pop out and let him swing around. Once he got to the front, the ITV camera van going along on the inside took his mind off things and he really relaxed. Usually horses gather momentum down that hill but he went down at a fairly sensible pace."

THE FINAL BATTLE

Ryan Moore has until now been looking on from the rear of the field but as the runners begin to climb back towards the stands, he moves Order Of St George up

▶ Big heart: Michael Bell with Big Orange and (left) the warrior fights off Order Of St George to win an epic Gold Cup

around his rivals and into a position from which to strike. While last year's St Leger hero Harbour Law is running another huge race, it is now obvious that this is going to be a duel up the Ascot straight between Aidan O'Brien's champion and Bell's warrior.

"I've always been a great believer that you should never try to make ground or use a horse uphill, and coming out of Swinley Bottom I felt we'd gone a reasonable enough gallop to ensure I wouldn't get attacked too early. Out of Swinley Bottom on the rise up to the home turn I just sat against him, tried to steady the race, fill him up and try to save as much energy as possible for the straight.

"When I let him go he quickened up really well and then he was quite lonely going into the last furlong. But when Order Of St George joined me he woke up and boom! He knuckled down well. I know it looked like Order Of St George just ran out of time to get me but, from the two pole to the one, Big Orange was going through the motions and then he surged to the line. It was an amazing feeling because usually horses just drop away. But I could feel him get lower and stretch and really want to win. He's an absolute warrior."

CELEBRATIONS The distance at the line is a short head and for the next few minutes the usual calm restraint of Royal Ascot gives way to scenes of unbridled joy as various members of the Bell and Gredley clans pretty much let it all go: trainer Michael embraces O'Brien, his nephew Oli – on duty for ITV Racing – tears off down the straight after Big Orange, cameras in laboured pursuit, and brother Rupert abandons any shred of impartiality in the TalkSport commentary box, screaming "you beauty!" as Big Orange lunges across the line. For the late substitute on top, the scenes are memorable.

"It was fantastic. I'm quite good friends with Gary and Craig Witheford [the equine behaviour experts] and a couple of weeks later Craig told me about walking back in ten paces behind Big Orange. He said the occasion and the reception we got made the hairs on the back of his neck stand up.

"I tweeted a picture of Big Orange afterwards saying it had been amazing to play even a small part in a fantastic day. I did the steering and that was literally all.

"It's one of the most famous, traditional races in the calendar and a great race to win and to knock off your CV. I've met the Queen plenty of times but to receive the trophy from her made it an unbelievable day, considering I didn't know I was riding him until the Tuesday morning."

ORDER OUT OF THE ORDINARY

Order Of St George lost out to Big Orange in the Gold Cup but in his second Ascot battle of the year he snatched an extraordinary victory from the jaws of defeat.

Aidan O'Brien's five-year-old was close enough in fourth straightening for home in the Group 2 British Champions Long Distance Cup in October but almost immediately found himself outpaced by Torcedor and Mount Moriah. Wandering under pressure, Ryan Moore's mount gave Duretto a nudge and was still only fourth entering the final furlong, at which point Torcedor looked home and dry, but then he surged to the front in the last 100 yards to win by half a length.

"He's unbelievably tough and hardy, and Ryan gave him a brilliant ride," O'Brien said. "He never stops. In every race he's ever run in he's always finishing. We saw the same thing in the Gold Cup. Sometimes the line comes too quick, but he doesn't stop."

This was a reversal of fortune for Order Of St George from his short-head defeat by Big Orange, who was a well-beaten 11th on this occasion, and completed another good campaign. His best performance came in the Group 1 Irish St Leger, where he left Torcedor trailing nine lengths behind in second, and he followed that with fourth place to Enable in the Prix de l'Arc de Triomphe, having been third in 2016.

"I'm hoping he stays in training. Nobody's told me that he doesn't," O'Brien said at Ascot, and top of the agenda would be a return there for a third run in the Gold Cup, which Order Of St George won in 2016. Among his opponents could be Torcedor, who was "possibly ten pounds above his previous best" in the Long Distance Cup according to jockey Colm O'Donoghue, and Ascot third Stradivarius.

Having won the Goodwood Cup from Big Orange and finished third in the St Leger, the three-year-old Stradivarius was the newest name to make a mark in a staying division that once again provided competitive and exciting sport.

And in Order Of St George and Big Orange, it is a division that continues to produce the sort of durable performers who endear themselves so readily to racing fans with their battling qualities.

▶▶ Ready for action: Order Of St George and Ryan Moore head out on to the track for the Irish St Leger

IN THE PICTURE

The Queen in a race to make Royal Ascot starting line-up

A CONVULSIVE year in politics led to business and pleasure mixing for the Queen in a hectic Royal Ascot week after the state opening of parliament was scheduled on the second day of racing.

The monarch, who has never missed a day of Royal Ascot since her coronation in 1953, gave the Queen's Speech in the House of Lords, finishing at 11.46am, before making the 30-mile journey from central London to Ascot for the start of racing at 2.30pm.

It was a tight squeeze to fit in both events after the clash was caused by prime minister Theresa May's decision to call a snap general election for June 8 and the fallout from the unexpected result of a hung parliament. The state opening of the new parliament had been scheduled for Monday, June 19, the day before the start of Royal Ascot, but had to be delayed while the Conservative Party negotiated with the Democratic Unionist Party to agree the legislative programme set out in the Queen's Speech.

Much of the usual pomp and ceremony was abandoned and for the first time since 1974 the Queen gave the speech wearing 'day dress' and a hat rather than robes of state and the imperial state crown.

Having worn purple for the morning formalities, the Queen changed to yellow for her sporting afternoon and arrived in time to lead the traditional carriage procession before racing. The Duke of Edinburgh was absent, however, as he had been taken to hospital with an infection the previous evening. The Queen was accompanied in the first carriage by the Prince of Wales, the Duchess of Cornwall and the Lord Fellowes, her former private secretary.

Dress, as ever, was a key ingredient of Royal Ascot and on the first day sweltering temperatures led the racecourse to relax its usual strict code. Normally men in the Royal Enclosure must wear black or grey morning dress with a waistcoat, tie and a top hat, but for the first time the jackets rule was not enforced after entry. The hottest spell of June weather since 1976 also led Ascot to deploy water barrels around the racecourse and on the walkways for horses, and thankfully no major problems were reported.

On the final day there were high hopes of a 24th Royal Ascot winner for the Queen when Dartmouth was sent off 9-4 favourite for the Hardwicke Stakes, but it was not to be. The Sir Michael Stoute-trained five-year-old, who had beaten Highland Reel in a thriller the previous year, was only fourth this time as victory went to Highland Reel's year-younger brother Idaho.

Picture: MIKE HEWITT (GETTY IMAGES)

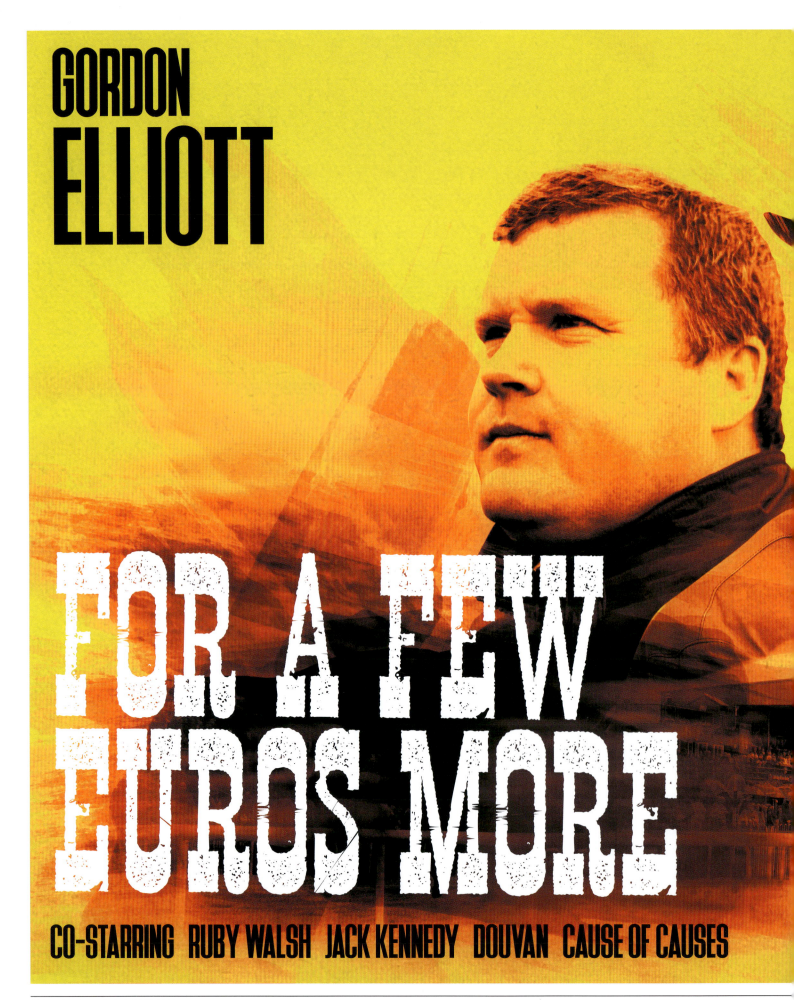

GORDON ELLIOTT

FOR A FEW EUROS MORE

CO-STARRING RUBY WALSH JACK KENNEDY DOUVAN CAUSE OF CAUSES

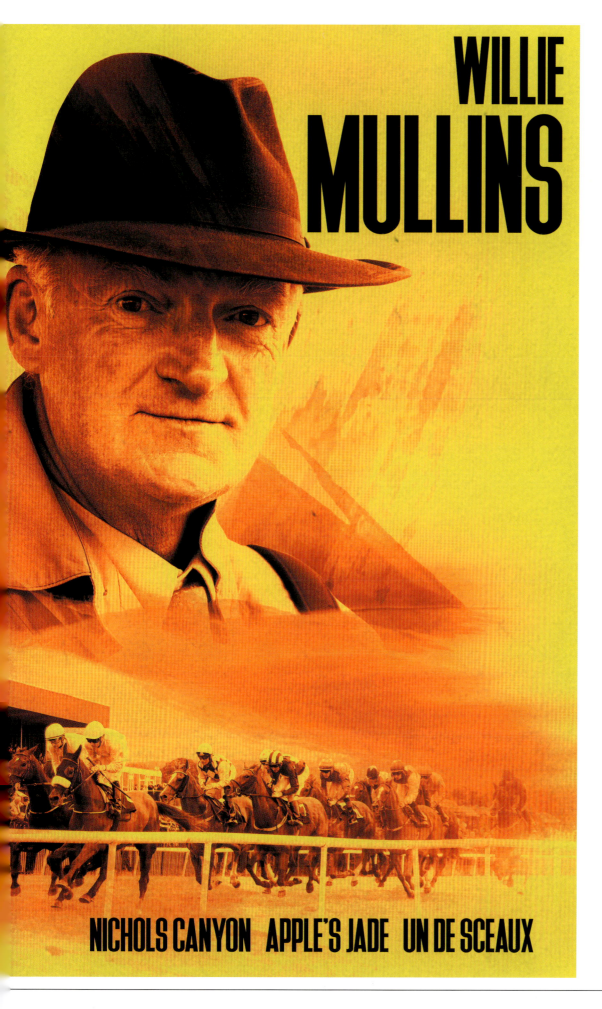

WILLIE MULLINS

NICHOLS CANYON   APPLE'S JADE   UN DE SCEAUX

Willie Mullins v Gordon Elliott was an epic battle of the 2016-17 jumps season complete with intrigue, plot twists and dramatic shootouts

By Steve Dennis

IT was a fresh, warm day, the first of May, the promise of spring bringing that old and irresistible feeling that anything was possible. The sheriff rocked back in his chair, feet on the table, gun on safety, hat tilted over his eyes. His silver star sparkled in a sunbeam, and he gave a happy sigh.

Things had been quiet in his little town for nine years, and he liked it that way. He began to think about having a little sleep, but just then he heard footsteps coming his way, and someone shouting. "Sheriff Willie, Sheriff Willie, El Gordino is coming with many, many horses."

It was his deputy, Rico. Sheriff Willie reached reflexively for his gun. By the time Rico burst through the door he was on his feet. "Sheriff Willie, it is El Gordino. He riding into town, he say he have enough ammunition to blow you clean away. He say this town need a new sheriff." The window was open wide, and from the street came the crackle of gunfire. A muscle flickered along the sheriff's jawline.

"El Gordino wants a fight, does he? Then that's what he'll get. Tell him Willie boy is here, and waiting."

▸▸ *Continues page 112*

****

ON MAY 1, 2016, Willie Mullins and Gordon Elliott started the Irish jumps season on level terms, no winners, no prize-money, and the two gunslingers wouldn't call it quits until April 29, 2017 when they both had more than four million euros in the bag. Their duel rumbled on throughout the campaign, now in the headlines, now in the small print, it would spread further afield and colour vividly the most important week of the jumping year, it would be aided and abetted by their main jockeys Ruby Walsh and Jack Kennedy, it would involve private feuds and public perception. It was quite a ride.

The purest distillation of their struggle, the moonshine that left everyone a little dizzy, was their rivalry at the Cheltenham Festival, which see-sawed this way and that before it was decided not by their winners but by their losers. The pair simply loaded their six-shooters and came out firing, and everything else got caught in the crossfire.

Elliott pushed all his chips into the middle of the table on day one, the serial reprobate Labaik getting him off to a great start in the opener. Later that afternoon Apple's Jade and Tiger Roll gave him three wins to Mullins' none, the man from Closutton's woe compounded by the eclipse of his headline stars Melon (runner-up to Labaik) and Vroum Vroum Mag and Limini (second and third to Apple's Jade). And Apple's Jade herself . . . well, that's another story.

The following afternoon Cause Of Causes and Fayonagh made the scoreline 5-0 in Elliott's favour; surely it was game over? Elliott fielded those questions with his habitual bonhomie – no it wasn't over yet, there was a long way to go, all to play for. We thought he was being polite. The following day we saw what he meant.

Mullins reloaded, took aim, hit the mark. Not once but four times, a crazy haul on a crazy day when the phrase 'forget everything you thought you knew' held particular resonance. Yorkhill, Un De Sceaux, Nichols Canyon, Let's Dance – Mullins had won four races in a day at Cheltenham before but not when he needed them quite so urgently as this.

By nightfall it was 5-4 and all to play for, just as Elliott forecast.

Friday dawned, and the show went on. Mullins levelled the score with Arctic Fire, then took the lead with Penhill, six unanswered victories turning the tables on Elliott in scarcely believable fashion. But Elliott had one last bullet to fire, and in the second-last race of the week narrowed his eyes, slowed his breathing, squeezed the trigger and made it count, Champagne Classic tying the scores at 6-6. On countback, Elliott's three runners-up gave him the Cheltenham crown over Mullins' two second places.

But yet – if the Mullins-trained Bapaume had finished second in the Triumph Hurdle instead of third behind the Elliott-trained runner-up Mega Fortune, the verdict would have gone the other way. The margin between Mega Fortune and Bapaume? A short head.

There, in microcosm, was

▶▶ Stinging blow: Apple's Jade (centre), one of the Gigginstown contingent switched from Willie Mullins to Gordon Elliott, beats erstwhile stablemates Vroum Vroum Mag (left) and Limini in the Mares' Hurdle on the first day of the Cheltenham Festival; (below) Arctic Fire strikes for Mullins on the final day

the season for Elliott and Mullins, a 12-month battle of marginal gains and losses that seemed to even out until the final analysis found a speck of evidence to tilt the scales this way or that. But as the spaghetti strands of the season wound around the two protagonists and drew us all in, three episodes stood out from the busy background. If for Mullins the Cheltenham Festival was the Bad (although describing six winners thus jars a little), then what happened during September was certainly the Ugly.

****

AFTER the Galway festival, at which Elliott won the Plate and Mullins the Hurdle, the reigning champion had a lead of just over €50,000 from his rival. On September 14, Elliott went back to the top of the table after victory in the Kerry National with Wrath Of Titans, an eerie augury of the next chapter in this unputdownable narrative.

▶▶ *Continues page 114*

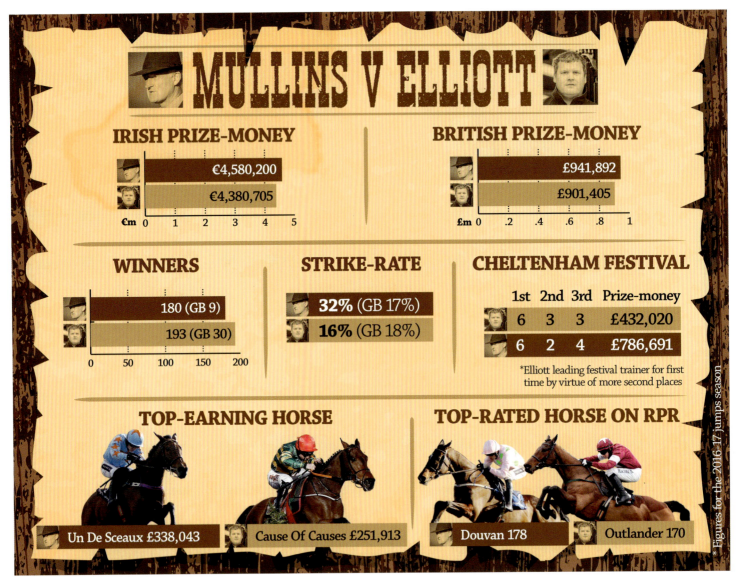

MULLINS V ELLIOTT

IRISH PRIZE-MONEY

€4,580,200

€4,380,705

€m 0   1   2   3   4   5

BRITISH PRIZE-MONEY

£941,892

£901,405

£m 0   .2   .4   .6   .8   1

WINNERS

180 (GB 9)

193 (GB 30)

0   50   100   150   200

STRIKE-RATE

32% (GB 17%)

16% (GB 18%)

CHELTENHAM FESTIVAL

	1st	2nd	3rd	Prize-money
	6	3	3	£432,020
	6	2	4	£786,691

*Elliott leading festival trainer for first time by virtue of more second places

TOP-EARNING HORSE

Un De Sceaux £338,043

Cause Of Causes £251,913

TOP-RATED HORSE ON RPR

Douvan 178

Outlander 170

*Figures for the 2016-17 jumps season

Two weeks later Mullins and one of his major owners parted company; the fallout was excessive.

Michael O'Leary removed all the 60 horses he had in training with Mullins and dispersed them around Ireland, with Elliott taking delivery of around 20 including Gold Cup prospect Don Poli and the star mare Apple's Jade. Other big names moving house were Valseur Lido, Outlander and Petit Mouchoir. The reason generally accepted for O'Leary's decision was Mullins raising his training fees, something he had not done for ten years.

"I'm not willing to try to maintain the standards I have without putting the fees up," Mullins said. "Losing the horses is a blow but it is also a challenge. Whoever gets the horses will present a big challenge to me

being champion trainer."

So as the core season began to find its stride, Mullins found himself shorn of a considerable portion of his stable strength. The horses were gone; within weeks the outstanding three-time Cheltenham winner Vautour was gone too, the victim of a freak and fatal accident in a paddock. That was a cruel blow, sharp and keen, to put with the ongoing dulling pain that was the continuing absence of Champion Hurdle winners Faugheen and Annie Power, who wouldn't see a racetrack all season.

These are things that happen to every trainer, naturally. Owners move, horses get injured. Yet all Mullins' troubles came at once, and at the

▶ Big earner: Outlander after his Lexus Chase victory for Gordon Elliott

same time his most dangerous rival for the title began to hit top gear on the racecourse. By November 1 Elliott was more than €250,000 ahead, and a month later he was twice that much in front (€1,913,832 to €1,405,507). Three days later he sent out Apple's Jade to win the Grade 1 Hatton's Grace Hurdle at Leopardstown; that must have stung Mullins. At the end of the month Elliott had the forecast in the Grade 1 Lexus Chase with Outlander and Don Poli, both former Mullins inmates. The Mullins-trained Djakadam was third. Insult was piled upon injury.

Added to which, the sheer quantity of horses emerging from Cullentra House made it plain that if it came down to a numbers game there would be only
▶ Continues page 116

Down Royal™ Racecourse

RACECARD 2018

Date	Raceday	Entrance Price	Time (approx)	Card Type
Wed 31st Jan	Race Day	£10	1.15-4.15pm	NH
Sat 17th Mar	Daily Mirror St Patrick's Day Race Meeting	£12	2.25-5.50pm	NH
Mon 7th May	Daily Mirror May Day Meeting	£12	2.20-5.20pm	NH
Fri 25th May	Barclay Communications Race Evening	£10	5.30-8.30pm	Mixed
Fri 22nd Jun	Tote Galway Plate Trial Race Evening - Summer Festival, Day 1	£12	5.45-9.00pm	NH
Sat 23rd Jun	Magners Ulster Derby - Summer Festival, Day 2	£15	2.10-5.15pm	Flat
Fri 27th July	Magners Race Evening	£10	5.50-8.45pm	Flat
Fri 31st Aug	Musgrave Retail Partners NI Race Day	£10	4.40-7.40pm	NH
Fri 14th Sept	West Coast Cooler Race Meeting	£10	4.00-7.00pm	Flat
Fri 2nd Nov	DR Festival of Racing - Day 1	£12	1.05-4.15pm	NH
Sat 3rd Nov	DR Festival of Racing - Day 2	£15	12.45-4.15pm	NH
Wed 26th Dec	Boxing Day Race Meeting	£12	12.30-3.30pm	NH

www.downroyal.com

Tel: 028 9262 1256

one winner. Elliott would eventually have 1,234 runners during the 2016-17 season, while Mullins saddled 'just' 571.

All that was keeping Mullins in the hunt was his exceptional strike-rate, at 32 per cent twice as efficient as Elliott, like the thin blue line of the Seventh Cavalry defending the fort against wave upon wave of Sioux. He had to make his bullets count and, with Douvan, Min, Vroum Vroum Mag and Un De Sceaux on his side, he kept the gap to Elliott from opening further, staunched the bleeding.

Such was the domination of the big two – in the Grade 1 Deloitte Novice Hurdle, for example, nine of the ten runners were trained by either Mullins (six) or Elliott (three) – that questions were asked about whether it was healthy for Irish racing to function on such a binary model, especially when small fields and vast resources led to the maroon and white colours of O'Leary's Gigginstown House Stud adorning nearly all the runners in certain races (all four in the Grade 3 Naas Directors Novice Chase).

All the while the gunfight rumbled on behind the scenes, occasionally exploding into a fireworks display when Elliott outdrew Mullins, as he did in, say, the Grade 1 Lawlor's Hotel Novice Hurdle with Death Duty beating Turcagua, or when Mullins did the same to Elliott in, say, the Red Mills Chase when Ballycasey beat Clarcam. Six of one, half a dozen of the other, and the sheriff and the rebel kept reloading their six-shooters. Who would misfire first?

****

AT the beginning of April, Elliott was €400,000 ahead (€3,680,117 to €3,274,112) and it became clear that only the Punchestown festival would settle the matter. It would be close, because the lesson of Cheltenham had taught us that – like a hustler at a Wild West poker table – each man could pull aces from anywhere. As Punchestown week dawned Elliott was 1-5 to prevail, Mullins 100-30. Everyone with any sense simply barricaded themselves into the saloon to wait until the gunsmoke cleared.

Mullins ate into the deficit on the first day with Grade 1 winner Cilaos

Emery, Elliott bit back a day later with Champagne Classic and Fayonagh, but now there was just €200,000 in it. At the end of day three the gap had shrunk to €130,000. Mullins was running Elliott to earth, but was he also running out of time?

As it happened, all he needed was 35 minutes on day four, and a little help from his deputy. When Wicklow Brave won the Punchestown Champion Hurdle in the hands of his son Patrick, Mullins was in front in the title race for the first time since September. With stablemate Arctic Fire sweetening the pot in third, Mullins finally had clear water.

"I didn't

realise we had gone in front until someone told me as I was coming off the stands," Mullins said. "It was the last thing on my mind. Patrick winning this means more to me."

It wasn't the last thing on anyone else's mind. Just over half an hour later Mullins jnr got Bacardys home by a short head in the Champion Novice Hurdle to give his old man another huge leg-up towards the top of the tree. Uproar, and a lead of €90,000.

The irony of one of the horses he'd lost coming through to deny Mullins at the last gasp was lost on no-one, so when Apple's Jade hacked up for Elliott in the Mares Champion Hurdle on the final

day there were plenty of wise old heads nodding.

But Mullins had mopped up all the place money down to fifth to defray matters, and when Bapaume – who, remember, could have garnered his trainer the Cheltenham crown had his nose been just a little longer – came home in style in the Champion Four-Year-Old Hurdle it meant he could get the party started. Open Eagle's victory later on the card was a bonus.

It was over. Mullins had won his tenth consecutive championship (11th in all) by €200,000, with Elliott's only consolation a final tally of 193 winners, a joint-record – with Mullins.

"Gordon has been magnificent all season and has been a gentleman about the whole thing," said Mullins, as relief crept into his voice. "It's been

a funny season for us and I can't say I enjoyed it all, but we got there in the end."

It meant a lot, of course, just as it meant a lot to Elliott, the Crisp to Mullins' inevitable Red Rum, that he was collared in sight of the finish line. It had been, by a colossal margin, his best season, yet it hadn't been quite good enough.

"I was broken-hearted leaving here on Friday night when I realised our chances of winning the title were all but gone," he admitted. "Willie is a legend but maybe we'll top the list next season. We'll be starting off the new season at Down Royal on Monday."

****

AS the dust settled, Sheriff Willie blew the smoke from his shooting iron, did that twirly gun/finger thing

▶▶ Late flourish: (clockwise from left) Willie Mullins finally seals a tenth trainers' title in a row with wins at the Punchestown festival for Wicklow Brave, Bacardys, Bapaume (pink) and Open Eagle (blue star on cap); Mullins celebrates with Ruby Walsh (centre bottom) and holds his trophy (facing page)

he'd learned from Jesse James and had El Gordino dragged off to the jailhouse. He was still sheriff, his star still gleamed.

He put his gun away, hung his hat on the hook and sank back into his chair. He remembered the ease and grace he'd felt on May 1 and found it hard to believe that only a year had passed. Then his eyelids drooped, and his head slowly fell forward until . . . "Sheriff Willie, Sheriff Willie!" It was Rico again.

"El Gordino, he escape! Meester O'Leary, he send him a cake, and there was a file in it. The hombre, he saw through the bars – he on the loose again. He vow to come back and get you next time!"

A huge smile spread across Sheriff Willie's face. "Well, Rico, a man's gotta do what a man's gotta do. And he knows where to find me."

By Nick Pulford

MARCH 18, 2017, the day after Sizing John's Gold Cup, and 350 miles to the north of Cheltenham thoughts are focused on the next big monument in the jumps season. With exactly three weeks to the Grand National, it is work morning at Lucinda Russell's Kinross yard and One For Arthur is let out into a field for a few moments of relaxation before getting down to the business of the day. Then the alarm is sounded: the National third favourite has lost a shoe.

This is serious. Every day counts so close to the big race and any interruption to One For Arthur's training routine is potentially calamitous. "It was a big work day for us and there was a huge panic," Russell recalls. "Everyone was trying to get hold of my farrier, Greg Crawford, but he'd gone to Dundee to be fitted for a suit for Aintree. He was in the changing room and his phone was going off. When he saw my number come up on his phone he knew it must be something about Arthur. He

answered immediately, half in and half out of his suit, then got back to the stables as soon as he could and put the shoe back on. Arthur had to wait an hour and go back into the next lot, but Greg saved the day."

The story, as we know, had a happy ending when One For Arthur bounded up the long finishing straight at Aintree to claim Grand National glory after a brilliant stalking ride by Derek Fox and, with the comfort of the record books having been written, Russell can recount the near ruination of the dream with good humour.

But the episode speaks volumes about the close-knit team she and Peter Scudamore, her partner in life as well as training, are so proud to have around them and the tightrope that any yard – especially one of the smaller ones for whom leading chances don't grow on trees – has to walk in the run-up to a big race.

October 4, 2017, and there are just over three weeks to go until One For Arthur's first appearance of the new season at Kelso in the 3m2f handicap chase he won so impressively 12 months earlier to

set the ball rolling towards Aintree. It had been decided in the summer to follow the same path to the National – Kelso, the Becher Chase at Aintree and the Classic Chase at Warwick – but disaster strikes on this October day and this time there is nothing that can be done to save the situation.

The next day Russell reveals on her website what has happened. "After his first piece of work, he was found to have disrupted fibres in his right fore superficial flexor tendon. He will miss the rest of this season," she says. This time the tightrope had not held the weight of their dreams, but that only served to illustrate how blessed they had been to make it to Aintree in the spring and taste National glory.

April 8, 2017 – that's the date they'll always remember. Nobody can take that away from them.

****

UNDERSTANDABLY, given what was to transpire in October, Russell fretted endlessly about One For Arthur in the 12 weeks between the impressive Classic Chase win at Warwick in January that marked him out as a leading

National contender and his date with destiny at Aintree. She knew a great opportunity lay in front of them, but any number of potential pitfalls too. "You'd go away from the yard and you'd think 'what happens if he gets a splint, what happens if he's lame, what happens if he's coughing?' And then you'd come back into the yard and go into his stable and he's such a noble, strong horse and he'd be standing there saying 'look, I'm fine, don't worry about it'."

More reassurance came ten days before the National when One For Arthur did his final serious prep under work rider Erin Walker. "Scu went up to watch and I was back at the yard, just thinking 'please come back sound, this is the last piece of serious work'. They came back into the yard and
▸ Continues page 120

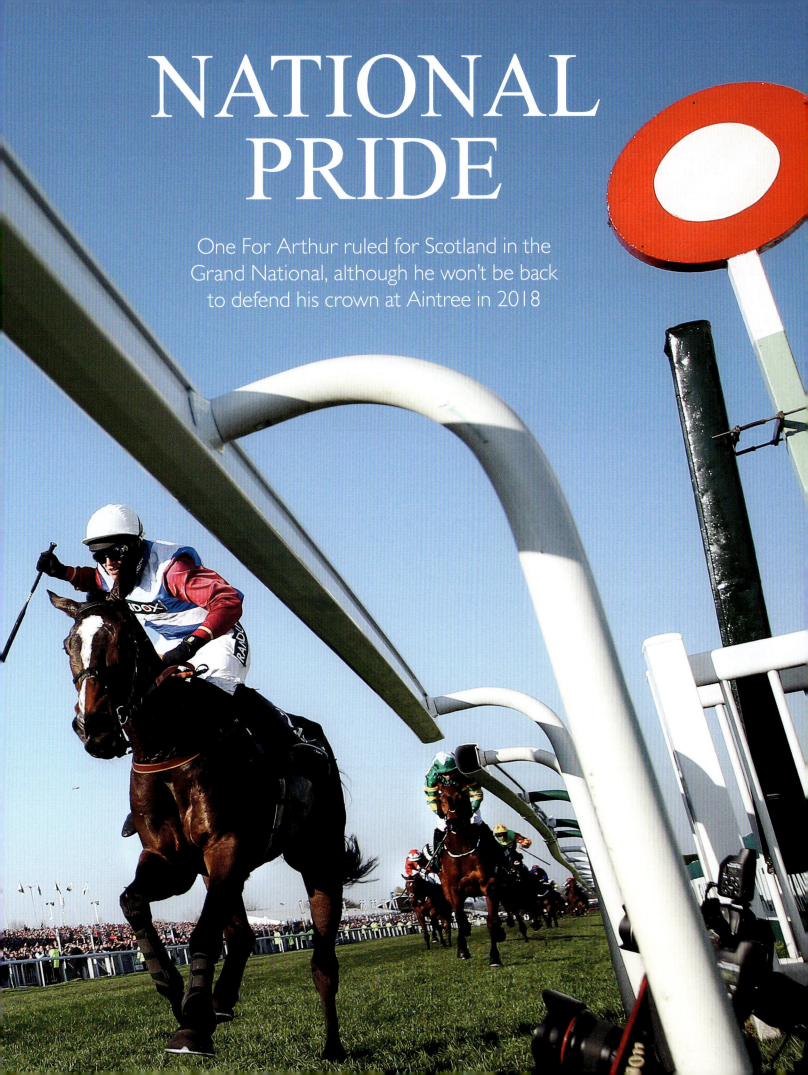

NATIONAL PRIDE

One For Arthur ruled for Scotland in the Grand National, although he won't be back to defend his crown at Aintree in 2018

ONE FOR . . . FRIENDSHIP

One For Arthur's National was a triumph for old-fashioned virtues: friendship, loyalty and the stamina of the traditional staying chaser.

The friendship belonged to owners Belinda McClung and Deborah Thomson, known as the Two Golf Widows as their other halves spend so much time golfing. The pair, who have been involved in racehorses individually over the years, are school pals who firmed up their friendship and went into ownership together to such great effect after "a few too many gins at Kelso".

The loyalty came when Derek Fox broke his wrist and was touch and go to recover in time for the National. Richard Johnson was put on standby but as Lucinda Russell said: "Fair play to the owners, there was no doubt in their minds that if Derek was fit he would have the ride. In an age when people can get their heads turned so quickly, it's nice there are some people who have loyalty."

And then there was One For Arthur himself. The Russell yard has built its reputation on staying chasers and the National was half in everyone's minds when he was purchased as a four-year-old for £60,000 at Cheltenham. "He won a few races over hurdles but we always knew he was going to be a chaser," Thomson said. "He's a fabulous jumper and he stays. We always hoped One For Arthur would be a National horse in the making."

With One For Arthur coming into his own over four and a quarter miles and Fox producing the ride of his life, friendship and loyalty had the ultimate reward.

▸▸National hero: (above from left) Lucinda Russell with One For Arthur; the Russell team line up with the Grand National winner; Derek Fox after his superb winning ride; (below) owners Belinda McClung (left) and Deborah Thomson; (below right) travelling head girl Jaimie Duff leads One For Arthur

I was anxious and asked Erin if he was okay, and she said 'listen, I can't believe it, that's the best I've ever felt him go'. And the relief floods over you, that not only is he sound but actually he's getting better."

The horse was ready, but the news wasn't so good for the jockey. On March 9, Fox – One For Arthur's regular partner both on the racetrack and the gallops – broke his wrist and dislocated his shoulder in a fall at Carlisle. He had just four weeks to prove his fitness for the ride of his life or lose his place in the saddle, with champion jockey Richard Johnson put on standby by Russell.

As One For Arthur completed his final serious gallop, Fox was still hard at work with the physios at Jack Berry House, the Injured Jockeys Fund rehabilitation centre in Malton. On medical advice he had left the wrist out of plaster, but it was still touch and go. On the Saturday before the National he was reunited with One For Arthur for a steady canter, but it wasn't until the Monday that he

received medical clearance to return to race-riding and the Wednesday before he competed again on the racetrack.

That same evening Russell and Scudamore rolled into Aintree in the campervan they had bought for the trainer's 50th birthday the year before. It has never been put to use for a holiday yet but it comes in handy on longer racing trips and at Aintree it gave them an on-site base for a little socialising and a lot of track walking. The concern now was the ground and, with Wednesday having been a drying day and more of the same forecast, it was felt that conditions might become too quick for One For Arthur.

"We walked the track on the Wednesday night, we walked the track on the Thursday morning and we kept walking it," Russell says. "We'd always agreed if it was good to firm we wouldn't run him. Good we were okay about, good to soft was fine, but we thought he wouldn't run as well as he would do on soft ground."

By Grand National day the official going was good to soft and Russell was happy. "Aintree had done a fantastic job and it was safe," she says. One For Arthur had slipped a little in the pecking order – he was now fifth choice in the betting at 14-1 behind 8-1 favourite Blaklion, Definitely Red (10-1), Pleasant Company (11-1) and Vieux Lion Rouge (12-1), the mount

of Scudamore's son Tom – but he was still well fancied.

"We decided to have a press day the week before and when I look back now at what I said about Arthur's chances I sound so cocky, I sound terrible," Russell says. "But when you have that belief . . ."

****

FOX warned in the Racing Post on raceday that "I'm very much aware it's possible I'll be further back than most Grand National winners come from" and he was true to his word. Anyone who had backed One For Arthur, whether on form or his name, would have had trouble locating him the first time round. As they galloped away from Becher's on the second circuit, 30 of the 40 starters were still standing and One For Arthur barely had a handful behind him.

Definitly Red was one of the departed but up front Blaklion, Pleasant Company and Vieux Lion Rouge were stalking the leaders Rogue Angel and Roi Des Francs, both in the Gigginstown colours. Fox could feel he had plenty of horse underneath him – "he took me there so easily," he said later – and Russell could see it as she watched the race on a TV monitor in a private box in the grandstand. By the Canal Turn, two fences after Becher's, Derek and Arthur were on the move.

"All you hope for once the race starts is that he stays safe and he doesn't run into any bad luck," Russell says. "When he jumped the Canal Turn he jumped past horses and I could see then he was travelling so smoothly. I knew that the last mile for him would be the easiest mile, whereas for some of the other horses it would be the hardest mile, and I was very optimistic at that point."

Fox sensed this was the moment. "After the Canal Turn my blood was up and I thought 'this is a horserace and I'd better get into it'. I really squeezed him and it looked like he'd just jumped in." He was 13th five out, up to 11th by the next and a little
▶ *Continues page 122*

ONE FOR . . . TEAMWORK

Even as she basked in Aintree glory amid a welter of media questions, Lucinda Russell was quick to say it was not all about her. "I'm the figurehead and I'm here saying what's going on, but actually it's everyone back home who has done so much. We've got a fantastic team behind us."

They were not empty words, and just one example of the camaraderie at the stable headed by Russell and partner Peter Scudamore came when travelling head girl Jaimie Duff was presented with her trophy for her part in One For Arthur's triumph. The trainer explains: "Jaimie travelled him down and led him up at the races, but she gave her trophy away to Ailsa McClung, the girl who looks after him at home. It was a very kind gesture." Ailsa is the stepdaughter of Belinda McClung, one of the Two Golf Widows who own the National winner.

Russell, who started training in 1995 having come from a show jumping and eventing background, adds: "When I started training I knew nothing about racing, not even what a handicap mark was. We've built up the yard and the team around us and that's what makes it so close-knit. That really means something to us."

One of the more recent additions to the team is assistant trainer Jamie Turnbull, who is credited by Russell as having brought about improvements that helped pave the way to One For Arthur's success. "He has put some really good systems into place and been a really good foil for Scu and myself," she says.

The bonds that knit the yard run deep and a much-missed member of Russell's team is never forgotten. At the yard is a tree planted in memory of Campbell Gillies, the stable's promising young jockey who died in a holiday accident shortly after Cheltenham Festival victory on Russell's Brindisi Breeze in 2012. "Of course our thoughts go back to Campbell and his family, and it's great that his sister Rita still works for us," Russell said the day after the National. "I think he'd be very proud of us."

closer again at the third-last. Crossing the Melling Road and turning into the straight, One For Arthur cruised up to the leaders and was second by the time Fox "winged" the second-last.

The 24-year-old jockey tried to contain himself and his bull-strong mount. "I took a small pull but could see the McManus colours [on Cause Of Causes] starting to pick up to my inner and while I tried to be patient I couldn't resist any longer." He pushed on and led by a length over the last. "The racket from the stands is unbelievable and almost pushes you back. I saw him flicking his ears and kept him right up to it. It's not over until it's over."

When it was over, One For Arthur had won by four and a half lengths from Cause Of Causes with Saint Are third and Blaklion fourth. Scotland had its second National winner – 38 years after Rubstic. "I'm so proud of the horse. He jumped fantastically and Derek gave him a great ride," the trainer said. "He has done us proud, he has done Scotland proud and he has done everyone at the yard proud."

****

BACK home was Walker, who had done such important work with One For Arthur but was unable to go to Aintree. Husband Barry was on duty as a fireman, so she was looking after their children, 11-year-old Emily and one-year-old Logan, at their home in Abernethy.

Along with other family members they watched on television, and Walker said: "It was hard to pick him out for the first circuit, but Derek was awesome. He's so patient and knows how to ride that horse. We were really nervous, but when he won there wasn't a dry eye in the house. Emily was screaming with us and Logan was clapping because we were clapping."

The celebrations of those associated with the yard had been in full swing for hours at the Thistle Hotel in Milnathort when One For Arthur arrived home around midnight to a hero's welcome from the revellers. Back in Liverpool there was also a rapturous reception for the owners and their partners, along with Fox and the trophy, when they went out into the city for what was described as "the traditional Liverpool Grand National party". Colin Dempster, the partner of Deborah Thomson, one of the Two Golf Widows who own One For Arthur, reported the following morning: "We walked into the Malmaison Hotel in Liverpool and Derek came in with us with the trophy and got a standing ovation. I think we drank most of the champagne in Liverpool last night." The trophy, as well as the drinkers,

▶▶Crowd-puller: the National effect is evident in the large turnout to see One For Arthur at Lucinda Russell's Kinross yard the day after his Aintree triumph

may have been a little the worse for wear by the end of the night.

That was all part of the 'National effect' and Russell has felt its force ever since. "One of the things I've noticed is the reception you get from people, even from outside racing. When they find out you've trained a Grand National winner their reaction is 'oh my goodness!' – it really means something to everyone. It's still a unique race and I'm extremely proud to have won it."

That's something that can never be taken from One For Arthur's connections, even if the opportunity to defend his crown in 2018 has been snatched away.

VICENTE'S SCOTTISH REPEAT

The tragic death of Many Clouds left a hole in the life of Trevor Hemmings and in his racing string, which the most successful owner in the modern-day history of the Grand National partially filled with the purchase of 2016 Scottish Grand National winner Vicente.

A fourth Aintree victory for the Hemmings colours was the aim a month after the purchase but the 16-1 shot proved unable to add his name to Hedgehunter, Ballabriggs and Many Clouds, making an ignominious course debut by crashing out at the first fence.

The early exit meant he could have another crack at the Scottish National two weeks later and Vicente became the first back-to-back winner since Andoma in 1984-85 with a brave neck victory over Cogry, conceding 18lb to the runner-up.

Aintree was disappointing but Ayr made up for it. "I had to replace the lovely Many Clouds," Hemmings said. "This was the horse I got and he has done me proud. This has justified it."

RANDOX
HEALTH

Proud sponsors of
The Randox Health Grand National

WORLD'S MOST ADVANCED HEALTH SCREEN

Includes up to 350 results, private consultations & repeat testing

EVERYWOMAN

EVERYMAN

SIGNATURE

We have more tests than anyone else

Search Randox Health • 0800 2545 130

Many Clouds died at Cheltenham in January, moments after a brave victory over Thistlecrack. At Oliver Sherwood's Lambourn yard the pain is finally giving way to pride and joy at a jumping life well lived

SUNSHINE THROUGH THE CLOUDS

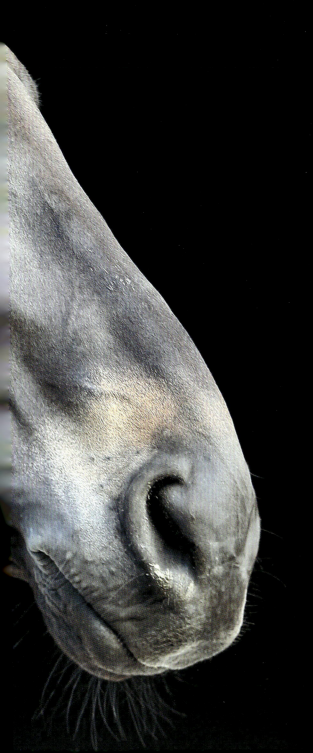

By Peter Thomas

CHRIS JERDIN stands at the door of the stable that once housed Grand National winner Many Clouds and the memories come back in a torrent of pride, pain and sadness. He still can't bring himself to go into the box, even after all these months, and he knows that the jumps season is getting back into full swing and old wounds will soon be opened up once more.

More than 50 years in racing plainly haven't inured the Stockport-born yardman to the grief caused by the loss of an old equine friend, and the bold warrior's death at Cheltenham in January is still as hard to bear as it was in the moment he collapsed and died on the wet winter turf.

Every racing fan has their abiding recollection of that afternoon, from the blood-pumping thrill of the duel between Many Clouds and Thistlecrack to the raising of the screens around his prone body and the awful silence that fell like a shroud over the roars from the grandstand. For 'CJ', however, after eight years of sharing a racing life with the son of Cloudings and nearly a year since his passing, one memory lingers above all others.

"The day before the race, a mother came up to me and said her six-year-old daughter was mad about 'Clouds'," he remembers, "so I told her to come up on Sunday after he'd run and I'd show him to her. It was heartbreaking to think of her having to tell her little girl he'd gone. That's the kind of horse he was, though. Every Saturday there was always a dozen people come up to see him and the old man [trainer Oliver Sherwood] never turned them away. We had two nuns here one day from Ireland, they knew their racing and so they loved him, the same as we all did."

If the story of Many Clouds tells us anything it's that from the most prosaic of beginnings can spring a tale capable of tautening and fraying every string of emotion, of bearing up the spirit and bringing it crashing to earth, of turning a sport into a proving ground for the human condition. If the Grand National is 'the people's race', then the €6,000 foal was 'the people's horse', and in this he was never failed by his friends.

"When he came to the yard he wasn't exactly nervous but he was always a bit suspicious," Jerdin recalls. "A big, tall, gangly horse who would jump six foot in the air if you said boo to him, which was amazing really when you think he jumped the National fences with no fear at all. I never shouted at him and he came round in the

▸▸ *Continues page 126*

end, although he always had that suspicion. I remember doing his bandages in the box one day last year and a couple of owners looked over the door, not knowing I was in there, and he flew back and nearly trampled me, because he didn't know what they were doing."

Even beset by wariness, Many Clouds quickly showed his talents by winning on his debut, in a bumper at Wetherby under lifelong partner Leighton Aspell, before being plunged into the white heat of Cheltenham's Champion Bumper – in the familiar green, yellow and white of owner Trevor Hemmings – and finishing ninth in a field that included winner Champagne Fever, The New One and Jezki. As ever he gave his all, even when physical maturity was a long way off.

"He started out as a bit of an ugly duckling, big ears, all legs, and a frame that didn't match," recalls Jerdin of the young Clouds. "I remember we nearly lost him swimming when he was a novice chaser. He'd got colic once in the pool but it wasn't bad, so you didn't think anything of it, and he was so brave and genuine that he went straight in the second time and it nearly cost him his life.

"He got colic again, really bad this time, and it was touch and go whether he'd come back from it. He was down the vets all tubed up, I went down there a few times to see how he was and finally he recovered, but it took him five days to get over it.

"Three weeks later he finished second in the Reynoldstown at Ascot [to subsequent RSA Chase winner O'Faolains Boy] – a hell of an effort after what he'd been through.

"He was a terrible traveller as well, and made a real mess of the box sometimes. He was a long horse and didn't like being cooped up, so he used to paw a lot and rub his tail raw, but he went all the way up to Kelso for his prep run for a second Grand National and it was called off, so he came home and then they put it back on again for him, so he went all the way back – 1,400 miles in a week, and he still won. It would have finished a lot of bad travellers but he came through it. That's how tough he was as a racehorse."

****

OLIVER SHERWOOD had known great success and top-class horses as an amateur rider and then as a trainer, but fashions come and go and the Chelmsford-born, cricket-loving master of Rhonehurst found himself on the fringes of the game and all but ready to draw stumps.

"When I started training I had a lot of success with good horses, then took my eye off the ball when I went through a messy divorce, going from being very spoilt to having some fairly average horses," explains the 62-year-old. "There were times when I wanted to get out, so a horse like Clouds gave me real confidence and meant everything to me – but that's also why he left such a huge hole when he went."

It doesn't take a professor of human nature to point out that good horses leave the biggest hoofprint on a yard. Had he been a run-of-the-mill performer, Many Clouds would have been missed when he died, but a series of extraordinary days on the racecourse ensured he would be remembered forever.

The first of these days was at Newbury for the 2014 Hennessy Gold Cup, a win made possible by a

LIFE AT THE TOP

Many Clouds in numbers

6,000 Purchase price (€) as a foal

6 Seasons in training

12 Career wins from 27 starts

174 Highest RPR recorded when winning Cotswold Chase in final race

928,000 Amount won (£) in prize-money

1 Only horse to win Hennessy and National in same season

1 Jockey in his entire career, Leighton Aspell

2 Jumps Horse of the Year titles

171 Official mark that made him champion three-mile chaser in 2016-17

meticulous strategy from the trainer, a 'fortuitous' early departure in the previous season's RSA Chase and a lenient reaction from the handicapper after his prep win at Carlisle.

"I really did start planning the Hennessy from the previous December," smiles Sherwood, "but nine out of ten great plans don't work out, and if he'd not been brought down in the RSA and had finished in the first three – as the form book says he would have – or if Phil Smith had put him up too much for a win that I hadn't expected, that would have been his Hennessy out of the window."

Raucous celebrations greeted Many Clouds' win at his local track. Sherwood, his wife Tarnya and their many staff and supporters greeted their return to the big time with gusto, little realising that even this mighty occasion would soon be dwarfed by the mightiest of all, when the trainer's reluctance to go to the well one more time, at Aintree in April, was overcome by an enthusiastic owner.

"If I'd had my way he wouldn't even have run in the National until the following year," Sherwood confirms. "He disappointed in the Gold Cup [sixth behind Coneygree] but

▸ Adored by all: (from left) Many Clouds with Chris Jerdin; surrounded by well-wishers as he parades through Lambourn after his Grand National victory; with Oliver Sherwood

Leighton was adamant he didn't turn up that day for some reason and when we couldn't find anything wrong, Mick [Meagher, Hemmings' racing manager] said it was either the National or out in a field, and I agreed we should go for it."

It was a decision that had seismic repercussions at Rhonehurst, both for the immediate high and the magnified impact of the low that followed.

"It changed my life," Jerdin says. "I'd rather win a National than three Gold Cups any day, because that's what people remember, the biggest race in the world. It was a bit of a blur, but coming home we got stopped in the petrol station because he had his name on the box and people knew what he'd just done. That's what the National does to you and it carried on until the day he died."

****

JERDIN is 63 and has had three jobs in racing, all of them in Lambourn: with Doug Marks for eight years, Fulke Walwyn for 18 years and Sherwood for 25 years. With Walwyn he was involved with horses of the calibre of Diamond Edge and Rose Ravine, "but Clouds was in a different stratosphere," he says. "With the

public as well, they adored him, he loved it and I loved it. That's what I miss most about him, the pleasure he gave to a lot of people."

When Many Clouds arrived at Cheltenham racecourse on January 28, 2017 his public were out in force. "He got off the box and all the drivers on the road past the racecourse stables could see his name on the side and they just stopped to look at him," Jerdin remembers. "We let them all take photographs, about 200 of them, and we could have been there an hour

'A GREAT PAL'

What they said after Many Clouds' death

"For 30 to 40 seconds he seemed absolutely fine. I was at my happiest for those 30 to 40 seconds because it was just an immense performance. Then he took a turn for the worse. It was very distressing. You're at your lowest then" *Leighton Aspell, jockey*

"I've had him since he was a foal. Many Clouds has given me and all those people who followed him a lot of great moments. He'll be sadly missed but I would rather remember him for all the successes because he became a great pal" *Trevor Hemmings, owner*

"Poor old Many Clouds. It's as sad as can be. He's a fantastic, lovely horse and beat us on the day. They went to battle and it's a tragic end to the race" *Colin Tizzard, Thistlecrack's trainer*

"He was a very public horse and everyone is very emotional. It's a blow for us all and all the people who have just cheered him on to such a brave win" *Michael Meagher, racing manager to Trevor Hemmings*

if we'd had the time. Once you win a National, that's everything for most people."

By 2.25pm that afternoon, Many Clouds was dead.

The Grade 2 Cotswold Chase had been expected to provide further confirmation that Thistlecrack was the best staying chaser in the country and a Gold Cup winner in waiting. He was sent off the 4-9 favourite and, despite stumbling three out, laid down a strong challenge to the leader Many Clouds from two out and perhaps narrowly headed him after the last, but was outbattled in the final strides, beaten by a head with Smad Place 17 lengths away in third.

The crowd was stirred to the point of hysteria. Many Clouds and Aspell circled on the track as the result of the photo-finish was awaited, and then the brutal tragedy struck.

"I watched it with Alan King and then charged out because I knew he'd won," Sherwood says with bittersweet recollection. "Then the phone went and it was Lisa [Kozak], my travelling head girl, and I knew he'd gone – she wouldn't have rung me otherwise.

"She said 'he's down'. I rang my wife straight away, I rang Mick

▸ *Continues page 128*

[Meagher], then I wandered out to where he'd dropped and saw Leighton and CJ and I knew he wouldn't get up. The screens were out and I didn't go and see him. I didn't have to. Leighton had seen him and was walking away with his saddle – and we didn't have to communicate.

"Leighton got changed and left straight away – he didn't want to see anybody and I understood that – but I'm sort of captain of the ship, and you can't just walk away. Deep down I was hurting like mad, but you have to look after your soldiers, have to be a bit stoic – a bit British if you like, in a good way?

"When Alice Plunkett from ITV asked me if I'd do an interview, I wanted to say something and I'm pleased I did. I don't know how but I got through it and I think it helped."

Sherwood's words poured oil on the deep and turbulent waters of anti-racing opinion, but there was no disguising the hurt being felt by those closest to Rhonehurst and to Many Clouds.

"I was at the last fence when he jumped upsides," Jerdin remembers, "then I was watching on the big screen and he was headed, then he got up to win and I was chasing after him but 50 yards before I got to him he was gone. I knew inside he'd gone. When you see a horse go down like that they don't get up and I knew he'd given everything. That's what he did and he paid for it with his life.

"I keep thinking about it even now. I wish Thistlecrack had made a little mistake and then he wouldn't have been in that battle. It's painful to watch a horse like him because once he's in a battle he goes through the pain barrier for you.

"I went to him because I knew it would be the last time I saw him. The one regret I have is that I didn't go and give him a pat. Leighton said he'd gone and I just turned away numb, and that was it."

****

IF the raw emotion of that afternoon at Cheltenham was hard to bear, then the aftermath, the eternal months missing a bona fide superstar and much-loved friend, were if anything worse. In a racing yard, the only

▸▸Champion at work: Many Clouds exercises at Newbury racecourse, shortly before his first run of 2016-17

practical approach is 'business as usual' but there's nothing usual about the loss of a great horse.

"I remember coming home in the empty box without him and it was terrible," says Jerdin, still moved even now. "If you ever think it's just a horse and it doesn't matter, you shouldn't be in racing. It still affects me after all these years and if you ever get used to it, you shouldn't be doing it.

"Monday morning was terrible. I was at Fulke Walwyn's when Ten Plus got killed in 1989 and it was the same feeling, it takes everything out of you, it kills the yard because the star's gone. It's great to have them but when they're gone you sometimes wish you hadn't had them because you don't want that feeling.

"If he'd gone through his life and retired a couple of years later to [Hemmings' yard on] the Isle of Man, ▸▸ *Continues page 130*

THE POST-MORTEM

The BHA took the unusual step of releasing the post-mortem result on Many Clouds, which revealed the ten-year-old had suffered a massive internal bleed. Although the horse had experienced wobbles due to post-race ataxia after his Grand National and Hennessy Gold Cup triumphs, "no significant underlying health issues were discovered in the autopsy", the BHA said.

The organisation's acting chief veterinary officer Tony Welsh said: "Episodes such as this are rare and can occur in horses who have no underlying health issues. Post-race ataxia and similar symptoms are linked to an increase in body temperature after exercise and can be treated by providing the horse with water. It is not uncommon in racehorses or other sport horses.

"Despite some reports following the incident [at Cheltenham], there is no existing veterinary evidence that links these symptoms with racehorse fatalities, and the post-mortem results have categorically proved the symptoms exhibited by Many Clouds in the past were in no way present or associated with his sad death at Cheltenham."

The BHA said the fatality rate in jump racing for horses suffering from similar episodes was 0.048 per cent of runners and the overall fatality rate in British racing has decreased by a third in the last 20 years owing to the sport's investment in equine health and welfare.

ROBERT COWELL
RACING
MULTIPLE GROUP 1 WINNING RACEHORSE TRAINER
Incorporating **BOTTISHAM HEATH STUD**

- Set within 180 acres of paddocks
- Private poly track gallop
- Stabling for 75 horses
- Quick access to Newmarket gallops; the HQ of horseracing
- Also full paddock boarding available all year round

Yard Sponsored by

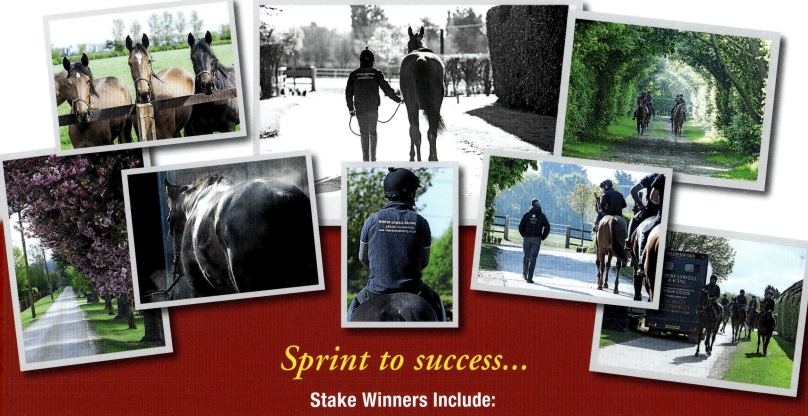

Sprint to success...

Stake Winners Include:
Encore D'Or | Goldream | Iffranesia | Justineo | Jwala | Kingsgate Native
Monsieur Joe | Prohibit | Prince Of Lir | Spirit Quartz | Visionary

Robert Cowell Racing Royal Ascot Winners

Bottisham Heath Stud, Six Mile Bottom,
Newmarket, Suffolk, CB8 0TT

Tel : +44 (0)1638 570330
Mob: +44 (0)7785 512463

Email: robert@robertcowellracing.co.uk
Website: www.robertcowellracing.co.uk
Twitter: @cowellracing

we'd still have been without him, but because it happened two years early, really quick, the feelings came all at once."

"You have another 60 horses to look after and you have to get up in the morning and get on with it," says Sherwood, searching for stoicism once more yet not immune from the anguish, "but the loss of a horse like him leaves a massive hole and I think it hits harder for the jumping people because the horses are around longer and you get to know them better.

"It's when you get home that the realisation sets in. I had a cry, my wife was in bits, and although you know you have to move on eventually, it still hurts. My job is to lift the team and find another Clouds, but it's no different to a friend or a family member dying.

"That night we went down to the George in Lambourn to toast him, no point sulking. My wife put it on social media, we asked the gallop guys who saw him every day, the farriers, the vets, just to have a quick drink. Trevor put a few quid behind the bar, plenty of other trainers and their staff dropped by and we gave him a good send-off.

"The mood on Monday morning was sombre, coming into the yard to an empty box. It was hard for everybody but I'm just glad he did what he did when he did, rather than breaking a leg on the schooling ground and having to be humanely destroyed. Leighton said he was dead before he hit the ground, and you have to take that as a positive."

****

RACING people emerged from the death of Many Clouds with dignity and credit. Sherwood pays tribute to his colleagues, friends, Cheltenham racecourse, the BHA, the vets, everybody who made the sad end of a wonderful horse more bearable.

The racing public offered their heartfelt condolences and those at Rhonehurst took heart from their sentiments. Even the inevitable critics of racing were slow to come forward.

"We got thousands of messages and answered every one, and only a dozen of them were nasty," the trainer says. "Even a couple of the nasties wrote

▸▸ Final act: Many Clouds (left) bravely defeats Thistlecrack in the Cotswold Chase before collapsing after the line

back to say thank you when we replied, because immediately after the race they'd equated the little post-race wobbles he'd had previously with what killed him, when it transpired they were nothing to do with it.

"It was just a dozen and I get more if we get an odds-on shot beat on a Saturday, so let's keep it in perspective, and I think 100 per cent we did everything right by the horse all through his career."

For Jerdin the end of his career in racing will come when he retires at 65, but the beginning of the end came at Cheltenham. The awards for Clouds keep coming – Horse of the Year, champion three-mile chaser, a tree on the downs, a bench in the village – but they only heighten the loss.

"I've lost my mojo for racing," he confesses. "My knee-jerk reaction was to pack it in, and although time's a great healer, it's still difficult. They'll play the race again when the season gets going and it'll all come back, and it still gets me. But I'm proud of what I did with him, what we all did with him.

"You only had to watch him jumping to know he loved it, and he never wanted for anything all his life. He was just happy, gentle and kind and would do anything for anybody. I know I won't see another one like him."

TOP OF THE POLLS

Posthumous honours continued for Many Clouds throughout the year and he was the public's overwhelming choice as the Racing Post Jumps Horse of the Year at the end of the 2016-17 season.

He took 65 per cent of the vote to win the award for the second time. The runner-up was Grand National winner One For Arthur.

Trainer Oliver Sherwood said: "It's a huge compliment and I can't thank all the voters enough. It's a huge accolade for the horse, the owner, the jockey and all of us at Rhonehurst."

Official recognition came in the Anglo-Irish jumps classifications when Many Clouds was named the champion three-mile chaser. He was given a mark of 171, the highest of his career, for his heroic victory over Thistlecrack in the Cotswold Chase. Cheltenham Gold Cup winner Sizing John was judged to be 2lb inferior to Many Clouds on 169, with Thistlecrack splitting the pair on 170. The overall chase champion was two-mile star Douvan on 174.

"You're joking?" inquired a genuinely shocked Sherwood when told of the official ratings, before offering a more considered appraisal of his late star. "We always rated the horse. You never dreamed he could do what he did but you always hope. You could see from the ratings he had improved from the season before. I've had one or two good ones like The West Awake and Large Action but he's definitely the best horse I've trained."

On Racing Post Ratings, Many Clouds (174) was behind Thistlecrack and Cue Card (both 176) among the staying chasers and joint-fourth overall – with Sizing John among those alongside him – behind top-rated Douvan.

Aintree, scene of Many Clouds' greatest triumph in the 2015 Grand National, inducted him into the hall of fame in April and unveiled a plaque in his honour in McCoy's Bar. Sherwood, owner Trevor Hemmings, jockey Leighton Aspell and groom Chris Jerdin attended the ceremony.

The 3m1f chase won by Many Clouds at Aintree last December on his penultimate start has been named in his honour after being promoted from Listed to Grade 2 status. The race, part of Becher Chase day, has become the Many Clouds Chase, worth £50,000.

HEROS Education

HEROS Charity is taking forward some exciting developments in Education and Training. In partnership with several well-established training providers it is introducing a range of courses and work experience opportunities for people of all ages.

Through its ex-racehorse retraining and rehoming scheme and its education and training programmes HEROS Charity is supporting the racing industry in its commitment to the welfare of racehorses by training high quality, skilled stable staff and by providing ex-racehorses with a secure future.

HEROS Charity is a registered charity and accredited 1st4Sport training centre based at North Farm Stud in Fawley near Wantage.

HEROS Education offers a variety of courses, which can be personalised to suit individual requirements based on time and experience.

HEROS Racing Staff Academy... in partnership with Abingdon and Witney College

This course offers learners a graduated approach to Racehorse Management. The programme includes weekly work experience in local racing yards giving learners a solid foundation in the racing industry.

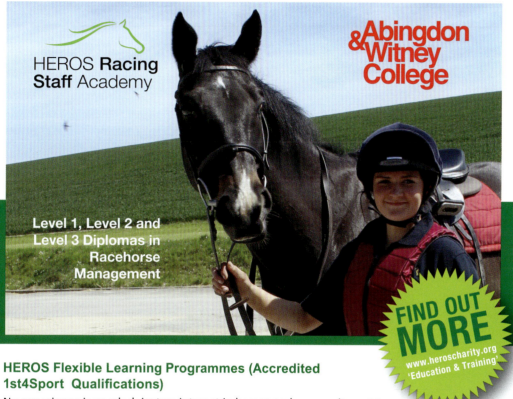

Level 1, Level 2 and Level 3 Diplomas in Racehorse Management

FIND OUT MORE www.heroscharity.org 'Education & Training'

HEROS Flexible Learning Programmes (Accredited 1st4Sport Qualifications)

No experience is needed, just an interest in horses and a commitment to being reliable, hardworking and motivated. Learners can join us on a long term or short course basis to complete their Entry level or Level 1 (depending on age and aspirations) horse care qualifications alongside functional skills.

The Flexible learning provision includes enrolment and delivery on Entry or Level 1 horse care Award/Certificate/Diploma on a 'roll on, roll off' basis.

1st4Sport Level 2 Certificate in Assisting with the Rehabilitation of Horses

This course will give the learner the higher level skills and knowledge required to assist with the development and implementation of rehabilitation programmes for retiring racehorses. The course is 12 weeks (1 day a week) and the units covered are:

- Carry out routine care and monitor the health and well-being of horses
- Assist with the rehabilitation of horses
- Develop and implement a horse rehabilitation plan

Full details and application forms are available at www.heroscharity.org/education-and-training

@HEROSCharityEducation | Tel: 01488 638820 | education@heroscharity.org | www.heroscharity.org

HEROS Charity, The Swallows, North Farm Stud, Fawley, Wantage, Oxfordshire OX12 9NJ | Charity No. 1115174

NOTE: All students follow a strict induction programme to ensure that safety remains paramount when working alongside animals. HEROS Charity Education does have a specific teaching, learning and assessment yard where all horses have been fully risk assessed to reduce the likelihood of an accident. All policies and procedures are available on our website or can be emailed on request – education@heroscharity.org

THE
BIGGER
PICTURE

Alpha Centauri (right) makes her way to the gallops at Jessica Harrington's Commonstown Stables in Moone, County Kildare, in May. The two-year-old filly won a Listed race at Naas on her next start and then was beaten a neck by Different League in the Group 3 Albany Stakes at Royal Ascot

PATRICK McCANN (RACINGPOST.COM/PHOTOS)

A SEASON TO REMEMBER
A MARCH TO FORGET

Cheltenham was disappointing for Colin Tizzard but everywhere else there were notable triumphs

By Peter Thomas

COLIN TIZZARD began the 2016-17 season with the summit of racing's highest peak in his sights amid sky-high hopes both within and without Venn Farm Stables. In his care were the favourites for the Cheltenham Gold Cup and King George VI Chase and the main rival for both crowns, along with a clutch of fancied contenders for many other of the biggest prizes to be contested through the campaign.

Where once he was a dairy farmer who trained a few horses, Tizzard had indisputably, by design not accident, become a fully fledged trainer who milked a few cows. It was a seismic shift that had fractured the crust and shaken the core of jump racing, but with

▶ *Continues page 136*

the earthquake came raised expectation and the 2016-17 season would be judged like none before it in the formerly sleepy backwater of Dorset.

When the time came to write the end-of-term report, assessment of whether it was an A* season or merely a B+ centred on how highly the Cheltenham examination is rated. For some there was a feeling of what might have been after the Tizzard stable faltered at what is widely regarded as the crucial moment. Having had a strike-rate throughout the winter of never less than 12 per cent and a peak of 28 per cent in a glorious November, Venn Farm managed only one winner from 53 runners in March at a measly two per cent.

For those who judge success through the prism of the Cheltenham Festival, Tizzard had fallen short; but for those who still rank the Hennessy, King George, Aintree and Punchestown as equally valued tests, his season was a rare triumph and it is notable that he was the only trainer to have as many as four of the top 20 earners in Britain and Ireland. Just as importantly, his stable continues to house some of the most exciting jumping talent around for the season ahead.

****

TO say the 2016-17 campaign began well would be an understatement. The village of Milborne Port became the epicentre of the jump racing universe as, bolstered by the arrival of high-calibre weaponry from leading owners Ann and Alan Potts, Tizzard annexed one big prize after another. By the time Native River bagged the Hennessy Gold Cup to put himself firmly in the Cheltenham Gold Cup picture, the yard had already won seven Graded and Listed races with seven different horses.

Most significant among them were Cue Card, who redeemed a moderate seasonal debut by taking the Grade 1 Betfair Chase, and the mighty Thistlecrack, who cemented his reputation as the second coming of equine Jesus with a Grade 2 novice chase victory earlier on the Hennessy card.

When Thistlecrack claimed Cue Card's King George title at Kempton

on Boxing Day – and Royal Vacation benefited from Might Bite's fall for a fortunate victory in the Grade 1 Kauto Star Novices' Chase – it seemed as though Cheltenham was Tizzard's for the taking, with his only taxing mental issue being how best to play a hand stuffed with aces.

For Tizzard's part, he handled the unprecedented pressure with dignity, fielding constant media interest with amused enthusiasm. He had owners to keep happy and a trainers' championship to win, which two ambitions sometimes butted heads, but the close-knit nature of the yard meant there was no sense of disharmony among the competing interests.

Tizzard, after all, is from a West Country hunting and point-to-pointing clan and has raised his closest allies, son Joe and daughter Kim, in the same vein. Venn Farm, despite its new,

▶▶ Trainer more than farmer: Colin Tizzard (top, and previous page) oversees proceedings at his Venn Farm Stables at Milborne Port, Dorset; (right) horses have become the main focus over cows as the racing operation continues to expand; (left) the Tizzard string returns from the gallops

state-of-the-art barn over the brow of the nearest of the Blackmore Hills, remains a traditional steeplechasing yard and they would never grumble about having two shots at the Gold Cup – even if aiming one of them at the Ryanair Chase might yield valuable extra pounds in the title race.

"I have input but the owners own the horses and we're talking about the Gold Cup, not a little novice hurdle at Wincanton where I might talk one of them out of it," said the trainer, realistic as ever.

As a novice stepping up from a sensational career as a staying hurdler, Thistlecrack was always likely to be the subject of much debate concerning the wisdom of pitting him against the best in open company instead of paddling for a season in shallower waters – although as an eight-year-old, rising nine, time wasn't on his side.

Clumsy jumping errors in his first two starts gave traction to the doubts, but by the time he bypassed the novice option to demolish his field in the King George, he was widely accepted as a valid hot favourite for the Gold Cup, with Tizzard no longer able to dismiss his own title claims as press speculation. "I'd say we're about a hundred horses short of being champion," he still suggested, although the quality of those horses he did have said otherwise.

Cue Card got back on the winning trail in the Grade 1 Ascot Chase, hard on the heels of rising star Finian's Oscar landing the Grade 1 Tolworth Hurdle and Native River the Grade 2 Denman Chase. Tizzard had Cheltenham possibilities coming out of his ears and might have been forgiven a hearty Dorset chuckle, were it not for the fact that he was long

▸Double cream: Colin Tizzard with two of his stable stars, Thistlecrack (right) and Cue Card

enough in the tooth to know that while class is permanent, form can come and go as it pleases.

First came the undoing of Thistlecrack, as exciting a chaser as had been seen in recent times and 4-9 to turn the Cotswold Chase at Cheltenham in January into a conclusive Gold Cup trial, yet overturned by the ill-fated Many Clouds in what proved to be a life-or-death battle up the hill. The favourite had stumbled at the ninth and pecked three from home, but he jumped the last still with every chance, only to be outdone, perhaps outstayed, by the 2015 Grand National winner.

Many Clouds suffered a massive internal bleed and collapsed soon after the line. A distraught crowd was united in disbelief, and by comparison the defeat of Thistlecrack was a minor

issue, a retrievable setback. Less than a month later, however, his Gold Cup chances had been reduced to rubble by a tendon injury that was deemed likely to keep him out of action until Christmas.

****

IF October, November, December, January and February were months of feasting, then March began to turn into what might best be described as an untimely famine, with the reality sinking as low as hopes had soared high. Native River and Cue Card were still first and second favourites for a Gold Cup already shorn of past winners Don Cossack and Coneygree, but the form of the Tizzard stable seemed to be dipping and there was little that could be done.

Come festival time, all that was left
▸Continues page 138

was to hope the dip had been a blip, but results soon dashed all such notions. By the time Aintree came around, Venn Farm would be rocking again, but at Cheltenham there was none of the customary spring in the step of its inmates. Cue Card fell for a second time in the Gold Cup as Native River snatched a gallant third behind Sizing John; it was success of a kind, perhaps an indication of a bright future, but hardly what had been hoped for.

Messrs Mullins and Elliott fought out the top trainer title at the meeting – the old master and the young pretender, with Tizzard watching on in dignified silence. If he were reflecting on a dismal denouement to a fine campaign, however, his mood was soon to be lifted.

On the second day of Aintree he landed a treble with up-and-coming Pingshou in the Grade 1 Top Novices' Hurdle, Fox Norton in the Grade 1 Melling Chase and Ultragold in the Topham, the first two owned by the Pottses and ridden by their retained rider Robbie Power. The following day brought a double with the Potts's Finian's Oscar in the Grade 1 Mersey Novices' Hurdle and Sizing Codelco, again with Power in the saddle.

If Tizzard had been looking for a way to end the season with a bang rather than a whimper, and cement his new-found alliance with a wealthy owner, he could have found worse ways than this. Follow-up wins at Punchestown for Fox Norton, in the Grade 1 Champion Chase, and Sizing Codelco, along with a welcome strike from Sizing Granite, simply reiterated what the racing world had already worked out for itself: that Tizzard was a pretender to the trainers' crown – if not a young one – and that even entering his seventh decade, he wasn't going away anytime soon.

Was his season a good one or a bad one? If success is measured by Cheltenham winners alone, then this was a campaign best forgotten; Thistlecrack never got there and the rest of the team misfired. If, however, one factors in 57 winners, more than £2 million in prize-money and third place in the trainers' table, it begins to look very much like the best season he has ever had.

▶▶ Family business: Colin Tizzard flanked by daughter Kim and son Joe, his assistant trainers

IT'S ALL LOOKING UP

The Tizzards are going all out to ensure that the 2017-18 season will be even better than the last campaign.

Hard on the heels of the arrival of 15 horses from the personal collection of Ann and Alan Potts in the autumn of 2016, assistant trainer Joe promised that up was the only way for Venn Farm and that their new barn would soon be joined by an even newer one; that Dad's instinctive focus on milk prices would take even more of a back seat behind the quest for more prize-money.

"People saw building the barn as a good business move and a major commitment," he explained. "It cost a lot of money but it told everybody we meant it, so we'll make it a bit bigger next summer, another barn and another step up."

True to his word, the latest building project has come to fruition, adding space for 20 more horses (with accompanying walkers and wash-off area) and taking the team into treble figures at a time when increased quantity won't mean a dilution of quality.

"We've never turned a horse away before and we're not about to do so now," insisted Joe, echoing the sound business sense of his father, with the added confidence that accompanies strategic success.

Judge them however you want to, but make no mistake, the Tizzards are on the up and the racing world now has to factor them into calculations whenever championships are up for discussion. Even the family has given up deflecting the inevitable questions.

"Whatever Dad says," insisted Joe, "I can tell you all of us go straight to the paper after every weekend to see where we are in the title race."

By Lewis Porteous

SOME wait a lifetime for a shot at redemption but for Lizzie Kelly the chance to put things right came just 20 days after the initial disappointment and girl did she make it count.

When it was announced Kelly was to become only the second woman, and the first for 33 years, to ride in the Cheltenham Gold Cup in March, everyone wanted a piece of the action. The 24-year-old and her partner Tea For Two were the feelgood story of the Cheltenham Festival but there was no happy ending, with the rider dumped on the turf after Tea For Two blundered his way through the second fence. She was down and out with the race a mere 30 seconds old.

"It was horrific," says Kelly, laying bear the anguish she suffered that afternoon. "My friends had a real job picking me up and dusting me off. That feeling is a tricky thing to master – it's like popping a balloon."

Amid the gloom, however, there was a glimmer of a silver lining; because their Gold Cup exit had been so premature, at least it meant a Plan B could be hatched as long as Tea For Two could prove his wellbeing after his Cheltenham mishap.

For a while, that was far from certain. "He wasn't himself at home afterwards," his rider says. "He's the type of horse who will come and stand at the front of his box and have a chat with you but he wasn't like that. It wasn't very nice to see him lose his confidence in that sort of way, so our main objective for his next race was to get him there and to enjoy it."

The race in mind was the Betway Bowl, a prestigious Grade 1 chase at the Grand National festival and Aintree's version of the Gold Cup. While it offered the opportunity of a second top-level success for Kelly – already the only woman to ride a Grade 1 winner over fences in Britain or Ireland thanks to Tea For Two's win in the Kauto Star Novices' Chase in 2015 – the duo were no longer in contention for back-page headlines after their Cheltenham anti-climax.

"From my point of view there was no media attention whatsoever, which was great," Kelly says. "I didn't even tell my dad. I stayed with a friend the

▸ Continues page 142

TEA PARTY

Bitter disappointment in the Cheltenham Gold Cup was followed by a momentous Grade 1 victory at Aintree for Lizzie Kelly and Tea For Two

▶▶ Pride and joy: Lizzie Kelly and Tea For Two are greeted after their Betway Bowl triumph (from left) by the rider's brother Chester Williams, mum Jane Williams, Fliss Spriggett, assistant yard manager at Nick Williams' yard, and yard manager Suzie Young

night before and didn't tell her either. Before Cheltenham it had got to the stage where I couldn't even step outside the weighing room without someone asking me for an interview. This time it was very different, which was very nice."

Instead the attention surrounded Cue Card, arguably the most popular chaser in training, who himself had fallen in the Gold Cup but was favourite to follow up his win in the Bowl the previous year. Silviniaco Conti, already a dual winner of the Bowl, was also in the line-up, not to mention promising young gun Bristol De Mai and proven warriors Smad Place and Empire Of Dirt. It was a worthy Grade 1 in all respects.

"I just wanted to go and ride him instinctively; strip it all back and ride him the way I knew how to," Kelly says. "Riding him is a dream and to be able to focus on that and the task in hand was very nice."

However, she and her mother Jane, who trains Tea For Two alongside husband Nick Williams, were unsure whether the horse's mental scars from Cheltenham had completely healed – and his demeanour at Aintree caused further anxiety.

"When he was walking around the paddock he wasn't himself," his rider says. "Normally it's really difficult getting on and getting him out on to the track but the fact I was able to sling my leg over and potter out on to the racecourse was a worry and Mum just said 'do what you can'."

The main objective was for horse and rider to negotiate the course

What they said about Lizzie Kelly's Aintree win on Tea For Two

Peter Scudamore, eight-time champion jump jockey
She was absolutely fantastic. I'm a big fan of her as a rider – she's a wonderful jockey. You've got to be on a horse that's good enough, but she's proved when she gets that she can deliver. She gave it such a great ride and it was a great race.

Carl Llewellyn, two-time Grand National-winning jockey
It was great for racing, great for sport and great for all the connections. Fair play to her, in a big race like that she was very cool. She was confident in her own ability, the horse's ability, and it was a lovely ride in such a big race. She was brilliant, always in the right place, and got it done.

John Francome, seven-time champion jump jockey
She gave him a great ride. He's a very good horse on his day – I backed him in the Gold Cup and what happened there was just one of those things, I'm afraid; that's the ups and downs of riding. She's very lucky, sometimes you have to wait a long time before something picks you up, but she didn't have to wait long.

▸ Aintree ace: Tea For Two sends the birch flying as he takes the last before sprinting to the winning line (below) for a memorable victory

safely, while making sure Tea For Two enjoyed the experience. "I jumped the first three and was happy with my place but coming past the stands he was still very unlike himself, still very quiet and travelling half-behind the bridle, whereas he normally pulls," Kelly says.

"Fearing the worst, I thought I'd better make some ground and when I did that leaving the stands, he grabbed hold of the bit and I realised there was plenty there. All that had happened was that he'd mentally grown up and I pulled him back to where we had been. I knew then we were okay and that he'd changed as a horse – it was brilliant to know he had grown up."

With confidence between horse and jockey rising, expectations started to stretch beyond merely a safe conveyance. "When I opened him up going down the back straight for the last time I made a couple of places," Kelly says.

"I started to look around and they were pushing along and slapping with their whips, yet I'd made that ground so easily. By the time we got around the bend, the only one left was Cue Card. We still had a long way to go but I was travelling well, while Paddy Brennan was shaking the reins a little bit. The best thing about Tea For Two is his jumping; he takes lengths out of horses and I thought if I could get alongside Cue Card, I'd get him on the jumping and that was the aim."

Cue Card started to wander to his left as Tea For Two piled on the pressure with his accurate jumping and approaching the last it was the

underdog who held a narrow advantage over the 2-1 favourite. Kelly knew this was a crucial moment.

"We got to the last and he was long but I didn't want to make the decision for him – he had to make the decision – so I let go of the reins, didn't move and just went with whatever decision he made and up he came. Someone said afterwards that was his apology for what happened in the Gold Cup. It was slightly unbelievable and I was just begging for the line to come from there. Cue Card was coming back but Tea For Two tries so hard and when we crossed the line his neck was as far out as it could possibly go."

The official margin was precisely a neck at the post, with Tea For Two having answered every call from Kelly's dynamic drive.

"There's no better sight in the whole world than my brother Chester running out to greet me when I've won a big race," she says proudly. "For me, that's the height of the joy I feel. He always comes sprinting out with a huge smile and that family association is what makes it so special.

"Tea For Two is Mum's horse. She bought him as a young horse and has trained and looked after him from the start, but she has the trust to hand him over to me on the track. She has to be sure that I'll make the right decisions and I have to be aware that if I make the wrong decision she won't be happy.

"Emotionally it was the most amazing feeling I've had, especially after the disappointment of Cheltenham. I then had to call round people like my dad and say 'I failed to mention I was riding in a Grade 1 – and by the way we won!'"

Asking Kelly which of her two Grade 1 wins on Tea For Two means the most is a bit like asking a parent to pick a favourite child, but there is little doubt which she thinks was the more significant in the bigger picture.

"The fact it wasn't a novice chase but the top drawer at Aintree is hugely important. Realistically the top three-mile chases of the year are the King George, the Gold Cup and the Betway Bowl, and to beat the names we did was great. Tea For Two has made my career and winning that Grade 1 on that day with this horse was just brilliant.

"When I won the Grade 1 the first time it was overwhelming and perhaps I didn't appreciate it like I should have. I've ridden in Grade 1s since and they're so high quality and so difficult to win. It's the best horses and the best jockeys and you're privileged to be there."

Kelly has no doubt been a pioneer for female riders and, while she would much rather be recognised as a jockey, rather than a female jockey, with time she is starting to accept her standing as a role model.

Even so, considering she is a dual Grade 1-winning rider, her services were hardly in Richard Johnson-like demand last season, when she had 11 winners from 112 rides, with all 11 winners coming from the 87 rides her family's stable provided.

"I'm very aware that it's difficult to get a lot of rides when you're not working for a big trainer but the job I have and the people I ride for outside of Nick and Mum are very good people," Kelly says. "If I had 30 or 40 more rides a season because of that win it would make a big difference to my career but I'm fully aware the times people want a second jockey are the big Saturdays when I'm riding for home anyway, so it's quite difficult as I'm not always available."

While she might have been the sole female rider to win a race at Aintree in April, there was plenty of success for women at the Cheltenham Festival and Rachael Blackmore took the Irish conditionals' title. And with Josephine Gordon making waves on the Flat in 2017, it could be argued the status of female riders is on the up.

"I think we're seeing more female conditionals and it's more of an open opportunity now than it ever has been," Kelly says. "For sure there's been a move in the right direction but the girls have to make the decision they want to be jockeys. There will always be fewer female riders than males because a lot of girls who work in racing don't want to be jockeys."

For those who do aspire to make riding a full-time profession, Kelly is adamant that fitness is fundamental. Her own dedication is clear from her use of a personal trainer and she adds: "I'll always be of the opinion that if you want to be a jockey and you're a girl, you'll have to try very hard and a lot harder than some females who are coming up through the ranks try."

Coming from a history maker, that is advice worth heeding.

'To beat the names we did was great. Tea For Two has made my career and winning that Grade 1 on that day with this horse was just brilliant'

WINNING STREAK

Female riders were unstoppable at the Cheltenham Festival as they completed a clean sweep of the three races for amateurs

L ISA O'NEILL is one of the unsung grafters who make the racing industry tick, as you can tell from Gordon Elliott's description of her role with his yard. "She's a star, who pre-trains horses, rides out each day, does everything. Fair play to her, she's a big part of our team," he said after celebrating three winners on the opening day of the Cheltenham Festival. By then, he could have added "festival-winning jockey" to O'Neill's CV after she had partnered Tiger Roll to victory in the National Hunt Chase.

O'Neill's own summary of festival week emphasised that, whereas most jockeys can turn up at Cheltenham and focus on the one job, riding Tiger Roll was only part of her duties. "It was hectic. On the Monday I came over in the lorry with eight of the horses, and it was non-stop for the next five

▶▶ Festival winners: (from left) Bryony Frost, Lisa O'Neill and Gina Andrews

days until I returned home with the horses on Saturday," she said. "It was an amazing achievement that Gordon ended up with six winners [for the week] and as leading trainer. I'm just so happy to be involved."

O'Neill, 30, has played a multi-tasking role in Elliott's operation over the past three years, combining a daily riding-out routine with three afternoons a week in the office and a variety of odd jobs into the bargain.

Last season she emerged from the backroom as a capable amateur rider. She first hit the headlines when partnering the Elliott-trained Wrath Of Titans to win the Guinness Kerry National at Listowel last September in the same Gigginstown House Stud colours she wore on Tiger Roll.

"If I'd been told at the beginning of the season I was going to ride the winner of the Kerry National I wouldn't have believed it, and if I'd been told after Listowel I was going to ride a Cheltenham Festival winner I would have thought it was a mad idea," she said.

The ride on Tiger Roll in the National Hunt Chase was a promise kept by Elliott once Jamie Codd turned down the opportunity and opted instead for the favourite A Genie In Abottle in the Gigginstown colours. "Jamie could have ridden him but I said to her, 'If you work hard you can ride him if Jamie doesn't,' and she did a great job," Elliott said.

Opportunities like that don't come knocking very often and O'Neill was the first to admit she was not exactly an overnight sensation. She had about 80 rides before landing her first winner – in a Britain v Ireland race for lady riders at Newton Abbot in 2010 – and managed only a handful of winners over the next few years but continued to acquire valuable race-riding experience, including internationally in Fegentri races.

"It's taken a while but I feel I'm riding with more confidence now. Of course a lot of it has to do with the fact Gordon and Gigginstown have allowed me to ride good horses," she said.

Gigginstown supremo Michael O'Leary has been more than happy to oblige. In the Cheltenham winner's enclosure, he said: "Lisa has been very lucky for us – she won the Kerry National for us on Wrath Of Titans and is a superb pilot. She's a lovely girl and tiny, but you could see Tiger Roll loved it, rolling along with her and having his own way of doing things."

In an era when the profile of female jump jockeys in Ireland has been raised by conditional champion Rachael Blackmore and top-level amateurs Nina Carberry and Katie Walsh, O'Neill added another high-profile victory to the list. "It's a very tough game and Nina has been an inspiration for any girl who wants to ride in Ireland and was definitely a big role model for me, as was Katie as well," she reflected. "They've set the bar very high but that's been a good thing because they showed we can compete successfully against the professionals. Rachael is more than holding her own as a professional and that's going to be a big boost to other girls in the future."

O'Neill provided her own source of inspiration. In grasping her opportunity on Tiger Roll, she set the ball rolling in a momentous Cheltenham week for female amateurs, before Gina Andrews and Bryony Frost picked it up and ran with it.

▸▸ *Continues page 146*

Andrews gets the party started

FROM the day she started race-riding ten years ago, Gina Andrews was gently admonished for setting her sights too high. "It has always been my ambition to ride a winner at the Cheltenham Festival," she said. "I was told it was pretty unrealistic but now it has actually happened."

Her victory at Cheltenham 2017 took some time to sink in. The driving finish that saw her force Domesday Book past Pendra in the Fulke Walwyn Kim Muir Amateur Riders' Handicap Chase was followed by a night of celebration with friends and family. Only when she awoke the next morning did reality dawn with the day.

Among the party that evening was her younger sister Bridget, who rode more winners than any other female rider in Britain in the 2016-17 season. But the gathering was brief. The following morning Andrews, 25, made the trek to Fakenham for a solitary ride.

Looking back on her festival win, she said: "I couldn't believe I was still in contention turning for home. Going to the second-last I was disputing the lead and thought I might win, but by the time we got to the last I was thinking I'd had a great ride and maybe I'd be in the first three."

Pendra was three lengths clear jumping the last, but then he faltered. "My horse rallied again up the run-in. I just kept going at the same speed and the horse in front of me wandered about and got lonely on his own. I caught him halfway up the run-in."

That Pendra was ridden by Derek O'Connor served to amplify Andrews' joy. O'Connor is one of Ireland's finest, an amateur in name only. She paid the price for over-zealously wielding her whip, copping a 13-day ban and £400 fine, but her determination was fuelled by her belief that Britain's amateurs are often overlooked by British trainers.

"British amateur riders find it very hard to get a ride at the festival," she said. "When Cheltenham comes around our trainers just reach for the Irish riders straight away, and I think that's wrong. I feel we're just as capable as they are. We're good enough on a day-to-day basis and suddenly when we get to the festival,

▶ Festival firsts: Tiger Roll (above) and Domesday Book (below) on the way to victory

apparently we're not. Hopefully I've done my bit to show we're up to it. I think British trainers should support British riders ahead of the Irish."

She is equally forthright about the status of female jockeys in racing. "If I'm perfectly honest, I think some girls are just as capable as the boys but a lot of them aren't. These girls give the better ones a bad name, so those who ride as well as the boys aren't given enough opportunity. Everyone knows that the more rides you get, the more experience you get and the better you get, but that process can't happen until you start getting rides in the first place. It becomes a bit of a hiding to nothing."

Andrews had never previously sat on Domesday Book before she met him in the paddock at Cheltenham. But she has known his trainer Stuart Edmunds for some time. A friend of her parents, Edmunds only welcomed Domesday Book into his yard from Ireland at the turn of the year. He ran the horse four weeks before the festival and soon after Domesday Book had finished an encouraging third at Leicester he rang Andrews to book her services.

"I didn't hear from him for some time afterwards," Andrews said. "After ▶ Continues page 148

RoR
Retraining of Racehorses

Racing to a new career at ror.org.uk

rorsourceahorse.org.uk

A new website for selling or loaning a horse directly out of a trainer's yard and for all former racehorses.

Bloodstock Sales

In addition to Horses In Training sales, RoR holds auctions dedicated to horses leaving racing.

Rehoming Direct

RoR has compiled a checklist to safeguard your horse's future when moved directly into the sport horse market.

Visit
ror.org.uk
for rehoming options and advice

Retrainers

RoR has a list of retrainers recommended by trainers who can start the retraining process and assess each horse.

Equine Charities

Retrain former racehorses for a donation, as well as care for vulnerable horses with the help of RoR funding.

RoR is British horseracing's official charity for the welfare of horses retired from racing.

a while I thought nothing would come of it but he stood by his word and put me up."

Horses were always going to be the pivot in Andrews' life. Both her parents were accomplished riders and she couldn't wait to be out of school – "I left when I was 16 and never looked back." Her husband Tom Ellis hails from similar stock; the couple have ridden more than 400 winners between them in points and under rules.

They now run a successful point-to-point yard, where Andrews' brother Jack also works, and they enjoyed an excellent season in that sphere. Gina became national champion lady point-to-point rider for a fourth time with 29 winners – beating fellow festival winner Bryony Frost by 13 – Tom was eighth in the trainers' list and Jack ninth among the male riders.

Plenty of cause for family celebration there, with a Cheltenham Festival winner the icing on the cake.

Frost keeps up family tradition

PAUL NICHOLLS' pupil-assistant Bryony Frost completed the clean sweep for female amateur riders when she partnered owner Andy Stewart's Pacha Du Polder to a memorable victory from stablemate Wonderful Charm in the Foxhunter.

"I was just willing the line to come and it came out right for me," Frost, 21, recalled. "At the top of the hill I had to pinch myself about how much horse I had underneath me. It was just a matter of getting those last two fences as well as he did the others and staying on up the hill, and he tried his heart out, put everything on the line for me.

"You can hear the other horses, they sound like a storming train coming up behind you and I knew it was Wonderful Charm because I recognised the cheekpieces. I thought, 'Oh no, don't you deny us today!' But Pacha was gutsy, he stuck his head out that extra inch for me, and a neck was enough."

Pacha Du Polder's success – a year after he had finished fifth in the same race in a high-profile spin with Victoria Pendleton – brought some adverse comment on social media.

"We got some griping about how it's meant to be an amateur sport and Paul coming in and picking up these races wasn't right but they were completely wrong. Paul's been in hunting since he was a kid and so have I, so it's a big thing for us," Frost said. "I want to stress that Pacha is a true foxhunter. He's been there and pointed – he wasn't one who was pulled out of the main yard and stuck in the race."

Frost – who had had just one previous ride at the festival – was following in a proud family tradition with Cheltenham success. Her father is West Country stalwart Jimmy Frost, who numbered Champion Hurdle success on Morley Street (plus a Grand National on Little Polveir) among about 500 successes as a jockey; Hadden, one of two older brothers, won the Pertemps Final in 2010 on Buena Vista.

"When I was little watching Hadden win the Pertemps and knowing Dad had won his, it was a massive ambition for me," she said. "But even getting older, it felt a little bit out of reach. Now I've been able to join them, it's huge. It's amazing all three of us have won at the Cheltenham Festival. Dad always said the races you win are probably the easiest to ride and he was completely right. It was so straightforward."

Joy was unconfined among those close to Frost and Pacha Du Polder after he galloped up the hill to victory. The rider's father and brother Hadden ran up the track in front of the stands to greet her and Pendleton, working for ITV Racing, was also quick to offer congratulations. Frost was embraced by Pendleton in the

winner's enclosure, with the Olympic champion cyclist saying: "You were amazing! You were really amazing there! Brilliant job!" She had offered encouragement to Frost before she went to post and was rooting for Pacha Du Polder all the way. "He's such a legend," Pendleton said. "I went and patted him this morning and was like, 'Go on. Have a good one. You can do it, Pacha'."

Frost started hunting aged four, pony racing at nine, did a lot of showjumping and then had her first point-to-point rides aged 16. She left home last year to become pupil-assistant at Ditcheat. "I'm under the wing of all the brilliant heads in that yard and I'm trying to pick up as much as I can," she said. "My riding career is extremely important to me first of all, but at the same time I'm adding another string to my bow by learning about training."

On the back of her festival success, Frost turned professional in July and was quick to make her mark, winning on her first ride as a 5lb conditional aboard the Nicholls-trained Black Corton in a novice chase at Worcester. "It's a big step forward, but very exciting to have the confidence and support of people to allow me to do something I've always wanted," she said. "I can't thank Paul enough. I certainly wouldn't have turned professional if I didn't have his support. He's given me massive opportunities."

It's one thing to have the opportunities, quite another to take them, but Frost has shown she is ready and able to seize the moment.

Reporting by Alan Sweetman, Julian Muscat, Nicholas Godfrey and Nick Pulford

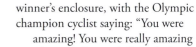

▶▶ Proud moment: Bryony Frost with the Cheltenham Foxhunter trophy

2018
Sales Dates

- CAPE YEARLING SALE

Mistico Equestrian Estate

25 February 2018

- NATIONAL YEARLING SALE

TBA Complex

24, 25 & 26 April 2018

- KZN YEARLING SALE

Sibaya

5 & 6 July 2018

- NATIONAL 2YO SALE

TBA Complex

16 & 17 August 2018

A Source Of Champions

Bloodstock South Africa • +27 31 303 1017 • +27 31 303 1200 • PO Box 78035, Avondale Road, 4101 • bsa@equine.co.za

www.tba.co.za/bsa

BSA 2018 Sales Strategy Returns R2 Million Back Into Breeders Pockets

MAJORITY RULE

Richard Johnson retained the British jump jockeys' title in a season highlighted by Native River, Defi Du Seuil and Menorah

By David Carr

STRONG and stable. That was a buzz phrase of 2017, but you can't escape the feeling that those using it were looking in the wrong place. Neither word would appear a fitting description for a transient, ineffectual government of whichever political hue. Forget Westminster, think the jump jockeys' weighing room.

Strength goes without saying. These are men and women persuading half a ton of horseflesh to carry them over occasionally fearsome obstacles. They do it seven days a week, 12 months a year, with just a nine-day enforced break in the summer – and it takes an awful lot to persuade them they are unfit to ride.

Yet despite the gruelling nature of the job, there is an incredible amount of stability at the top. Since the days of Gerry Wilson before the second world war and Tim Molony afterwards, generally one man has led the pack for several seasons.

The Fred Winter era was followed by multiple titles for Josh Gifford, Terry Biddlecombe and then John Francome, Peter Scudamore and Richard Dunwoody. You could not ask for more stability than Sir Anthony McCoy's 20 straight championships – and it looks as though his successor has booked in for a decent stay in the number one spot as well.

Delight at a good man eventually getting what he deserved was the prime emotion when 16-time runner-up Richard Johnson finally clinched his first championship in 2015-16. Marvel at the quiet determination and supreme effectiveness of a top-notch jockey was the feeling as he repeated the feat 12 months on.

McCoy used to blast out in front in the title race, bound clear with a clutch of early-summer winners and hose up by a wide margin, rather like Slip Anchor in the 1985 Derby. Johnson is more like Reference Point two years later, setting off in front, never appearing to do anything spectacular but never looking at all likely to be caught – and
▸▸ *Continues page 152*

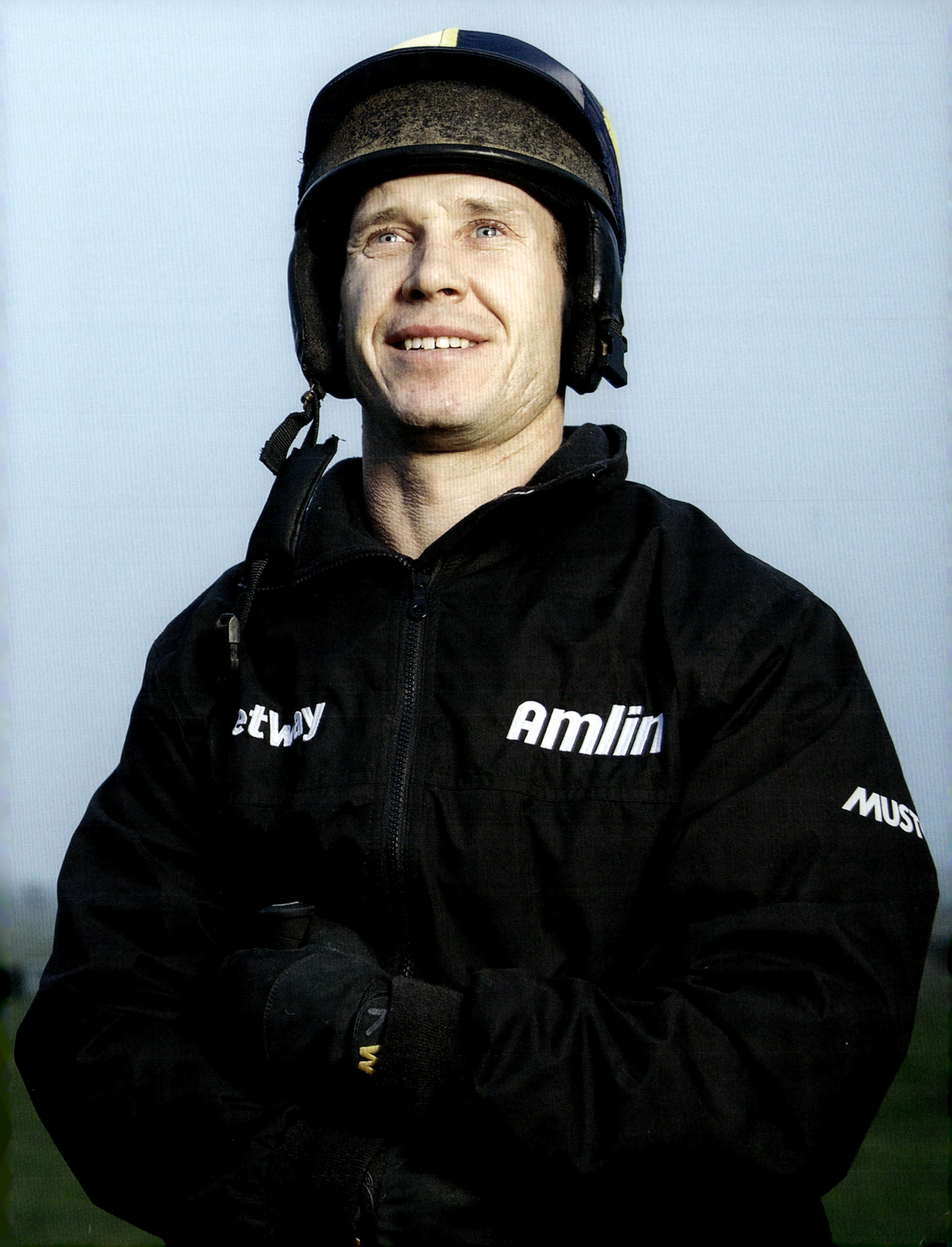
etway
Amlin
MUST

undeniably he is a high-class performer.

His second title was secured with 189 winners, down on the 235 he achieved the previous term but still the second-best of his career. The drop was partly down to a quiet February when he had to take six days off due to a shoulder injury.

Illness also meant he missed the Gold Cup warm-up ride on Native River, the progressive Colin Tizzard-trained seven-year-old who was unquestionably the best chaser he partnered through the season. Victories in the Hennessy Gold Cup – the jockey's first success in the very last running under that branding, before Ladbrokes took over sponsorship – and the Coral Welsh National were followed by a gutsy third place behind Sizing John under a typically forcing Johnson ride at Cheltenham.

Johnson's sole Gold Cup success came on Looks Like Trouble for his future father-in-law Noel Chance in 2000 and it is a measure of his longevity and quality that the only other jockey from that race who is still riding over jumps is Ruby Walsh. He has won all the big races at the festival at least once and, after landing a first Fred Winter Juvenile Handicap Hurdle on Flying Tiger in March, he collected a third Triumph Hurdle on Defi Du Seuil. That took his festival total to 22, behind only Walsh, Barry Geraghty, McCoy and Arkle's rider Pat Taaffe on the all-time list.

That Triumph success, when Johnson stood in for JP McManus's sidelined rider Geraghty, was yet another high spot in his enduring relationship with Philip Hobbs. Trainer and jockey have enjoyed success together for the best part of 20 years and emotions understandably ran high when their old stalwart Menorah galloped gloriously into retirement by landing the Bet365 Oaksey Chase at Sandown on the very day his rider was crowned champion.

Menorah, who took the Supreme Novices' Hurdle way back in 2010, has won every running of the race and earned the comment 'retired with honours' from the otherwise strictly factual Racing Post close-up writer.

▸▸ Continues page 154

NORTHERN GRAFTERS

Gaining a championship contender but losing another man who had been a permanent fixture for nearly a quarter of a century – it was a life of two Brians in the northern weighing room in 2017.

Not since the days of Jonjo O'Neill and Ron Barry four decades ago had there been serious thoughts of an assault on the jump jockeys' title from the north, but that all changed thanks to Brian Hughes, who enjoyed a breakthrough season in 2016-17.

Having ridden just over 100 winners for fifth place in the previous two campaigns, Hughes stepped up to second behind Richard Johnson with a tally of 144 – an astonishing effort given he started slowly and drew a blank through the whole of September.

Riding 31 winners in November alone, including five on one day at Musselburgh, thrust him into the spotlight and made him even more the go-to jockey for anyone needing a rider in the north, to such an extent that he won races for three dozen different trainers.

▸▸ Life of Brians: Brian Hughes (left) has become the go-to jockey for anyone needing a rider in the north; (top) Brian Harding is given a fitting send-off by his weighing-room colleagues on the final day of the Perth festival

The numerous relationships that Hughes, 32, and agent Richard Hale have built up in recent seasons really paid off but this was no overnight success story. Hughes has been grafting hard since he moved from Northern Ireland – it was in 2007-08 that he became champion conditional jockey while based with Alan Swinbank, who died in May.

He famously rode out on the morning of his own wedding and is renowned for doing his homework. Malcolm Jefferson, his main source of winners since the pair teamed up five years ago and supplier of his four Graded winners in 2016-17, quipped: "I think he lives in the form book."

Brian Harding is now a reader of the form book rather than one of its leading characters, having retired from race-riding on an emotional afternoon in April to start a new life running a pre-training livery yard and as a jockey coach. He had made the decision early in the season but kept it quiet for months before enjoying a fittingly emotional farewell on the final day of the Perth festival.

Harding had been part of the fabric of northern jump racing since moving from Ireland in 1992 to join the late Gordon Richards, for whom he won the Queen Mother Champion Chase in 1998 on the great One Man – less than four months after returning from a year out of action with a fractured skull suffered in a fall. That was one of more than 600 winners in a career whose other major highlight was victory in the Irish Grand National on Granit D'Estruval in 2004.

Age never appeared to catch up with him and, nearly two decades after One Man's triumph, he rode a personal-best 56 winners in 2014-15 and might have beaten that again the following season had injury not intervened.

But he turned 45 in September and reasoned: "No matter who you are, at some stage you've got to stop. I would rather stop when I'm going well than get to the stage where you have to stop because nobody wants you any more."

Hobbs supplied 67 of Johnson's winners but you don't become champion without having a healthy supply from other yards too and Gordon Elliott, Charlie Longsdon and Tim Vaughan each contributed more than a dozen to the tally. Nor do you come out on top without being prepared to put in the miles. In each of Johnson's championship seasons his most successful course has been Perth – and no British track is further from his Herefordshire base.

Aintree is nearer but its biggest race remains unconquered territory. Second place on What's Up Boys in 2002 remains the closest he has finished in the Grand National and he did not even have a ride in 2017, although it might have been his year had the cards fallen differently because he was on standby to partner One For Arthur had Derek Fox not recovered from injury. He professes insouciance at his lack of success in that once-a-year lottery, a race that curiously also eluded four of the previous seven champions – Scudamore, Francome, Jonjo O'Neill and Ron Barry.

But the title means an awful lot – "The most important thing is to be champion again," he said as he started

▶▶King Richard: a guard of honour from his fellow jockeys at Sandown as Richard Johnson is crowned champion jockey; (bottom, from left) punching the air on Defi Du Seuil after their Triumph Hurdle success; in the Ascot changing room; with his championship trophy

out on his 2017-18 campaign – and he hopes to keep it for a while longer. He was 40 in July, the age at which McCoy retired, but reasoned: "I'm quite fortunate with my weight, and I'd say that if AP had been my size he would have carried on longer. I'm loving doing what I do, especially when riding nice horses."

What price an assault on McCoy's seemingly unassailable British jumps record of 4,204 winners, by a man who sailed past 3,000 in January 2016? That would make a hell of a story for the 2021 Racing Post Annual.

Defi Du Seuil dominated the juvenile division with a perfect 2016-17 season, raising the inevitable question: will he be more than a fleeting sensation?

By Keith Melrose

A TRIPLE crown for juvenile hurdlers became truly conceivable only in 2005, when the Anniversary Hurdle at Aintree joined the Finale at Chepstow and the Triumph at Cheltenham at Grade 1 level.

They are the only three such races for juvenile hurdlers in Britain and Defi Du Seuil won them all in the 2016-17 season, becoming the first to do so as he completed a perfect seven-race campaign for trainer Philip Hobbs and owner JP McManus.

For an older novice hurdler, such a dominant season would have inevitably brought summer favouritism for the Champion Hurdle and excited talk of their autumn return would have pushed up through the Flat season like moss between the flagstones.

The perception is different for juveniles, especially those bred in France. The received wisdom is that French-breds are more precocious. Like a well-shaken bottle of champagne, after the pop and the fizz and the spray you are left with half of the wine and even fewer of the bubbles.

Others see a self-fulfilling prophecy. Those believed to be precocious, goes the argument, are rushed and over-raced as juveniles. They subsequently struggle to develop at the same rate as late-maturing store horses and ex-pointers. Fait accompli.

Defi Du Seuil makes up the smallest possible sample size but is the closest to a perfectly isolated variable we have yet seen. Put frankly, not before has a French-bred champion juvenile emerged from a yard with equal proficiency in hot-housing youngsters and nurturing more traditional National Hunt types.

Hobbs has been associated with widely disparate performers, from Detroit City through to Rooster Booster, Menorah and Balthazar King. All types of horses seem to come alike to him. If it turns out Defi Du Seuil cannot maintain his early effervescence, it would be difficult to pin the blame on a pushy trainer.

Judging by Hobbs's post-race reaction at Cheltenham the relationship might be better described as doting. Few horses have so obviously misted the eyes of a trainer whose competing guardedness and candour usually gives him the air of a kindly headmaster.

Abashed by his reddened eyes, Hobbs explained: "It's the relief! He's been favourite all year and it's great when it goes right." He added: "You shouldn't get too bullish too early, but he has a fantastic attitude and fantastic ability, so he has everything going for him." Later, at Aintree, the trainer described him as "a lovely horse to deal with in every way".

It had been clear from the beginning that Defi Du Seuil was well regarded. Bought privately from Emmanuel Clayeux in France after winning the second of two bumpers, he was sent off at 1-4 on his British debut in the McManus colours at Ffos Las in October. He then won the juvenile hurdles at the Open and International meetings at Cheltenham, making him the leader on the road as far as the division went, but connections remained unsure about his suitability for faster ground and so were keen to keep going through mid-winter.

That explains his run in the Finale, often bypassed by serious Triumph Hurdle horses who are

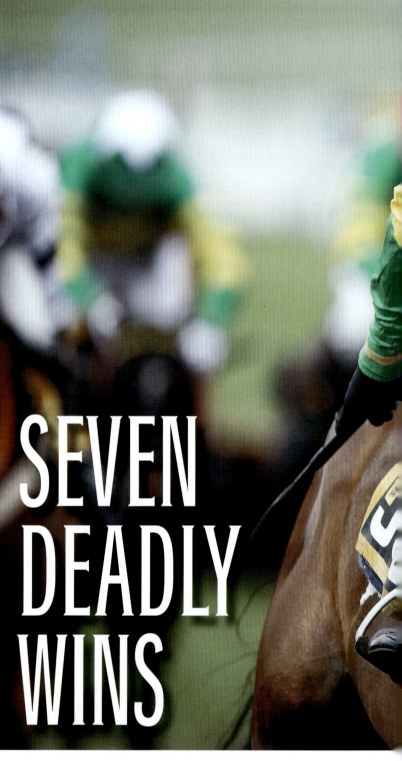

SEVEN DEADLY WINS

spared the worst of the winter ground. There he won by his biggest margin all season – 13 lengths – but also showed his only real sign of weakness, clouting the last two flights after Richard Johnson had seen no point in keeping him with the others any more.

A quick return to Cheltenham to mop up another Grade 2, this time on Trials Day, finalised his Triumph Hurdle preparation, but still the unease about his ground preference persisted. The

emergence of Charli Parcs, a nippier juvenile in the same silks, also tested Defi Du Seuil's dominance in the Triumph betting. These misgivings lasted right up until post time and he was sent off at 5-2, one of only two occasions all season that he was odds-against.

Johnson said afterwards he was "a passenger all the way, to be honest" but the champion jockey is not shy when it comes to self-effacement and he once more undersold his role, but only a little.

He played expert enabler, keeping Defi Du Seuil as far away from trouble as possible and allowing class to tell. His mount travelled beautifully throughout, led before the last and skipped five lengths clear from Mega Fortune. Charli Parcs, the 9-2 second favourite, was sixth. This was Defi Du Seuil's first encounter with good ground since his Ffos Las debut, in much lower class, and his dominance of the division was intact.

There was still the small matter of Aintree and the Anniversary Hurdle, and a small matter was all it proved to be. Many Cheltenham combatants stayed away and it was a couple from the Fred Winter who posed the biggest challenge, which was nowhere near as strong as the length and a half between Defi Du Seuil and Divin Bere would imply.

Doubts about the strength of last season's juveniles were often cited alongside the usual caveats when it came to assessing Defi Du Seuil's chances of making an impact in better company as a senior. His rare dominance and his atypical yard stand on the other side of the argument, along with his atypically impressive physique.

"He's definitely the best juvenile hurdler I've trained," Hobbs said at Aintree. "The thing about juvenile wonders is that they've usually been in training since they were yearlings. This horse had a couple of AQPS bumpers [in France] but that's a bit different to a Flat horse who has been in training for a long time, and he's by a jump stallion [Voix Du Nord]."

Evidently a perfect match with Cheltenham to boot having won four times there as a juvenile, on both the new and old courses, Defi Du Seuil has the racing profile of one who may fade away but all the long-term promise of one we will be seeing at festivals for years to come.

Cheltenham 2018 will be the first proving ground and his journey there might be one of the big hooks of the jumps season. He may even upset some received wisdom along the way.

TEENAGE KICKS

By David Jennings

IT WAS going to happen sooner or later but Jack Kennedy has always done things sooner. Later is never worth the wait. He was champion pony rider in Ireland at 13, rode his first racecourse winner soon after he turned 16 and a few months later he was winning the Troytown Chase in JP McManus's famous colours. He had three rides that day at Navan and left with a 147-1 treble. He never let age ambush him.

So his first winner at the Cheltenham Festival seemed only a matter of time. When it came, however, the name of that winner could hardly have been more surprising. Labaik came into the Supreme Novices' Hurdle, the first race of the 2017 festival, with form figures of RR6. His undoubted talent was being submerged in waywardness. He wouldn't budge on the beach at Laytown on his first start for trainer Gordon Elliott in September 2016 and it was a similar sorry tale at Fairyhouse and Navan in December. Sandwiched in between were stylish successes at Punchestown and Navan. He thought about the game: some days he fancied it, other days he didn't.

On this day, on jump racing's biggest stage, Kennedy made sure he fancied it. In winning his first festival race on the 25-1 shot, the 17-year-old not only reached an important milestone but did so with a ride that justified all the bright hopes long held for him.

****

KENNEDY had a hell of a job on his hands simply to get Labaik into the race, let alone have a chance of winning. His first task was to get the grey to move. Once he moved, the next task was to settle him. If that happened, he had to bury him towards the rear of the pack and, if all of those impossible tasks were completed, the final aim would be to swoop late and fast. All of that is well and good when you are talking about a normal thoroughbred, but Labaik was anything but normal. He was, to many eyes, a lunatic.

Looking after the lunatic was the responsibility of a 17-year-old. Luckily for Labaik, this was not any normal 17-year-old. Elliott hails him as "amazing" and he has drawn praise from Barry Geraghty and Cheltenham Gold Cup-winning rider Conor O'Dwyer, now a trainer. These men spot talent quicker than Simon Cowell ever could.

"Jack is a lovely, quiet rider," says Geraghty, first jockey for McManus. "He gets in the right place through a race. Horses jump and travel for him. I'd heard about him a good few years ago when there was plenty of talk about him coming from the pony circuit. He's just a natural. He wins on everything he should be winning on and he's very level-headed."

Jack Kennedy, the riding sensation of Irish jump racing, took another big career step with his first Cheltenham Festival victory on Labaik

O'Dwyer, speaking last season, had even more lavish praise. "I cannot think of any other jockey of that age – ever – who does what he does the way he does it. I can safely say I've never seen anyone so complete at 17. He's a fantastic natural talent."

Elliott spotted that natural talent early and snapped up Kennedy to ride for his stable. Decisions like that have got Elliott to where he is. Finding talented riders is every bit as important as being able to spot thoroughbreds with the potential to go to the top.

"What Jack has done since he came to me is amazing," Elliott says. "He's a very hard worker. He's laid-back and has his feet firmly on the ground. He doesn't say much

and he just does what he's told. If he stays in one piece and his attitude continues to be as good as it is, he can go right to the top."

****

ENOUGH of the compliments for now. Back to the start of the Supreme. Labaik is looking around as the runners are called in. He walks in with them, aided by Elliott's assistant Ian 'Busty' Ammond, whose persuasive skills work wonders. "Labaik in the orange has jumped away perfectly well with the rest of the field," reveals course commentator Ian Bartlett. Kennedy's first and toughest test is passed, although he jumps the first hurdle with just one behind. He doesn't panic,

though, he never does. Leaving the back straight he has three behind. The picking-off process has begun.

"Labaik has come through cantering," bellows Bartlett as the final flight approaches. The grey crashes through the hurdle but momentum carries him over the line in front, two and a quarter lengths ahead of main Irish hope Melon. The 17-year-old, having only his sixth Cheltenham ride, did not only get Labaik to start, but he got him to finish faster than anything else.

"The main worry was getting him to start, but everything went smoothly. He didn't even think about it," Kennedy said. "Secretly I thought he would jump off but I didn't want to jinx it, so I didn't

say much. Once we got him going I knew we had a fair chance. When I was 12 or 13 I always watched Gordon's horses in their races and Paul [Carberry] or whoever was riding them was always very cool. I always enjoyed watching Cheltenham and it was great to get a taste of what it's like for real. It's a dream come true."

****

KENNEDY was in dreamland for most of the 2016-17 season. He helped himself to 68 winners, a significant rise from 44 in his first season and putting him second in the Irish jockeys' table behind Ruby Walsh. Labaik was his third Grade 1 winner of the campaign,

▸▸ *Continues page 160*

THE RIGHTS AND WRONGS OF LABAIK

The delinquent carried out crime after crime. The first offence was at Lingfield on his only start for Owen Burrows. The stalls opened and he stood still. The same thing happened on the beach at Laytown on his first outing for Gordon Elliott. He was robbing races of their intrigue and causing consternation at the start.

Perhaps a tape instead of stalls and hurdles instead of open spaces would sort him out. It did at Punchestown in mid-October 2016 as he ran out an emphatic winner of a maiden hurdle. He followed up in a Grade 3 novice hurdle at Navan, displaying an impressive turn of foot to beat stablemate Mick Jazz. Rehab was obviously working. Or so we thought.

The temptation to stand still was too strong in the Royal Bond at Fairyhouse as his first appearance in a Grade 1 was a brief one. He never moved at Navan next time either. Three strikes and he would be out – and it was almost the end of Labaik at Naas in February. He was up to his old antics but Jack Kennedy was patient and the pair proceeded to take off a few furlongs after the rest of the pack. It was that shrewd move that allowed him to line up in the Supreme Novices' Hurdle.

Labaik was like a prized child at Cheltenham. He was beautifully behaved and stormed to success in the Supreme. "I don't mind if he never jumps off again," beamed Elliott afterwards.

Punchestown was his next port of call. A rematch with Melon was the big talking point on day one but Labaik didn't fancy it, refusing to jump off until it was too late and finishing a distant last.

He did take off at the right time in the Punchestown Champion Hurdle later that week and got within two and a half lengths of Wicklow Brave in finishing fourth. That performance was all the more admirable when you consider he damaged his off-fore suspensory.

We might never see Labaik again, according to Elliott. What a shame. It could have been the 'start' of a hugely successful career.

▶▶ No-go: Having won the Supreme Novices' Hurdle (previous page), Labaik plants himself at the start of the Champion Novice Hurdle at the Punchestown festival

following Outlander in the Lexus Chase at Leopardstown and Death Duty in the Lawlor's Hotel Novice Hurdle at Naas.

Yet there is one other notable achievement that cannot be seen in the form book, only by those who know him well. One of those people is Elliott's former assistant Olly Murphy, who reveals that Kennedy remains a grounded teenager despite his meteoric rise.

"Plenty of lads think they're too good once they get going, but Jack's far from that," says Murphy, who has

made a blistering start to his own new career as a trainer in Britain. "He knows where his bread is buttered and he stays in the yard in the rain come 4.30pm, helping to feed 150 horses when there's no racing. If he keeps going the way he is, he has the world at his feet."

Not even top-class teenagers with the world at their feet can withstand serious injury in this game, though, and Kennedy suffered a bad break of his left femur from a fall off Bobbie's Diamond at Punchestown in May. Months were spent on the sidelines

QUICK-FIRE

Jack Kennedy was 17 years 326 days old when he won the Supreme Novices' Hurdle on Labaik. As a comparison, Ruby Walsh was 18 when he had his first winner at the Cheltenham Festival, while Sir Anthony McCoy and Richard Johnson had to wait until the age of 21 for their breakthrough successes

recovering but you would have sworn he had never been away judging by his never-say-die ride on A Toi Phil in the Grade 2 PWC Champion Chase at Gowran Park at the end of September. He was back and better than ever, it seemed.

Kennedy turned 18 in April. In two and a half years he has achieved more than most jockeys do in a lifetime. Sooner or later he will become one of the best in the business. That is, if you don't think he is already. We did say he preferred to do things sooner rather than later.

No 1 Choice in Fencing! Do it Once... Do it Right...

- 30 Year Guarantee • Average Cost £3.50 per meter per rail
- Safety & Security • No Maintenance
- Electrifiable • 2 ton breaking strain per rail

www.horserail.org.uk | horserail@mmg.ie | 0808 2344766

Cause Of Causes landed a remarkable third Cheltenham Festival triumph and added second place in the Grand National for good measure

HAT-TRICK HERO

By Nick Pulford

EVERY year some big names fluff their lines on Cheltenham's grand stage, while others rise to stardom in the famous amphitheatre. And then there are players like Cause Of Causes, who handle the occasion with such aplomb that they return year after year to rave reviews and ever greater acclaim.

Cause Of Causes may not be a Grade 1 performer but he is no ordinary horse. Three wins over fences, all three at the Cheltenham Festival, and each time in a different race. That is the remarkable little battler's record after his latest festival victory in the Cross Country Chase, which made him only the fifth horse to win three different chases at the festival – and the first in more than 60 years.

The other four names on that list – 1920s winner Dudley, Medoc from the war years, Gold Cup hero Silver Fame and Kim Muir winner Arctic Gold – may have receded into the mists of time but not these three: Flyingbolt, Bobs Worth and Vautour. Cause Of Causes also stands alongside that trio with the feat of having won three different races at the festival, following his victories in the 2015 National Hunt Chase and the 2016 Fulke Walwyn Kim Muir Handicap Chase.

Completing the hat-trick brought understandable pride to his connections. Jamie Codd, the amateur who has ridden him to all three festival wins, said: "In the build-up to Cheltenham it gives me a lot of confidence to know I have a horse like Cause Of Causes to ride. He's been a remarkable horse for my career. To win three different races, three different trips, he's a great horse and we're all lucky to have him."

Codd's view was echoed by trainer Gordon Elliott: "I'm so lucky to train him. He's a favourite in the yard, everyone loves him, and he's as quiet as a lamb at home, a gentleman."

The person who knows that better than anyone is Georgie Benson, who looks after Cause Of Causes and has the remarkable distinction of three festival wins to her name at the age of 17. The groom said: "He's been 'my' horse for the last three years – this was the first time I haven't had to take a week off school to go to Cheltenham with him. I was so proud of him, I couldn't believe he did it for the third year running. I watched the race at the last fence with all the other lads and when he jumped it in front I went a bit mad, started running up the hill after him.

"He has a big personality, plenty of character and he can be really grumpy sometimes – he puts his head over his door and his ears are back, but when I go in his box he cheers up, he likes a cuddle. And he'll eat anything, carrots, mints, whatever you've got."

Cause Of Causes' vanquished rivals are the ones in need of some comfort at the festival, where his latest victory came by nine lengths. He had been beaten into fifth on his first attempt over the cross-country course six weeks before the festival, but once again came good when it mattered most.

"When you need him, when you set him alight, he's always there for you. He's very idle and not the biggest at just over 16hh, but he jumps very efficiently, he knows what he's doing and he's never going to let you down," Codd said.

"At this stage of his career he wants a trip because he's idle in his races. He has that turn of foot from his two-mile days and he's still able to save it up and produce it at the end of a race. Over the last three years he has done that remarkably well."

Just to prove his ability, versatility and fighting spirit, Cause Of Causes followed Cheltenham with a crack at the Grand National, just as he had after his first festival win in 2015. On that occasion he got round in a distant eighth, but this time he ran a corker to chase home One For Arthur in second place. That was his biggest payday and he might be back at Aintree in 2018, but the main destination will be Cheltenham in March. Perhaps it will be in a fourth different race, with the Foxhunter and Ultima Handicap Chase among the potential targets.

As to why Cause Of Causes performs so well at the festival, Elliott says: "That's a hard question to answer, but he comes alive at that time of year and at Cheltenham especially. Perhaps he likes the undulating track or the rhythm of the races, but whatever it is we know he loves it there and we train him for that week. He's only nine, although it's hard to believe, so if we mind him and train him accordingly he could easily be back in the next couple of years."

A thought to send shivers through his growing army of fans, and to put a chill in the hearts of his rivals.

▶▶Easy as 1-2-3: Cause Of Causes and Jamie Codd are led back to the winner's enclosure by Georgie Benson after the Cross Country

THE
BIGGER
PICTURE

A glorious summer scene at Wexford in July as the ten runners in a 3m1½f handicap chase make their way around a bend. Victory goes to Rachael Blackmore on the Conor O'Dwyer-trained Prosperity Square (blue colours, racing in fifth)
PATRICK McCANN (RACINGPOST.COM/PHOTOS)

BREAKING THE MOULD

Rachael Blackmore made history as Ireland's first female champion conditional jockey

By David Jennings

RACHAEL BLACKMORE is not your typical champion conditional jockey. She was the wrong sex – no woman had ever won the title before. At 27 she was the wrong age – most previous winners were in their teens or early 20s. She came from the wrong background too – only 11 point-to-point winners in seven seasons before she turned professional.

It was Shark Hanlon who suggested the idea. He saw something. He spotted a raw talent that could be nurtured into something special. Just because she wasn't an ace amateur didn't mean she couldn't progress into a successful professional. Try it, he urged.

"A lot of people said it wouldn't be the thing to do, but I didn't have anything to lose. It wasn't like I was leaving behind a fantastic career as an amateur," Blackmore explains. "When you have a trainer like Shark saying he's going to support you, it would be silly not to have a go. I wouldn't have done it without him."

Ten of Blackmore's 32 winners in her title-winning season were trained by Hanlon, but 94 other trainers supported her too. They used her because she was good. She got results. Six winners for Ellmarie Holden, six more for Denise O'Shea and two for Paul Gilligan. She was also successful for Michael Bowe, Liam Cusack, Finian Hanley, Pat Kelly, Dot Love, Andrew McNamara, Mouse Morris and Michael Mulvany.

There were plenty of contributors to the shock title success that put her name alongside previous champion conditionals such as Robbie Power, Bryan Cooper and Jack Kennedy.

Blackmore was in demand on the big days too. She was on board Ex Patriot for his maiden hurdle win at Fairyhouse and finished fourth on him in the Triumph Hurdle at Cheltenham. She won the Leinster National on Abolitionist as well as being placed on him in the Troytown Chase at Navan and the Irish Grand National at Fairyhouse.

"There have been loads of little highlights," says Blackmore, who had only 12 jumps winners to her credit before last season. "To be coming there with what you felt like a good engine under you in a Triumph Hurdle was great, and Abolitionist was absolutely fantastic in the Irish Grand National.

"Ellmarie [Holden] and her assistant Ray Cody do a great job and I'm privileged to be riding for people like that. You can't ride winners unless you're on the right horses and I've been very lucky with the people I've been riding for."

Blackmore and Katie O'Farrell are the only two professional female riders in Ireland. "It's weird. Some of my friends who don't know about racing are like, 'Oh wow, you're professional – you must be really good!' But it doesn't work like that," Blackmore says. "You take Derek O'Connor, the champion amateur rider – he's as good as Ruby Walsh. People just go with what suits them. It suited

me to become a professional but just because I did, it doesn't make me a better rider than Nina [Carberry] or Katie [Walsh].

"Katie and Nina have both won the Irish Grand National. How many other amateurs have even won an Irish Grand National? They're able to compete at that level without it mattering whether they're amateur or professional. They never needed to turn [professional].

"I did it because I was going badly as an amateur. I needed to try something different, I needed to get more rides and better rides. For other jockeys, the career path is to do really well as an amateur, move up the ranks and turn professional. For me, I wasn't doing well as an amateur, so it was a case of trying something different or give it up altogether. I didn't have much to lose."

Blackmore might not have had much to lose but she had everything to gain. Now 28, she has firmly established herself as a popular professional and is already well on the way to surpassing last season's total of 32 winners. There is no resting on laurels here. She rode out her claim at Wexford in June and now the only thing trainers can be attracted to is her ability. This season she is into double figures for the number of new trainers who are on her winners' list, including Conor O'Dwyer, John Joe Walsh and Seamus Fahey. Her popularity grows with every winner she rides.

So what does the brains behind the Blackmore operation make of it all? "Rachael's a great girl. She's a very good rider and she does

everything right," Hanlon says. "I was delighted to see her win the conditionals' title and then to ride out her claim. I remember she said to me a few years ago that she was worried she would never ride out her claim. She should never have worried."

He continues: "I put her up on her first ride ever on the track and point-to-pointing. She's come a long, long way since then. She's a hard worker and deserves all the luck she gets. I had no jockey for a race at Thurles one day and Davy Russell recommended her to me. Since that day she's been with me. That's how it all started."

Word of mouth got her going, but ability has kept her going. She isn't finished yet either.

RISING STAR

Born July 11, 1989

From Killenaule, County Tipperary

First winner Stowaway Pearl (trained by Shark Hanlon), Thurles, February 10, 2011

First professional winner Most Honourable (Shark Hanlon), Clonmel, September 3, 2015

Winners before 2016-17 12

Winners in 2016-17 32

Prize-money before 2016-17 €158,860

Prize-money in 2016-17 €671,656

Finishers in first four in 2016-17 37%

Biggest win Leinster National on Abolitionist (Ellmarie Holden), Naas, March 12, 2017

By Julian Muscat

DISNEY FAIRYTALE

GUY DISNEY likes to play it down, but he did something remarkable and unique in February. Then, just for good measure, he did it again three weeks later.

The Royal Artillery Gold Cup, a three-mile chase at Sandown confined to riders who serve or have served in the armed forces, has something of a reputation for producing emotion-tugging stories and Disney wrote a chapter of his own in the 2017 edition aboard Rathlin Rose.

Disney is a former captain in the Light Dragoons but what distinguished him on this particular day was that he became the first rider to win a race under rules in Britain with a prosthetic leg when Rathlin Rose passed the post four and a half lengths clear. Disney lost his right leg below the knee when a grenade detonated in his armoured vehicle in Helmand province, Afghanistan, in July 2009 and his return to the saddle in the face of overwhelming odds was a triumph in itself.

Winners, though, make the best headlines and Disney's achievement featured on the national television evening news programmes. To cap it all, Disney then posted a second victory aboard Rathlin Rose in March, this time in the Grand Military Gold Cup over the same course and distance.

For Disney, however, the defining feature of his success was not his injury but that he had broken his duck under rules. He makes light of his prosthetic leg, maintaining that it does not compromise his ability to ride. "People assume that it's something it isn't," he said. "To be honest, I don't ride well enough for it to make much of a difference. I'd got very bored with people coming up and slapping me on the back after I'd ridden in a race without winning.

"As far as I'm concerned I'm on a completely level playing field [with able-limbed jockeys]. But that's what I love about racing in general:

it's such a great leveller. Just because you ride the hot favourite doesn't mean you're going to win."

Rathlin Rose was the hot favourite in both races at Sandown and Disney would be the first to acknowledge how the fates had aligned for him. For starters, he was helped in securing the ride aboard Rathlin Rose by Tom Scudamore, stable jockey to David Pipe, who trains the nine-year-old. Disney and Scudamore went to school together. Their respective fathers, John and Peter, forged

their own friendship through John's former role as the racecourse doctor at Cheltenham. But the man who did more than anyone to return Disney to the saddle was Dr David Carey, and fate played a part there too.

"After my initial recovery process I sat on some horses and felt that the prosthetic leg wasn't really an issue where riding was concerned," Disney recalled. "So I applied for my jockey's licence. I did it quite rashly and Dr Michael Turner [then the British Horseracing

Authority's medical officer] gave me three pretty fair reasons why not. If he'd denied it because I had a fake leg, that would have been the end of it. But because he gave me three specific reasons, I was able to work on them."

That's where Dr Carey came in. Disney was preparing for an expedition to the North Pole when he met Carey, who was then attached to the Royal Navy.

"David had an interest in racing," Disney said. "He'd owned a few racehorses, he'd been a

The traditional military chases at Sandown saw rider Guy Disney make history after his remarkable return to the saddle

medical doctor on racecourses and he thought my case was interesting. At the time he was retraining to be a barrister and said he'd like to take my case on a pro-bono basis. It took us four years to put it together. There's no way I could have afforded to do it on my own, never mind employ anyone to argue my case."

One of the reasons Disney's application was denied was the concern that his foot might get stuck in his iron when he fell off a horse. "I had a fitting done which means that if you dragged me around the floor, my leg would stay on," he said. "It also allowed me to regain an iron if my foot slipped out, which David Carey and I filmed on Kim Bailey's gallops. Eventually I got my licence back." The rest, as they say . . .

Disney is now hoping to raise his sights. He would like nothing more than to ride in the Foxhunter Chase at the Cheltenham Festival. "That would be an amazing experience but I'd want to be competitive rather than on a no-hoper. I've ridden at Cheltenham once before, when I was third in a hunter chase, but really I'm just very lucky to be riding in races at all. I'm massively smitten by it, although I'm aware it can't last forever. I do wonder what I'll do when that day comes; I think the feeling is irreplaceable."

The winning feeling is best of all. "You have this moment of complete exhilaration as you pass the line. The annoying thing is that you can't bottle it. You just want to feel it again and again."

And those 15 minutes of fame? Disney doesn't quite see it that way. "I think people had assumed mine is a completely debilitating injury and I can't do anything because of it, which is clearly not the case," he said.

"I now realise that everyone in life has a story. Mine got a bit of attention but to me it was a chance to say thank you to everyone who has helped me out. There are so many of them, especially in racing. They made it happen for me and I will always be grateful."

The death of stalls handler Stephen Yarborough cast a dark shadow over the sport

By Jon Lees

RACING was united in shock and grief in July after a senior stalls handler was killed while working at Haydock racecourse.

Stephen Yarborough (*left*), aged 60, was the leader of the RaceTech team of handlers working at the start during the track's Friday afternoon meeting on July 21 when he was run over by the stalls unit before the fourth race.

Runners coming into the paddock for the race were sent back to the stables and an air ambulance was called to the scene of the incident at the mile-and-a-quarter start. Screens were erected while Yarborough received medical treatment before being flown to Whiston Hospital on Merseyside, but he could not be saved. His death is believed to be the first fatality involving a handler since stalls were introduced in Britain in 1965.

Yarborough, a widower with two children, Christopher and Sheriden, lived in Great Habton near Malton, North Yorkshire. He had worked as a stalls handler for 30 years, having started in racing as a teenager and worked for trainer Peter Easterby, where he met his late wife Molly. Too heavy to become a jockey, Yarborough ensured he stayed in racing by taking a job with the northern stalls team.

His death highlighted the unsung role carried out at every race meeting by the stalls handlers. Speaking the day after the tragedy, former Flat champion jockey Paul Hanagan, who has been based in the north for most of his career, summed up the bond between jockeys and handlers.

Respects are paid at Newbury, where the stalls team was led by Arnie Jones (below)

'When someone goes to work you expect them to come home. We're in shock'

"People don't realise how close we are to these lads," he said. "Everyone knows how dangerous it is. We've been in some pretty scary situations in those stalls. The lads have always got your back. They're always there to drag you off a horse or to get the horse's head up. We have so much respect for them.

"When I first started out as an apprentice Steve was there," Hanagan added. "He's been there since day one. He didn't change from day one either. He would acknowledge me with a smile and ask me how I was doing. I'm gutted, absolutely gutted. The whole weighing room is in shock.

"It's incredibly sad. I'm speaking for everyone when I say Steve was a pleasure to deal with at all times. He was an absolute gentleman."

Haydock abandoned the rest of the card on the day of the tragedy but resumed racing the following evening, having consulted with the Yarborough family. Before the first race there was an emotional minute's applause as Yarborough's colleagues, jockeys and their wives, and valets lined up beside the winning post to pay tribute.

Six of the 11 stalls handlers who had been at Haydock the day before were back on duty. "We're

all determined to continue, though some of the guys couldn't face coming back here today," said RaceTech's racing operations and safety manager Andy Peverell as he fought back tears.

Around the country jockeys and officials wore black armbands in memory of Yarborough. Arnie Jones, the stalls team leader at Newbury that day, said: "It's devastating. I would have worked with Steve only about a dozen times but he was a great lad, always outgoing, always happy. He was a lovely lad who would do anything for you. When someone goes to work you expect them to come home. We're in shock. It's tragic. You expect the horses to be the risk, not the starting stalls."

Kieran O'Shea, Newmarket's starter on the same day, said: "I was working with Steve at Leicester on Thursday. To say

good night to someone on that afternoon, and for them to be dead the following day, it's too much to take in. I've known him for 14 years and he was a great lad. My thoughts, and those of the handlers here at Newmarket today, are with his family."

BHA chief executive Nick Rust said: "This is a tragic incident and we are all shocked and saddened. Stalls handlers carry out a brave and important job each day looking after the safety of the horses and riders and we are grateful for their work. British racing will come together in grief at this incident – we are one family and today we have lost one of our own."

At a memorial service held at York racecourse in August, Tom Phillips, speaking on behalf of RaceTech, said: "Steve was with us for 30 years and was a dedicated and highly regarded member of the northern stalls team. His death has hit us all hard."

Dale Gibson, of the Professional Jockeys Association, said: "Steve was a great guy, I knew him well in my riding days. You can go for weeks, even months, without an incident and then a horse kicks off and as jockeys you are reliant on the expertise of the handlers. Steve was one of the best."

Perrett groom Ken Dooley dies at Kempton

Racing was hit by another tragic death among its core workforce on October 14 when Ken Dooley, a groom with trainer Amanda Perrett, died at Kempton while working in the stable area.

Dooley, who was in his 50s and married, is believed to have suffered a kick from a horse and was found lying in the entrance to the stable yard with what was described as "a serious blow to the face". He had been with Perrett's stables in Pulborough, West Sussex for seven years and had a wealth of experience in racing, having worked in yards in the US and Japan as well as other training centres in Britain.

Perrett said in a statement: "Ken was a very special member of our family business at Coombelands. He was an excellent employee, very experienced with racehorses, having worked all of his life with them as a jockey, trainer and jockey coach around the world.

"He was always first into work in the morning, hugely enthusiastic and dedicated to his horses and a very much valued and integral member of our team."

Despite the attention of doctors, paramedics and other staff, Dooley died before he could be taken to hospital. Among those who helped was Pete McCulloch, travelling head lad for Hugo Palmer, and he was widely praised for his efforts.

Later, speaking on At The Races, Perrett said: "The whole racing industry is feeling it. I've had condolences from Japan, America, every corner of the globe has been in touch, and I hope that will be some comfort for his family."

George McGrath, chief executive of the National Association of Stable Staff, said Dooley's death highlighted the risks of working with racehorses.

"Ours is an incredibly dangerous job," McGrath said. "I've always likened what we do to almost working with Formula One cars. These are highly strung thoroughbred racehorses. At the point they're racing they're at their fittest and most volatile, and the experience and skill that goes into looking after these animals and keeping them calm is considerably underestimated by the general public, and probably by some in the racing industry as well."

THE
BIGGER
PICTURE

Pedal power meets horse power as a cyclist
watches the runners go by in a 1m4f fillies'
handicap at Goodwood in August. Leading
the way is the James Fanshawe-trained Lady
Bergamot, who goes on to win by a head
EDWARD WHITAKER (RACINGPOST.COM/PHOTOS)

MONEY
MONEY
MONEY

Arrogate's five-month romp from the Breeders' Cup to the 2017 Dubai World Cup via the Pegasus was the most lucrative in racing history, making him the global leader both on rankings and earnings

By Nicholas Godfrey

"Here comes the 'Big A'! Arrogate swoops up on the outside. America's King Croesus of horseracing went to the front with 200 metres left to go. Arrogate has drawn away from Gun Runner. A is for Arrogate, A is for absolute superstar, A is for anointing. Have we seen the anointing of the Man o' War of the 21st century? Arrogate, a brilliant winner of the Dubai World Cup."

NOBODY could accuse long-serving racecaller Terry Spargo of underplaying his final effort after nearly two decades at the microphone at the Dubai Carnival. Fortunately, the 'Voice of Meydan' had something special to work with in a sensational World Cup as the American four-year-old Arrogate overcame serious adversity to confirm his status as the best horse on the planet with a spine-tingling,

never-to-be-forgotten last-to-first display worthy of any number of hyphenated adjectives.

A two-and-a-quarter-length margin over the estimable Gun Runner, destined to prove himself one of America's top horses in the months to follow, was superlative in more ways than one. Arrogate was not only the world's highest-rated racehorse, he was also the richest: in a few short months, the strapping roan colt with the distinctive blue noseband had become the highest prize-money earner in the history of the sport. Hence Spargo's "King Croesus" line.

Thereby hangs a tale, however. Arrogate's status reflected the beginnings of what appeared little short of a financial arms race straddling the globe; the Juddmonte colt may have been in first place in money terms, but the Dubai World Cup no longer was, its $10 million prize fund having

been overtaken by the $12m attached to the inaugural Pegasus World Cup, a new concept with innovative entry conditions – $1m a throw for a place in the starting gate – dreamed up by US-based racetrack magnate Frank Stronach. In January, the first Pegasus had taken place at Gulfstream Park. Arrogate won that too, adding to his laurels from the previous year's Breeders' Cup Classic, where he had established himself as the world's number one.

Arrogate's connections took home $7m in Florida, while the winner's share at Meydan was another $6m, which took his total earnings to almost $17.1m – clearly North America's leader ahead of old rival California Chrome, who retired after the Pegasus on a total of $14.7m. More significantly, Meydan meant Arrogate's career earnings also rocketed past all the Japanese-
▸ *Continues page 176*

trained horses clustered at the top of the earnings charts owing to that nation's inflated prize-money structure.

In less than a year, with only a handful of runs, Arrogate had come from nowhere to lead the world. As such, cynical souls might have been tempted to point to a dictionary definition of his name – arrogate: "verb, to take or claim (something) without justification" – but any such smart aleck sentiments would have been unjust. Arrogate had indeed run only eight times by the time he won in Dubai, his first outing – a defeat on his career debut at lowly Los Alamitos – having come only in April 2016.

Yet his race record, abbreviated as it was, featured a series of brilliant victories that led to his name being mentioned in the most rarefied company, which means Secretariat if you're American (or Man o'War if you're Terry Spargo) and Frankel if you're from Europe. Okay, Arrogate wasn't quite up to that standard – no-one was seriously suggesting he was – but he did enough in his pomp to suggest he was perhaps just one level beneath such luminaries, even if he was found wanting upon his return to California after Dubai.

****

A SON of Unbridled's Song, Arrogate was purchased for $560,000 at the Keeneland September Sale in 2014, one of a slew of potentially high-class dirt performers sent to training legend Bob Baffert by Juddmonte in the past few years as they renewed their presence on the west coast.

After Arrogate's low-key debut, the 2016 Triple Crown came and went without him, though he went on to complete a hat-trick in the minor leagues during a two-month period over the summer. His breakout performance came in the Travers Stakes at Saratoga where Arrogate absolutely thrashed the cream of the three-year-old crop in a stunning all-the-way victory by 13½ lengths in track-record time; following a break, Arrogate then overhauled California Chrome inside the final furlong of a dramatic Breeders' Cup Classic. "That winner is the real McCoy," said the runner-up's trainer Art Sherman. "I

KER-CHING

How Arrogate went from third in a maiden to all-time prize-money leader in less than a year

17 Apr 2016 maiden	Los Alamitos *3rd $5,400*
5 Jun 2016 maiden	Santa Anita *1st $33,600*
24 Jun 2016 allowance	Santa Anita *1st $34,800*
4 Aug 2016 allowance	Del Mar *1st $40,800*
27 Aug 2016 Travers Stakes	Saratoga *1st $670,000*
5 Nov 2016 Breeders' Cup Classic Santa Anita	*1st $3,300,000*
28 Jan 2017 Pegasus World Cup Gulfstream	*1st $7,000,000*
25 Mar 2017 Dubai World Cup Meydan	*1st $6,000,000*

Total earnings by that stage: **$17,084,600 (£13,347,744)**

knew he was the one we had to beat, but I didn't know how good he was."

Good enough to become the de facto world champion at the World Thoroughbred Racehorse Rankings unveiling in London in January, the month in which the Arrogate team were lured by the attractions of the first Pegasus World Cup. "It took $12 million to get me off the couch," grinned Baffert, in reference to the prize-money on offer at Gulfstream, while the identity of his jockey could hardly have been more appropriate: veteran Mike Smith, known as 'Big Money Mike' for his tremendous record in high-value races.

Indeed, only filthy lucre can explain why both Arrogate and California Chrome went to Florida for a much-publicised rematch after their epic Breeders' Cup battle. Under Stronach's novel entry procedure, a dozen initial 'stakeholders' were required to stump up $1m to purchase a position in the starting gate for what was designed as a 12-runner race. The entrant then had the right to race, lease, contract or share a starter, or sell their place in the gate; California Chrome's owners were among the initial 'stakeholders' whereas Arrogate got into the race only after a deal was struck with Coolmore for their place.

'In less than a year Arrogate had come from nowhere to lead the world'

As well as a staggering $7m prize for first place, $1.75m was on offer to the runner-up and $1m to the third-placed horse. Every other runner was to receive $250,000; Pegasus entrants were also set to receive an equal share in the net income from the event (ie profit from betting handle, sponsorship and media rights revenues). As Gulfstream had actually paid NBC for a 90-minute broadcast, it always seemed likely the media-rights element would not amount to a big hill of beans; post-race reports suggested it was no more than $100,000 per runner, which meant 'also-rans' dropped $650,000, a hefty loss that raised obvious questions about the event's long-term viability. Nevertheless, all Pegasus shares were sold within a week of the initial announcement of the race; a full field of 12, six of them Grade or Group 1 winners, competed at Gulfstream.

The plain fact is if it hadn't been for the existence of what immediately became the world's richest race, California Chrome would already have been at stud, while his Santa Anita conqueror would have been enjoying his winter break. "These races can change the dynamic – California Chrome would have gone to stud last year if it wasn't

▶▶ *Continues page 178*

for Dubai," admitted Frank Taylor of the horse's part-owners Taylor Made Farms.

Taylor said there was disagreement among the owners about whether to retire California Chrome or continue chasing the cash for another year – to the extent that he put in a cheeky call to Meydan to see if they fancied upping the ante. "I said, 'Surely, you want to bump it to $15m,'" he told reporters. "You don't want the Americans to outdo you."

As for the Pegasus, in the event it was a lap of honour for Arrogate, the very definition of a one-horse race as Arrogate totally overwhelmed his so-called rivals. California Chrome exited the scene for stud duties after a thoroughly downbeat showing in the worst performance of his career as he beat only three home, virtually pulled up nearly 30 lengths behind the winner, with an ashen-faced Sherman left clutching at the straw of a minor knee issue.

The imperious Arrogate – Arrogate the Arrogant – was utterly dominant, powering away with a ground-devouring stride before being eased down inside the final furlong, with the on-track racecaller barely able to contain his fervour. "What a race! What a horse! What a sport!" he shouted as Arrogate scored by nearly five lengths from subsequent Santa Anita Handicap victor Shaman Ghost. "Is it time to call him Arrogreat?" asked Blood-Horse magazine, and you could see why.

****

WHETHER the Pegasus concept can sustain is anybody's guess – even for rich folk, $1m is a lot to spend for your horse to be rendered a no-hoper crushed into the dirt behind a superstar. But surely among those watching with more than a smidgen of interest were the racing authorities in Dubai, whose own World Cup had been usurped as the richest race in the world. Ironically, at its inception in 1996, the Dubai race had also been labelled something of an eyesore in terms redolent of criticism now directed at the Pegasus. As a result, the now 21-year-old Dubai World Cup found itself in the unlikely position of relying on concepts such as history,

tradition and status in the face of an attack from a vulgar parvenu.

Mind you, if Arrogate had ducked the issue in Dubai, they would have been struggling. Despite the usual cosmopolitan presence – well, four horses from Japan – the race was dominated by US horses, among whom Arrogate was the only proper star attraction at the time. He was enough on his own, though. "It's like I'm bringing Usain Bolt to Dubai," said Baffert. "People love to see greatness, no matter what sport it is. I think this horse is like the dirt version in the States of Frankel."

Gun Runner's subsequent exploits may suggest this was a tougher assignment than it appeared at the time, but even if the race looked slightly lacking in depth, it was to lack nothing for drama after Arrogate completely blew the start. Racing outside the US for the first time, with no Lasix, and with a wet track also a new experience, Arrogate

▸ From last to first: Arrogate is towards the rear of the field in the Dubai World Cup (top) before sweeping through in sensational style to lead a furlong out and score easily; the victory followed Arrogate's win in the $12 million Pegasus World Cup under elated rider Mike Smith (below)

was so slowly into his stride that it briefly looked as though he'd be pulled up. In a scenario eerily reminiscent of Zenyatta's notorious Breeders' Cup Classic run at Churchill Downs, the favourite was travelling with no fluency whatsoever in the early stages, leaving him trailing at the back of the entire 14-runner field in the back straight, where he finally began to pass horses.

Still eight lengths adrift on the turn for home, Arrogate was only fourth as he entered the Meydan straight, only for his long, raking stride to totally overwhelm his rivals. It was a truly astounding performance: he won going away from the gallant Gun Runner, with Pegasus third Neolithic completing a 1-2-3 for the US. Somehow, the winner missed the Meydan track record by only 0.32sec.

Though he was to temper his comments in succeeding days out of

▸ Continues page 180

RIGHT PLACE

RIGHT PEOPLE

RIGHT TIME

Send your message to a local audience.

With Racing Post's digital targeting services, you can hit the right people, in the right place, at the right time.

And with Racing Post's extensive reporting and market insight, we'll give you all the information you need.

RACING POST.com

loyalty to his Triple Crown winner American Pharoah, an ecstatic Baffert was in no mood for understatement. "That's the greatest I've ever seen," he marvelled. "That's unbelievable. That is a great horse right there. When he turned for home I said to myself 'if he wins this will be the greatest horse we've seen since Secretariat'.

"Everybody who was here tonight is going to say, 'I'm glad I was here to see that,'" added the trainer. "If anybody wasn't super impressed with that, they just don't like horseracing. I still can't believe he won the race."

Neither could anybody else – including, presumably, the race's organisers, who could not have written a more desirable script. At a stroke, the same horse who put the Pegasus World Cup on the map had enabled its Dubai predecessor to trump the upstart newcomer.

That, however, was by no means the end of this story of financial oneupmanship. In the run-up to Arrogate's Meydan triumph, Sheikh Mohammed vowed to increase the Dubai purse to regain the number-one slot in prize-money terms. Then, in the first week of April, the Stronach Group announced that the 2018 Pegasus World Cup would be even richer, a $4m boost taking its value to $16m.

Yet all went quiet after that announcement – to the extent that just four months before the scheduled date of the second Pegasus, some were openly questioning whether the first edition might turn out to be the last. Or at least the last at Gulfstream, as speculation about a possible move to Santa Anita persisted.

Meanwhile, in Sydney, plans were announced for a sprint over 1,200 metres (six furlongs) to be called The Everest and run at Randwick in October 2017. Entry procedures were broadly similar to those of the Pegasus; with a total prize fund estimated at $A10m (£6m/€7.1m), the Everest would immediately become the world's richest turf race, outgunning anything in Dubai or Japan, or anywhere else.

Unlike Arrogate, due to be retired after his four-year-old campaign, this incredible money race looks set to run and run.

JACKPOT FOR 'EVERYDAY AUSTRALIANS'

The Everest, the new richest turf race in the world, may have been modelled on its dirt equivalent, the Pegasus World Cup, but the two races could not have been more different when it came to their winning connections.

Whereas the first running of the Pegasus went to Khalid Abdullah's global racing operation with Arrogate, the Everest winner Redzel is owned by a syndicate described as "everyday Australians" and his victory in the six-furlong race at Randwick, Sydney, in October sparked wild scenes of celebration from the owners.

Representing trainers Peter and Paul Snowden, the five-year-old gelding held off the late run of the favourite Vega Magic by three-quarters of a length to claim A$5.8m (£3.45m), the winner's share of a A$10m prize fund bettered only by the Pegasus and the Dubai World Cup, both of which are run on dirt.

Redzel went into the Everest on a four-race winning streak for his owners Triple Crown Syndications, who bought him for A$120,000 at the 2014 Magic Millions Yearling Sale. According to Sydney's Daily Telegraph, brothers Chris and Michael Ward, who run Triple Crown, then syndicated Redzel to "a group of 17 owners from all walks of life", among them policemen, schoolteachers, a doctor, taxi driver, builder, electrician, pharmacist, a former New South Wales cricket coach and a security guard.

Following the template pioneered by the Pegasus, 12 'shareholders' paid A$600,000 (or £355,000) for a place in the Everest starting gate. Redzel occupied the slot held by James Harron Bloodstock, who teamed up with the owners to run the horse.

"It's a dream come true," said Triple Crown's Michael Ward. "There are about 30 people in the horse all up. It's hard to put into words."

Harron spoke of his "wonderful experience", according to the Sydney Morning Herald. "When you have to find a horse to fill the slot, I couldn't have found a better group to join," he said. "Look at these people, they're going crazy and it's a race everyone will want to win now."

This financial arms race was more about Sydney v Melbourne rivalry than attracting international interest and the Everest was mainly an Australian affair, although Jamie Spencer turned up to ride Brave Smash into third place.

Coolmore, whose $1m Pegasus slot eventually ended up in a deal with Arrogate's connections, were among the initial dozen shareholders for the Everest. Although Caravaggio was mentioned as a possible, the Irish team's slot was taken by their part-owned Australian-trained filly Tulip, a 50-1 shot. She finished fifth.

Winning jockey Kerrin McEvoy, who gained so many admirers during a lengthy stint in Britain as Godolphin's second jockey behind Frankie Dettori a decade ago, was certainly excited to be part of the occasion.

"The horse has performed unbelievably – woohoo!" he exclaimed. "He's a little star, isn't he? He had a dream run outside the leader and I'm over the moon. It's so exciting to be a part of it, such a huge buzz."

▶▶ Going wild: Celebrations for Redzel's owners (above) and jockey Kerrin McEvoy

Yarmouth blunder as 'winner' turns out to be wrong horse

YARMOUTH was the scene of an embarrassing mix-up in July when the 50-1 winner of a two-year-old race was later identified as her year-older stablemate who had been due to run later on the card.

Mandarin Princess had appeared to cause an upset when winning the 6f novice auction stakes for Newmarket trainer Charlie McBride and jockey John Egan from 4-6 favourite Fyre Cay (right). However, when the horse (blue colours) was later checked at the sampling unit, where race winners are taken for a blood or urine sample, she was revealed to be Millie's Kiss, a three-year-old stablemate scheduled to run in the fourth race, a 1m1f handicap.

By that time the weighed-in announcement had been made by officials and the racecourse stewards had no power to amend the embarrassing result, which officially stood for betting purposes, although some bookmakers paid out on the horses who finished first and second.

It was the first time such a situation had occurred on a British racecourse since the introduction of microchip identification in 1999 and McBride called the error a "genuine, honest mistake".

He said: "I went to the weighing room to get the saddle. I like to weigh my horses out early but I had to wait over 20 minutes for the saddle. The filly was already out when I got back and as I was stressed and rushing I didn't look that closely – I just assumed it was the right horse."

The matter was referred to the BHA and McBride's runner was officially disqualified at a hearing a fortnight later, with the trainer fined £1,500. The disciplinary panel, led by Patrick Milmo QC, found McBride guilty of a "high degree of carelessness". They said they had "some difficulty accepting what Mr McBride told us as Millie's Kiss has distinct white markings on her forehead and hind leg. Mr McBride had plenty of opportunity to notice this and the only conclusion is he never bothered to look closely. He has a small 25-horse stable and therefore must be familiar with the horses in his yard."

The BHA did not push for a more severe sanction as it accepted McBride had made a genuine mistake. An integrity officer noted there were no suspicious betting patterns surrounding either of the two races in which McBride's fillies were due to run.

In an attempt to prevent a repeat, the BHA moved quickly to introduce a second microchip scan on racedays for horses after they had been saddled, described as an "interim measure" while further consideration was given to longer-term policy.

Picture: ROGER HARRIS

CLOUD NINE

By Steve Dennis

WHEN you're starting out it's all about making an impact, all about doing something to set you apart from the crowd. Competition is fierce, results are important, publicity is vital. In track-record time, Richard Spencer sent his profile soaring.

Spencer chose the perfect stage to train just the ninth winner of his career, saddling Rajasinghe to land the Group 2 Coventry Stakes on the first day of Royal Ascot. Little wonder the second-season rookie faced the cameras with a grin and said "it's all downhill from here". For now, though, Spencer is heading in the other direction. Twenty years earlier Aidan O'Brien had got off the mark at the royal meeting by winning the Coventry, and although coincidence and comparison are not the same thing at all there are worse precedents to follow.

"It isn't very often a trainer in my position would be able to have a runner in one of the big races at Royal Ascot, let alone one with a winning chance," he says. "I only have nine two-year-olds, so for one to be good enough to win at Ascot is fantastic.

"Since I started training in April 2016 my horses had been involved in so many photo-finishes, and so many of them went against us. It began to become frustrating, because I needed winners to get my name out there. When the Coventry went to a photo-finish, I couldn't celebrate. I thought he'd won, I hoped he'd won, but I'd thought that before about a few horses. So when the result was announced it all got a bit emotional."

There were tears, but the heat of the spotlight soon dried them up. Rajasinghe's head success, in two-year-old track-record time, had thrust 28-year-old Spencer into the big time. Everyone loves it when a plan comes together, although in this case it was Plan B after the son of Choisir missed the break and left jockey Stevie Donohoe with plenty to think about.

Spencer praised Donohoe for his cool head, yet it was another part of the jockey's anatomy that had been on ice just hours earlier.

Never mind Luke, here's Cool Hand Steve.

"I'd dislocated the little finger of my left hand at Windsor the night before – I broke the knuckle too," says Donohoe, for whom it was also a first winner at the royal meeting. "African got rid of me down at the start and when he was galloping by I caught him, and then I realised that my finger was on upside down. I quickly snapped it back in, because I was afraid that if the doctor had come over and seen it I might be stood down. It hurt a lot. That'll teach me to stop a loose horse – but he won, I knew he would, he was so well handicapped. It was worth it."

It wouldn't have been worth it if Donohoe had been stood down from Rajasinghe – "Imagine sitting at home and watching a Royal Ascot winner you should have been riding. It'd haunt my career" – so he iced his hand, strapped it up, didn't let on about the pain.

"I couldn't bend it that much. I was holding him going down to the start and it didn't feel great, but I knew the adrenaline would kick in, so I decided to pull off the strapping. I didn't feel it during the race but when I pulled up it was killing me.

"William Buick rode over, went to high five me, and for some reason I put out my left hand and he hit it . . . it was agony. But I got away with it. Imagine how far he'd have won if I'd had two hands!"

Spencer can trump his jockey's medical record. His own riding exploits were a source of fun rather than the foundation for a career in the saddle, but their sudden conclusion left him with no alternative but to separate pleasure and business.

"I enjoyed myself in point-to-points and hunter chases, and won a Royal Artillery Gold Cup," he says. "I rode 20-odd winners, but I broke my back in the spring of 2015 in a fall at Warwick – it was bad enough without having to be operated on. I was laid up in hospital with plenty of time to think, and I decided there was more to life than galloping around a field jumping 18 fences.

"Just over a year later I had my first runner as a trainer, so breaking my back might have been the best thing that could have happened for my career."

Some people wait ages for Royal Ascot success, for many it never comes, but Richard Spencer lived the dream with just the ninth winner of his fledgling training career when Rajasinghe landed the Coventry

Spencer started young, turning his summer job at Peter Bowen's yard into a permanent stay at the age of 16. Two years later he moved to Lambourn and to Barry Hills, arguably a fearsome prospect for a raw youngster but an invaluable grounding that was completed by two years as assistant to Michael Bell.

"Working for Barry Hills was amazing. I'd learn stuff simply from spending time around him, soaking it up without knowing. I learned how to take a bollocking too, which is always useful. When you work with the likes of Barry and Michael Bell you're surrounded by so many good horses year in, year out, and it's easy to take it as the norm. You only realise that isn't the case when you start out on your own."

A connection to the past shaped Spencer's future. Phil Cunningham – owner of dual Guineas winner Cockney Rebel – advertised for a trainer for his Rebel Racing outfit,

and Spencer, who had met him during his time at Hills's yard, sent in his CV. Cunningham liked what he saw and set Spencer up in the historic Albert House stables at the foot of Warren Hill in Newmarket.

"Phil told me what he wanted to achieve, and one of those things was a Royal Ascot winner," says Spencer. "This is a great location, a great yard, and there's scope to expand if we want to. There's a lot to look forward to. Some people have to wait a lifetime for a Royal Ascot winner and I've got one in my second season. It's a dream come true."

▶▶ Landmark win: Rajasinghe (fifth left) heads to victory in the Coventry Stakes at Royal Ascot under Stevie Donohoe for a jubilant Richard Spencer (right)

FIRST TEAM

Aclaim's Group 1 victory on Arc day was a notable milestone for trainer Martyn Meade and jockey Oisin Murphy

By Lee Mottershead

BY the time the Prix de la Foret brought down the curtain on Chantilly's second and last Arc day, some racegoers had already departed for the train station, keen to avoid overcrowding on platforms not accustomed to such popularity. As those fans began their journeys back to Paris, Martyn Meade and Oisin Murphy were also experiencing something to which they had not been accustomed.

For the young jockey and rather more senior trainer, Aclaim's Foret strike broke both their Group 1 ducks. It was only two weeks later that Murphy won his second. Meade has a horse he believes could at the very least double his own tally in 2018.

In the autumn of 2013 Meade paid £2.95m to buy Newmarket's Sefton Lodge Stables. Although wonderfully located, right by the heath, the stables had not been used since December 2008. The historic yard has been revived by the impressively young 70-year-old, who in the spring had high hopes of Classic success with Eminent. Those hopes were dashed but it would be wrong to say Eminent had a bad year. Meade most definitely did not.

Across the final day of September and the first day of October, Meade enjoyed a weekend to remember. At Newmarket on the Saturday he sent out Dolphin Vista to spring a 50-1 shock under George Wood in the Cambridgeshire.

On the Sunday, Aclaim struck gold on the biggest afternoon

in the European Flat racing calendar.

"Our main objective of the weekend, and indeed of the weeks preceding, had been the Foret," Meade said. "That had to be the race for Aclaim, a race we had been waiting to run him in for a long time. Winning it was mission accomplished. We started the year with the ambition of landing a Group 1 with him. It's always nice when you make a plan and it works out. So often it doesn't."

As for Dolphin Vista, who was having only his second run from Sefton Lodge, Meade added: "As we got into the final fortnight before the Cambridgeshire it was obvious he was getting better and better. I suddenly thought: 'Blimey, this horse is going to run a big race.' I then saw the odds and wondered how he could be

such a big price. I realised that nobody else knew what I knew."

In the spring, the successful entrepreneur, who sent out the first winner of a stop-start training career back in 1972, knew he had a smart three-year-old colt. Eminent proved him right when landing the Craven Stakes and, though he was unable to turn Classic trial victory into Classic glory in the 2,000 Guineas and Derby, he ended the campaign on a high, bagging the Group 2 Prix Guillaume d'Ornano before posting a fine front-running third in the Irish Champion Stakes.

"He never put a foot wrong," Meade insisted. "He progressed and progressed. We couldn't have been more thrilled with him. He gave us enormous excitement by allowing us to take part in races you can normally only dream

about. The disappointment was simply that he turned out to be a bit immature. The upside of that is I can't wait for his four-year-old career.

"I have no doubt there's a Group 1 in him. We'll go back and revisit some of the races he ran in this year but this time with a stronger horse. We'll bring him along slowly and hopefully start off at Royal Ascot. To have a winner there would be fantastic.

"The really big one is obviously the Arc. Maybe that's a dream too far at this stage, but I certainly do think Group 1 success at Royal Ascot is very much within his grasp."

For Murphy, there was a first success at Royal Ascot in 2017, courtesy of Godolphin's Group 3 winner Benbatl. Qatar Racing's retained jockey remained without a first top-flight triumph at that point and he continued waiting through the rest of the summer, although you may not have realised given how enthusiastically he celebrated winning the Group 2 Celebration Mile on Lightning Spear, standing in his stirrups and punching the air on the walkway back to the paddock.

That left Murphy slightly embarrassed but he had nothing to be embarrassed about when steering Aclaim home in France, nor when exporting the Grade 1 EP Taylor Stakes at Woodbine aboard Blond Me for former boss Andrew Balding.

"Oisin has come a long way in a very short space of time, but at the same time it's taken him a little while to ride a Group 1 winner considering he's had a few chances," Balding said. "It's great for him and I'm sure this is only the second of many Group and Grade 1 wins."

Balding believes Murphy has every reason to aim high. Meade believes the same is true for his racing stable. "I have a burning ambition to go on and on," he said. "Once you start to taste a bit of success you want more and more of it.

"I have bags of energy. There are so many things I'm keen to do, so that I can have a proper business for the family to go on with afterwards. At this stage age doesn't cross my mind. I'm sure one day it will and that I'll decide I've had enough – but I'm certainly a long way off that at the moment."

▶ High flyers: Oisin Murphy celebrates his second top-level win with Blond Me (above), just two weeks after sharing his first with Martyn Meade (below)

YOUTH OPPORTUNITY

Amateur jockey Ellie Mackenzie is just one of the young riders who have boosted their profile with success in Arabian racing

WINNERS open doors and nobody knows that better than amateur rider Ellie Mackenzie, whose success in Arabian racing has led to a move to Lambourn, a new job there with trainer Mark Usher and a new ambition to ride over jumps as well as on the Flat.

All that stemmed from a racecourse gallop at Kempton on an Arabian three-year-old called Riyam, followed by a winning ride on his first run in Britain on the Wathba Stallions Cup card at Chelmsford in mid-July. That card was part of the Sheikh Mansoor Festival that takes Arabian racing around the globe and puts strong focus on opportunities for young riders in general and women in particular. In Mackenzie's case,

that win was just the opening she needed.

Two weeks later Mackenzie and Riyam took another big step with a Group 2 victory on the prestigious Dubai International Arabian Raceday at Newbury. Many of the top jockeys turn out for this day and behind Mackenzie as she won the seven-furlong event on Riyam were Olivier Peslier, Jim Crowley and Tadhg O'Shea – all on better-fancied mounts.

"It was amazing, words can hardly describe it. I crossed the line and I couldn't believe it," says Mackenzie, 24. Soon afterwards, she began to notice the difference her winning association with Riyam had made. "It's really boosted my profile. I've found that a lot more people have contacted me and taken me more seriously.

Even professional riders have heard about the win and said 'well done'. It has helped me out so much."

In late September, Mackenzie moved from David Evans – who had provided her first two wins on the Flat – to join Usher's Lambourn yard full-time. She hopes that will lead to more opportunities and is doing all she can to make that happen. "It's great being in Lambourn because people see more of you on the gallops, and in my spare time and my lunch hours I ride out for as many people as I can.

▶▶ Winning riders: (from left) Ellie Mackenzie on Riyam (right); Tadhg O'Shea on the grey Mith'haf Athbah; Rikke Bay Torp; Milly Naseb; (below left) Mackenzie with her trophy at Newbury

Pictures: DEBBIE BURT

This winter I'm going to try my hand over jumps as well, so far it's just been Flat rides."

Proof that the top Arabians can produce exciting finishes came in the HH Sheikh Zayed Bin Sultan Al Nahyan Cup, the first Group 1 race (Arabian or thoroughbred) to be staged at Chelmsford. O'Shea came out on top aboard the Phil Collington-trained Mith'haf Athbah, who prevailed by a nose over Kalino, trained by Alban de Mieulle. This was a high-class race, with Kalino having won the 2015 edition of the prestigious HH Sheikh Zayed Bin Sultan Al Nahyan Jewel Crown.

The Zayed Cup was the main event on the Chelmsford card, which also featured the HH Sheikha Fatima Bint Mubarak Ladies World Championship and HH Sheikha Fatima Bint Apprentice World Championship. Again these races were all part of the HH Sheikh Mansoor Bin Zayed Al Nahyan Global Arabian Festival, which travels the world throughout the year before concluding with a hugely valuable finals night at Abu Dhabi in November featuring the HH Sheikh Zayed Bin Sultan Al Nahyan Jewel Crown, the world's richest race for purebred Arabians.

The races for female and apprentice riders offer invaluable opportunities and Milly Naseb,

who is based with Newmarket trainer Stuart Williams, was quick to seize her chance with a front-running victory aboard Storm Troupour in the apprentice race. Naseb, 24, represented Jordan and was delighted with her victory, which secured her a place on finals night. "Although I've had nearly 150 thoroughbred rides in my career so far, I've only had three on Arabian racehorses and this was my first win on an Arabian. It'll be really exciting to ride in the finals in Abu Dhabi," she said.

The riders in the Ladies World Championship race on the Chelmsford card included Cheltenham Festival winner Lisa O'Neill for Ireland and Mackenzie for the UK, but victory went to Danish amateur Rikke Bay Torp, who led from start to finish on Madjanthat.

Winning trainer James Owen said: "Madjanthat is ridden by girls at home and they get on really well with him. Rikki gave him a great ride, letting him take charge, and she's absolutely delighted that she'll be going to the finals in Abu Dhabi."

Owen, whose Newmarket yard is also a pre-training facility for several top Flat stables, went on to take the Arabian trainers' title for the second year in a row. Having crowned his season with four winners on the final day at

Huntingdon in September, he thanked his principal owner, Sheikh Hamdan, for his support. "It's been wonderful with his young horses coming through, and exciting with three-year-olds like Al Kaaser and Rafeef for next season," he said. "I'm really pleased for all my staff at home, they work really hard, they enjoy coming racing and their parents come along too. We're a happy team."

David Turner secured his first Arabian Racing Organisation jockeys' title and Joanna Mason, closely linked with the Owen yard, was champion lady jockey. "It's thanks to James that I've been able to ride nice horses," she said. "It's amazing to get ten winners, I'd never have dreamed that was possible at the start of the season."

The final word must go to Mackenzie, whose memorable season in Arabian racing finished with the ARO champion novice jockey title. "It's been absolutely fantastic to be given the opportunities that I have and I'm so lucky. I never expected it to be such a great season and to win a Group 2 race was incredible."

With the determination she showed to beat the professionals at Newbury and has brought to her new life in Lambourn, Mackenzie has every chance of further success in the amateur ranks in both Arabian and thoroughbred racing.

THE
BIGGER
PICTURE

Racegoers arrive for the final day of the Ebor meeting at York in August

EDWARD WHITAKER (RACINGPOST.COM/PHOTOS)

Our selection of the horses and people – some established, some up-and-coming – who are likely to be making headlines in 2018

ANNUAL
20

HAPPILY

Family pride was finally restored on October 1 when Happily took care of some unfinished business by recording a victory that was denied to her brother.

Gleneagles was first past the post in the Prix Jean-Luc Lagardere in 2014 but was stripped of victory after drifting and cutting across the two horses who chased him home. Three years later there was no argument as his full-sister Happily took on the colts and beat them decisively, scoring by a length and a quarter from Olmedo.

She became the first filly in 31 years to land France's most prestigious juvenile race and, while that may say something about an overall lack of quality among the juvenile colts, it certainly said a lot about Happily's ability.

A Racing Post Rating of 112 was a mark of how far Aidan O'Brien's filly had come from seventh place on her debut in June. On that occasion she was behind stablemate September (another Group 1-performing filly for the Ballydoyle team) but she progressed at a rate of knots, landing a Group 3 on her third start and a first Group 1 on her fifth when she took the Moyglare Stud Stakes at the Curragh – this time ahead of September. In between them, in a Ballydoyle 1-2-3, was Magical, who had previously beaten Happily in the Group 2 Debutante Stakes.

A high temperature put paid to another Group 1 mission in the Fillies' Mile but there was no doubt Happily had proved her worth in her first term.

Where the daughter of Galileo ranks among Ballydoyle's fillies next season remains to be seen but family history bodes well, with Gleneagles becoming a dual Guineas winner and sister Marvellous landing the Irish 1,000 Guineas.

ELARQAM

The Classic picture for colts was blurred in the autumn by the injury layoff of ante-post 2,000 Guineas favourite Gustav Klimt, a setback for National Stakes winner Verbal Dexterity that ruled him out of the Dewhurst and odds-on Expert Eye's flop in the Dewhurst. That could leave the way open for others and, on pedigree, there is no better candidate than Elarqam.

Sheikh Hamdan's colt, who cost 1.6 million guineas as a yearling, is a son of Guineas-winning parents, by the great Frankel out of Attraction. His juvenile career was nowhere near as glittering as either of them but the genes had mixed well enough to take him to an easy Group 3 win at Newmarket on only his second start.

That victory put him high up the Guineas betting and trainer Mark Johnston, who won five Group 1s with Attraction, admitted: "It's the most nervous I've been since his mother ran. It's not the size of the race that makes me nervous, it's when nothing but coming first will do."

Dane O'Neill, who rode Elarqam to his debut victory over seven furlongs at York in September, distilled the excitement around the colt to its essence, saying: "Forget his breeding, forget his price tag, he rode like a good horse." O'Neill is a good judge and his words may be worth heeding.

YORKHILL

Enigmatic, exuberant, exhilarating and as wayward as he is wonderful. There are few horses in training with the allure of Yorkhill *(above)*, who has been beaten only twice under rules – officially by other horses but most probably by his own character – in an 11-race career. He could give Might Bite a run for his money in the quirkiness stakes but has such rich ability that trainer Willie Mullins has a wealth of options with him.

Top of the wishlist might well be the Cheltenham Gold Cup, which Mullins has yet to win, but Graham Wylie's livewire is speedy enough to have had connections looking at the Champion Hurdle after his electric win in the Neptune Novices' Hurdle in 2016 and versatile enough to prompt Ruby Walsh to say "he'd win an Arkle with his mouth open" if they went novice chasing instead.

The switch to fences was the decision but the 2017 Cheltenham Festival target ended up being the JLT Novices' Chase over 2m4f and Yorkhill gave a spectacular display, winning more impressively than the one-length margin over Top Notch suggests. Significantly he jumped much more accurately than in previous races, although his tendency to idle was apparent once again on the run-in. Mullins was putting it mildly when he said "he's not the easiest of rides".

That was evident the following month when Yorkhill gave another spectacular display in the Ryanair Gold Cup at Fairyhouse, but this time of the wayward variety. Having pulled his way to the front and jumped violently left, he still looked set to win until virtually refusing at the last and handing the spoils to Road To Respect.

Which way will Yorkhill go? Not even Mullins seemed sure after the exasperating Fairyhouse defeat, as he openly pondered a switch back to hurdling. "He looks like either a Champion Hurdle horse or a Gold Cup horse. At home he seems to jump straight enough."

One thing is for certain: wherever Yorkhill ends up, you will want to be watching.

NICOLA CURRIE

Richard Hughes knows a thing or two about race riding and in Nicola Currie, his up-and-coming apprentice, he recognises ability as well as a strong work ethic.

"She has come on in leaps and bounds and I know how much Nicola wants to be a successful jockey," the trainer says. "Due to an enormous amount of hard work she has started to make significant progress. She comes into the yard at 5.30am every day. She is always asking me questions and is desperate to learn."

Currie is in a good school at the Hughes yard in Upper Lambourn. "Every race I ride I go into the office and go over it with him, whether it's style, whip or racing tactics," says the 24-year-old.

From a farming background on the Isle of Arran, Currie rode ponies at a young age and was involved in showjumping before switching to racing in her late teens. She was a slow starter – she didn't ride her first winner until her fourth year as a jockey and thought about packing it in – but 2017, her fifth year, marked a coming of age.

The highlight of her fledgling career came in September with victory on Kryptos in a mile handicap at Doncaster on St Leger day, John Berry, trainer of Kryptos, described her as "outstanding" and added: "She claims 7lb and I'd happily use her without a claim."

Currie models her style on Josephine Gordon as the pair are of similar build, and her stated ambition is to emulate Gordon by becoming champion apprentice.

It's an ambitious goal, but with Hughes in her corner Currie could not have better guidance.

OUR DUKE

It is a decade since stablemates Kauto Star and Denman fought one of modern steeplechasing's most famous proxy wars, culminating in what the fullness of time allows us to call a damp squib of an eventual meeting in the 2008 Cheltenham Gold Cup.

Now it looks as though there might be an Irish version, with defending Gold Cup winner and reformed two-miler Sizing John up against the resolute galloping, brawn and bustle of big-handicap graduate Our Duke. They'll remake anything these days.

"He does look like a Gold Cup horse and we'll keep him and Sizing John apart," said trainer Jessica Harrington after Our Duke had carried near top weight to a 14-length success in the Irish Grand National on Easter Monday. "I've never seen a horse win a race like that so easily – I couldn't believe it," she added.

That was just Our Duke's fourth start over fences in a transformative campaign that had until then been marked by haphazard jumping. He took several fences with him on the way to a Grade 1 success at Leopardstown and could not shrug off the errors when dropped in trip in the Flogas on his next start, finishing second to Disko in that Grade 1 novice chase.

What is so exciting about Our Duke is that by the end of his novice season he had run only twice at three miles or further and they were his two most visually impressive performances. It can only be hoped that the Harrington stablemates make it to Cheltenham unscathed, and with any luck they will provide a fitting spectacle on the biggest stage.

SAXON WARRIOR

"He has the pedigree on top and bottom," Aidan O'Brien said after Saxon Warrior *(right)* won the Group 2 Beresford Stakes at Naas in September, and the top and bottom of it is that he did enough as a juvenile to back up that pedigree with racecourse performance.

Saxon Warrior's sire is Japanese superstar Deep Impact and he is the second foal of Maybe, a Group 1 winner as a two-year-old for O'Brien before being beaten favourite in the 1,000 Guineas. "When you run those horses you're always hoping you'll find something," the trainer said after the colt's winning debut in a 1m maiden at the Curragh in August.

A Racing Post Rating of 90 for that first run indicated that O'Brien had found something worth having and that impression was confirmed in the Beresford four weeks later when he scored easily in a five-runner contest to record an RPR of 111 and move to the head of the Derby betting. "He's a Classic horse for next year," O'Brien said simply.

Saxon Warrior was the trainer's 17th winner of the Beresford, and the seventh in a row, although only a handful of the others have covered themselves in glory as three-year-olds.

Hopes are high for Saxon Warrior, not least because his wins at the Curragh and Naas came on yielding and soft ground. O'Brien reported that Ryan Moore, who rode him in the Beresford for the first time, felt better ground would be in his favour.

Moore also felt there was pace in the locker and it is not cut and dried that Saxon Warrior will go straight up to middle distances as a three-year-old. "We'll wait and see which way we'll go with him next year," O'Brien said. The trainer will be hoping the main way is up.

DESERT SKYLINE

About 30 years after Desert Orchid was at his best, another 'Desert' hit the headlines for veteran trainer David Elsworth, although the son of Tamayuz has more in common with another Elsworth legend, Persian Punch, than Dessie.

Desert Skyline *(red star on cap)* emulated Persian Punch by winning the Doncaster Cup (a gelding operation prevented connections considering him for the St Leger 24 hours later) in the style of a potential Gold Cup winner at Royal Ascot.

Perhaps a busy season and soft ground took their toll next time in the British Champions Long Distance Cup but Elsworth is confident Desert Skyline will improve with maturity. "I'm sure you might be hearing of him again next year – he's going to be around for a while," he said.

While Desert Skyline has some way to go to match Persian Punch's record of 13 Group victories, it would be some story if he could win the Gold Cup, which always eluded that staying legend, for a trainer two years away from turning 80.

FINIAN'S OSCAR

Even with all the talk about Colin Tizzard's established stars early in the last jumps season, the whispers about Finian's Oscar were loud enough to identify him as the potential next big thing and he did not waste any time in putting actions to the words.

Tongues had been set wagging by his price tag of £250,000 at the 2016 Cheltenham November sale – three weeks after an Irish point-to-point win – and less than two months later he was a Grade 1 winner in the Tolworth at Sandown on his second run over hurdles. A minor setback ruled him out of the Cheltenham Festival but he won another Grade 1 at Aintree and then finished a short-head second to Bacardys at the Punchestown festival.

That was a good six months' work and the progress continued with a Listed victory on his chasing debut at Chepstow in October. That course is favoured by Tizzard as a stepping stone – Cue Card and Thistlecrack also had their first runs over fences there – and this season the aim is to be at the Cheltenham Festival. "That's where we want to end up with him," the trainer said.

On board, all being well, will be Bryan Cooper, who was signed by owner Alan Potts to ride his British-based string shortly before Finian's Oscar made his chasing debut. The Cheltenham Gold Cup-winning jockey had lost his job with Gigginstown in the summer and Potts was quick to snap him up.

In Oscar and Bryan, Potts has a couple of gems.

OLLY MURPHY

Olly Murphy was bred to be a trainer and, after four years learning with a man who has taken the sport by storm, it was no surprise that he started his training career with a bang.

His first runner, Dove Mountain, was a winner on the Flat at Brighton in early July and a few days later his first two jumpers finished first and second at Market Rasen. Murphy had arrived, but he did not stop there. The same month he had an across-the-card four-timer at Stratford and Newton Abbot, and on it went as he racked up 16 winners in his first three months with his relatively small number of "summer horses".

The fledgling trainer is the son of Anabel Murphy, nee King, who has been training for 35 years, and Aiden Murphy, the master bloodstock agent who buys many of the Philip Hobbs horses. He had spells with Brian Meehan and Alan King before heading west to complete his training education by becoming assistant, right-hand man and friend to Gordon Elliott.

In May he moved back home to the 400-acre family farm in Warwickshire and now trains close to his mother but with his own purpose-built facilities. He admits he is lucky – "I would never dispute I've been given a leg-up" – but that brings its own pressure and he knows the only way to prove himself is by training winners.

"I have no interest in training racehorses and finishing second," he says. "In my eyes I've worked for the best, so I want to be the best. I want to be as good as anyone in England."

Murphy has a long way to go but he could not have made a better start.

MONARCHS GLEN

The attraction of John Gosden's yard to leading owner-breeders is clear from his expert nurturing of talents such as Enable and Cracksman, which brings great prizes and prestige on the track and hugely enhanced value in the mating game that follows their racing careers.

Monarchs Glen is an up-and-coming older horse for Gosden and Enable's owner Khalid Abdullah in 2018 but, as he is a gelding, the game plan will be all about maximising his prize-money haul on the racecourse. That should mean he is kept busy and the signs towards the end of his 2017 campaign were that he could take high rank.

He is well bred, from the first crop of Frankel, but was not so well behaved and after five runs that brought two wins and a Racing Post Rating of 100, he was gelded in the early summer. His progress after the operation was eyecatching, starting with second place in a 1m2f Sandown handicap on his return from three months off the track.

Three weeks later he won a Goodwood Listed race over the same distance, then dropped back a furlong for a Group 3 success at Newmarket.

The graph of his RPR went to 107, 111 and 117 in those three runs, meaning he has already improved more than a stone for the gelding operation. That puts him on the fringes of Group 1 class and, with further improvement expected after another winter to strengthen up and settle down, he could be in the thick of the action next summer.

GEORGE SCOTT

September was quite a month for Newmarket trainer George Scott. First he got married to Polly Gredley, followed by a snap honeymoon in Mallorca, and a week later he enjoyed the biggest success of his career thanks to James Garfield in the Group 2 Mill Reef Stakes.

More excitement lies ahead in 2018 with James Garfield as the spearhead for his third full season in the training ranks and plans afoot for a new base that will be up and running by the end of the year.

Scott's father-in-law Bill Gredley, a Group 1 winner in 2017 with the Michael Bell-trained Big Orange and also owner of James Garfield, has given him the best wedding present a trainer could wish for with the building of a 130-box yard at Fitzroy Paddocks, a disused six-acre area adjacent to Bell's stable at Fitzroy House.

Scott, who four years ago was headhunted from California to become assistant trainer to Lady Cecil at Warren Place, will be coming back to his roots as he was previously a pupil assistant to Bell at Fitzroy House. He started training in November 2015 and is currently at the 50-box Saffron House Stables on nearby Hamilton Road.

The 2018 season will be a vital one before moving to the new yard, as Scott acknowledges. "I'm incredibly grateful and excited to be given this opportunity to train from a new yard, but the hard work starts now as we want to have as many winners as possible so we get the horses to fill it. There's a lot of work to do but the ambition is one day to become champion trainer."

FAYONAGH

Proof that Jamie Codd is a top rider – amateur in name only – and that Fayonagh is a first-class jumps prospect came at the very end of day two at the Cheltenham Festival. Not everyone stays to watch the Champion Bumper bring down the curtain on the Wednesday card but those who did were treated to quite a show.

In a messy standing start, Fayonagh was left flat-footed, knocked sideways and then set off behind her 21 rivals. All hope appeared to have gone and trainer Gordon Elliott later admitted: "I wanted to run on to the track and tell Jamie to pull up." Codd patiently made up ground, however, and on the home turn a place looked possible. That would have been a good result in the circumstances but what happened next was extraordinary as Elliott's mare *(above, red cap)* stormed up the hill to score by a length and a quarter.

"It was a bit surreal," said Codd, who works for Tattersalls Ireland and bought Fayonagh there for owner Maura Gittins before recommending Elliott as the trainer. "She got a fright at the start and I thought that was her chance gone but it's pure ability. When I got a belt into her, God she quickened. She's exceptional."

Fayonagh did nothing to change that opinion when she followed up with another Grade 1 bumper win under Codd at the Punchestown festival, nor when Davy Russell guided her to victory on her hurdling debut at Fairyhouse in October. Elliott's long-term target is the mares' novice hurdle back at the Cheltenham Festival.

With the two-years-younger Cheltenham runner-up Debuchet another to watch, the 2017 Champion Bumper should be a race worth looking back on for some time to come.

SAMCRO

"The Neptune looks an obvious target if he was to progress throughout the season, but he'd have the pace for a Supreme and I'd say he'd stay the trip in the Albert Bartlett – he's just a very good horse." Gordon Elliott's assessment of Samcro in the Racing Post's Stable Tour series marks him out as one of the most versatile novice hurdlers around as well as one of the most talented.

With a price tag of £335,000 at the inaugural Goffs UK Aintree Sale last year, Samcro has always carried a weight of expectation but he has borne it lightly. He was unbeaten in three bumpers last season, although Elliott deliberately steered clear of the big festivals to avoid pushing the five-year-old too hard.

His early profile is strikingly similar to Elliott's Cheltenham Gold Cup winner Don Cossack, right down to the fact that both of them ended their bumper career with a 17-length victory in the 2m race on Irish Grand National day.

There is no doubt Elliott hopes Samcro will take big strides this season. "Everyone knows I rate him very highly, but with horses like him you'd rather let them go and do their talking on the track."

What Samcro has done so far speaks volumes.

LORCAN MURTAGH

You can safely say horseracing has been a permanent fixture in Lorcan Murtagh's life. He was reportedly riding ponies aged two, has competed at the Horse of the Year Show and the Royal International Horse Show and rode his first winner, Busy Bimbo on the Flat for Alan Berry, in October 2014 while still at school. His father is ex-jockey turned trainer Barry Murtagh and his younger brother is talented apprentice Connor Murtagh.

While Connor is making waves on the Flat having, amazingly, undergone three major heart operations, northern-based Lorcan, 19, switched his attention to the jumps shortly after his sole Flat victory.

Medical setbacks have also interfered with Lorcan's progress. He broke his leg a couple of months after a breakthrough win on the Rose Dobbin-trained Rocking Blues in the 2016 Eider Chase and was out for six months, but he is making real progress in the 2017-18 season and surpassed his best seasonal total by August, the majority of his winners coming for his boss Donald McCain, whose stable is back on the up.

In what looks an open year, Lorcan ranks a big contender for the conditional jockeys' title.

BACARDYS

Willie Mullins was nervous before Bacardys made his hurdling debut at Leopardstown last Christmas. Not because he wasn't confident that the Grade 2 bumper winner was ready enough to do himself justice, but because the six-year-old had twisted a shoe on his way to the track. "My lads had his foot in a bucket of ice all morning," he reported. "We were wondering how he would be when asked to jump on it but thankfully adrenaline kicked in."

Bacardys' battling victory there marked him out as a tough cookie and he went on to bolster his reputation with two narrow Grade 1 wins, finishing his season with a short-head success over Finian's Oscar in the Champion Novice Hurdle at the Punchestown festival. He couldn't have done much more as a novice hurdler, having lost his chance in the Neptune at Cheltenham when badly hampered by a faller, but as Mullins said at Punchestown: "He was bought as a chasing prospect. He's a good stayer and he's tough. We're looking forward to seeing him jump fences next."

Bacardys has class aplenty and, if the difference among the top novice chasers comes down to a willingness to go through the pain barrier, he will be hard to stop.

BRAIN POWER

"Brain Power is not living up to his name. He's really stupid and doesn't concentrate." So said owner Michael Buckley – a little harshly – after his horse had won a Kempton hurdle in March 2016. "He has lots of ability but thinks he's on holiday in his races."

Well, the holiday's over. Nicky Henderson's stellar team of novice chasers were pivotal in wresting the trainers' title from Paul Nicholls last season and, with the likes of Altior, Might Bite and Whisper now mixing it in the top tier, it is time for Brain Power to step up.

"We schooled Brain Power over fences this time last year and nearly went chasing, but I just thought he didn't know enough," Henderson said. "He's quite a timid horse and running in those big handicaps over hurdles did him good."

Horses aren't stupid – fact – but Brain Power (above) has certainly been infuriating. He won on his debut, followed by a 26-length tenth place next time out in the Aintree bumper – albeit behind future Grade 1 winners Barters Hill, Bellshill and stablemate Buveur D'Air. Last season he progressed from a Listed hurdle victory to win an Ascot Grade 3 by five lengths, only to finish 30 lengths adrift of Buveur D'Air in the Champion Hurdle.

"He has been an entertaining horse to say the least," Henderson said. Nevertheless, the trainer hopes Brain Power will provide a seamless handover from one generation of top novice chasers to the next and the Arkle Chase prospect now has the chance to show he is quick of mind and nimble of feet.

DYLAN HOGAN

Promising Irish apprentice Dylan Hogan hails from Newmarket, but not the one you might expect of a racing talent as he was raised in Newmarket-on-Fergus, a small town in County Clare.

Having ridden ponies from an early age, Hogan, 23, enrolled in RACE (Racing Academy and Centre of Education) before

WILLIAM COX

Andrew Balding's famed Kingsclere apprentice academy appears to have produced another talented young jockey in the shape of 18-year-old William Cox.

The nephew of trainer Clive Cox received a positive appraisal from Balding, who described him as "a very good horseman, very intelligent in a race, level-headed". The young Cox is happy to be under the wing of Balding, saying: "There's always lots of very good young riders there; it keeps you on your toes, keeps you hungry."

A graduate of the pony racing circuit, where he rode around 25 winners, Cox took out his licence in 2016 and his career stepped up a gear in the latest season when five winners in September put him on course to achieve his aim of riding out his 7lb claim by the end of 2017. Next year should be even better.

earning a placement with the legendary Kevin Prendergast on the Curragh, and his links with the famous racing family don't end there as he has successfully teamed up with Kevin's nephew Patrick.

Hogan had something of a breakthrough

JAMES BOWEN

The latest Bowen to make headlines is 16-year-old James, who, having set a British record for point-to-point wins in a season by a novice rider, went on to have a glorious summer under rules, taking his winning total into double figures and securing a job with Nicky Henderson.

Older brother Sean, champion conditional in the 2014-15 season, is part of Paul Nicholls' team of riders, so you can imagine there will be no rivalry spared between the pair, although they will be on the same team when it comes to supporting their father, trainer Peter.

Bowen says of his role with Henderson: "It's a really good opportunity for me as it's probably the best place to be at the moment." He could be in for some winter if he maintains his current rate of progress.

year in 2017, with his number of winners clearly surpassing his totals for the previous three seasons combined, and he has caught the eye with his bold rides from the front, notably on the John Feane-trained Not A Bad Oul Day and Patrick Prendergast's Hailstone.

Keep an eye on him at Dundalk this winter before he mounts a bid for the Irish apprentice title.

LAURENS

In his short time as an owner, John Dance has built up a string of more than 30 racehorses, plus 22 broodmares, and acquired around 30 more yearlings in 2017. In Laurens, he has his first Group 1 winner and an exciting Classic prospect for 2018.

Dance, 42, founded Vertem Asset Management in 2010 after cutting his teeth in City finance and his fast-growing company has allowed him to make rapid inroads since he switched from race sponsor at Newcastle to highly enthusiastic owner – he treated TV viewers, and appalled wife Jess, by performing the robot after Laurens won the Group 2 May Hill Stakes in September.

Laurens went up another notch the following month by landing the Group 1 Fillies' Mile at Newmarket by a nose from Aidan O'Brien's September, with Ballydoyle favourite Magical well beaten in fourth. That success – also a first Group 1 for Dance's retained rider PJ McDonald – rounded off a four-race juvenile campaign that yielded three wins and second place in a Deauville Group 3.

With plenty of stamina on her dam's side, the £220,000 yearling purchase should be suited by middle distances and trainer Karl Burke, well aware that O'Brien's massed ranks of fillies will stand in Laurens' way again next year, nominated the Prix de Diane as a Classic target, while adding that the 1,000 Guineas would be a live option if it came up soft.

If they choose wisely in 2018, Laurens might well spark some more Dance dancing.

Reporting by Katherine Fidler, Jack Haynes, Daniel Hill, Keith Melrose, Maddy Playle, Nick Pulford, Colin Russell, Brian Sheerin, Kitty Trice and Zoe Vicarage

THE
BIGGER
PICTURE

An eventful start to the Grade 1 Frank Ward Solicitors Arkle Novice Chase at Leopardstown in January as the Henry de Bromhead-trained Identity Thief unseats David Mullins in spectacular fashion at the first fence. De Bromhead still claims victory, however, when Some Plan is the only one of the four runners to complete the course
PATRICK McCANN (RACINGPOST.COM/PHOTOS)

Final Furlong

Stories of the year – from the serious to the quirky

Cobden enjoys season of firsts

HARRY COBDEN had a season to remember in 2016-17 with a runaway win in the British conditional jockeys' championship, a first Grade 1 success, victory over Aintree's famous fences at his first attempt in the Topham Chase and a completed round in the Grand National. Not bad for an 18-year-old.

Cobden, part of the competitive coterie of young riders at Paul Nicholls' Ditcheat stable, has a century of winners as his next target, having claimed last season's conditionals' title with an impressive total of 60 that put him 24 clear of runner-up David Noonan.

"I'd love to be champion one day and I'll try to get 100 winners [in the 2017-18 season]," he said. "That might not happen but if I could do it in the next five years, that would be great. There's a good set of lads at Paul's. We're all good mates but you strive to be better than the others, which can only help."

Cobden started the new season

without a claim but still with the support of Nicholls and several other West Country trainers, most notably Colin Tizzard, and soon had another valuable success with the six-length victory of the Tizzard-trained Tempestatefloresco in the Listed Summer Cup at Uttoxeter. Asked after that win about his increasing use of Cobden, Tizzard said: "Harry comes in to ride out for us every Wednesday and we'll use him as much as we can when he's not required by Paul Nicholls."

The link with Tizzard goes back a decade to Cobden's early days in the hunting field alongside the trainer and they enjoyed an even bigger win together at the Grand National meeting when Cobden partnered Tizzard's Ultragold to a 50-1 triumph in the Topham.

"I was looking forward to this all week and I

fancied him," Cobden said in the winner's enclosure. "Even though he was a 50-1 shot I thought he had a little squeak. I had a lovely run down the inside most of the way. He jumped like a buck, was very clever and was a dream horse to ride around there. The fences ride better than they look."

Tizzard was impressed by the youngster's calmness on his first ride over the National fences. "Harry hunted alongside me as a little boy for a long time and I was thinking three out, just sit still, but I didn't have to say it because he did it. He's got a brain on him," he said.

The following day Cobden rode another

outsider when the Nicholls-trained 33-1 shot Just A Par lined up in the National and, although there was no fairytale success, he negotiated the 30 fences safely to finish 14th.

Cobden's biggest win for Nicholls came in the Fighting Fifth Hurdle on Irving, his first ride in a Grade 1 race and exactly three weeks after his 18th birthday. He was unable to claim in that contest but saw off another tyro, Jack Kennedy on the favourite Apple's Jade, by a nose.

His roots with Nicholls run deep too. He went to school with the trainer's daughter Megan and competed against her in pony racing before graduating to the point-to-point

field, where he was the leading novice rider in 2014-15. Cobden, whose parents are beef farmers at Lydford-on-Fosse, ten minutes from Ditcheat, started riding out for Nicholls at the age of 13.

His progress was rapid last season. Celebrating his title success, he said: "I'm delighted. I was miles away last year and then in the last month I rode 11 winners and only just missed out, and after that it was my goal to be champion conditional. I've ridden some big horses in big races thanks to Paul. Irving was massive – it was my first ride in a Grade 1 and to win it was pretty special."

More special times lie ahead for the talented Cobden.

▶▶ Golden moment: Harry Cobden lands the Topham Chase on Ultragold

Uninvited guest puts himself in big picture

A NOTORIOUS interloper made the Racing Post front page in Cheltenham Festival week when he was pictured alongside Sizing John as the Gold Cup hero was led into the winner's enclosure.

The man was identified as Richard Melia, 56, from Colchester, Essex, and his actions led to a security review at Cheltenham and other racecourses in an attempt to prevent a repeat.

Melia was not easily deterred and led in a winner at Yarmouth's eastern festival in September, after which he was ejected from the racecourse.

Melia, who works as a driver and is a keen gambler and racing fan, said his gatecrashing of major sporting events started more than 20 years ago.

"I know it's naughty but I've done it at loads of places," he said. "I've been on the grid at Silverstone, I was in the ring at the Dubai World Cup the year Animal Kingdom won, and I've been in the ring after a Floyd Mayweather fight in

Vegas and shook hands with him."

Among his racing 'moments' are joining Collier Bay's Champion Hurdle celebrations in 1996, appearing next to Frankel after the legend's last race in the 2012 Champion Stakes at Ascot and going out on the Aintree track as Auroras Encore was being cooled down after his 2013 Grand National triumph.

"It's only for a laugh – it's nothing serious," Melia added. "I always keep out of the way

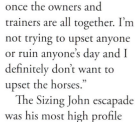

▶ Gatecrasher: Richard Melia (below) helps lead in Sizing John at Cheltenham (above)

once the owners and trainers are all together. I'm not trying to upset anyone or ruin anyone's day and I definitely don't want to upset the horses."

The Sizing John escapade was his most high profile yet, according to Melia.

"It's not trying to find fame but just to get people talking about it. It's been much bigger [after the Gold Cup], probably because of social media."

There was a similar if more low-key incident

at Newbury in April when a man dressed as a jockey briefly made it into the parade ring. Newbury head of communications Andy Clifton said: "A guy who appeared to be on a stag do tried to walk in with the jockeys and was politely asked to leave."

As for Melia, he was promptly banned from all Arena Racing Company tracks after being rumbled at Yarmouth. Following that incident, Melia said: "I think the racing authorities are on to me now and I'll have to go abroad. Maybe I'll try the Breeders' Cup."

●Kangaroo jumps to it

A HUMAN interloper like Richard Melia is one thing but 2017 also brought some strange animal antics on the racecourse.

None more so than the kangaroo who almost caused chaos at an Australian provincial track in May.

The kangaroo appeared in the midst of the ten-runner field (right) at the halfway point of a ten-and-a-half-furlong race at Cessnock, New South

Wales, and ran along with them for about a furlong. Having shown good speed on the inside rail, the unscheduled runner then veered through the pack and headed off the other side of the track.

With the kangaroo out of the way, victory went to Cunning As A Tiger – who was definitely a horse.

Somewhat tamer – in a manner of speaking – was the hare who intruded upon a race at Southwell, also in May,

and narrowly avoided a calamitous clash with the nine runners, who had just entered the home straight.

Showing a blistering turn of foot that marked him down as a real Fibresand specialist, the hare shot across the track before seemingly having a change of heart, putting in a U-turn and sprinting back across the path of the runners.

Luckily no animals were harmed in the making of this story.

Carberry back with a bang after childbirth

NINA CARBERRY has done some incredible things in her riding career – Irish Grand National victory on Organisedconfusion, seven Cheltenham Festival winners – but surely nothing can beat the top amateur's winning return to the saddle only four months after giving birth to her first child.

Eleven months had elapsed since Carberry's last race ride but it was like she had never been away as she steered the Noel Meade-trained Cask Mate to a 12-length success in a bumper at Ballinrobe in September. Her smile said more than words ever could.

"It's so great to be back – I've missed it," she said after hopping down off the 9-4 co-favourite. "Noel gave me a great horse to ride and I managed to steer him in the right direction. I remember the way to go around [the track] anyway."

Carberry, 33, who is married to Ted Walsh jnr, added: "I've had a wonderful couple of months and little Rosie is doing great, so I wouldn't swap that for any winner, but it's certainly good to be back.

"I couldn't believe how well I was travelling turning for home. I was wondering to myself 'have we got another lap to go?' Noel quietly fancied him and it was great to come back with a winner."

Meade, the man who knows Carberry better than anyone, said: "That was just marvellous. She was very excited about coming back.

"She's a magic person and it's brilliant to have her back."

▶ Mother of all comebacks: Nina Carberry with Noel Meade after Cask Mate's win

● Well, you did ask

RTE's special 'Ask Ted' segment during the Punchestown festival, in which viewers sent in questions for Ted Walsh to answer live on air, moved into unexpected territory when the trainer was asked by presenter Robert Hall: "What's your favourite Kardashian, and why?"

Looking totally perplexed as Hall bellowed with laughter, Walsh responded: "I never ate a Kardashian. What's a Kardashian?"

As Hall suggested a Kardashian might be an American celebrity, Walsh added: "It sounds like something you get in a Chinese restaurant. I wouldn't eat it!"

● Meat and drink

ONE racegoer's plan to smuggle vodka into Southwell racecourse got full marks for ingenuity but none for execution after a steward thwarted her sandwich-based plot.

During routine searches on the gate at the Nottinghamshire venue, a lady's lunchbox was searched by a steward, who became suspicious about the weight of one of her sandwiches.

The offending butty was opened up and the £7.29 bottle of vodka was discovered, partially wrapped in tomato and salami, as a picture (above) posted on Twitter revealed.

● Filly goes off course

FOUR-YEAR-OLD filly Rosamaria did not make any headlines on the track but she became a viral sensation following her post-race antics at Redcar in May.

Having finished fourth in a mile handicap, the grey made a detour on the way back to the stable yard and appeared behind the counter in the stable lads' canteen. News of the incident spread quickly after the video was shared on Twitter by trainer Simon Waugh.

Explaining how the unusual event unfolded, Steve Brown, husband of Rosamaria's trainer Julie Camacho, said:

"The filly shied away from a camera and got loose, ending up in the canteen. It could have been bad but there was no harm done. Of all the things I've seen on a racecourse this is a new one – it was very bizarre."

Redcar racecourse manager Amy Fair praised the kitchen staff's calm response. "What helped is that the ladies who run the kitchen work at a number of racecourses in Yorkshire and are comfortable with horses and know how to deal with them – they didn't panic."

▶ Wrong turn: Rosamaria in the stable lads' canteen at Redcar

RACING POST
ANNUAL
AWARDS

Our pick of the best of 2017 – plus the results of a Racing Post readers' poll in the top four categories

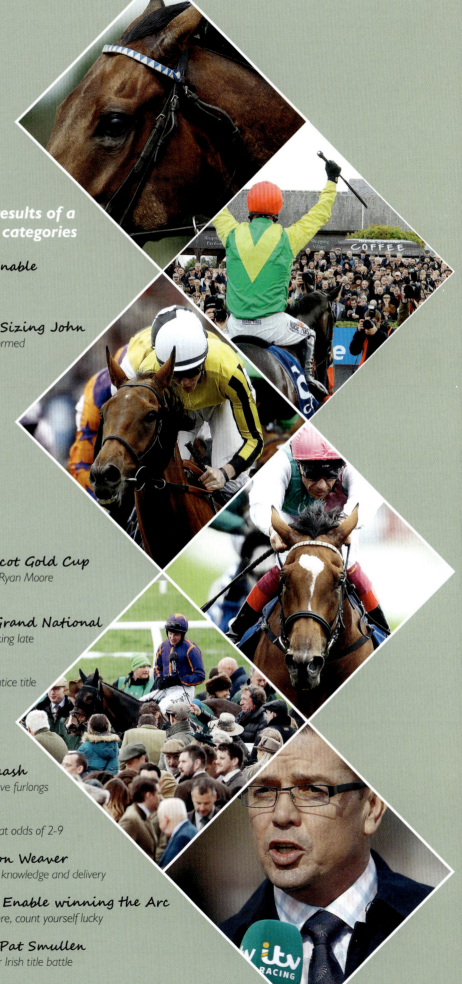

HORSE OF THE YEAR (FLAT) OUR CHOICE *Enable*
Dominated the season from Classics to King George to Arc
READERS' CHOICE *Enable*

HORSE OF THE YEAR (JUMPS) OUR CHOICE *Sizing John*
Speed, stamina and spirit in equal measure from a chaser transformed
READERS' CHOICE *Sizing John*

RACE OF THE YEAR (FLAT)
OUR CHOICE *Ascot Gold Cup*
Battle royal between Big Orange and Order Of St George
READERS' CHOICE *Ascot Gold Cup*

RACE OF THE YEAR (JUMPS)
OUR CHOICE *Punchestown Gold Cup*
Sizing John, Djakadam and Coneygree in a hell-for-leather thriller
READERS' CHOICE *Cheltenham Gold Cup*

RIDE OF THE YEAR (FLAT)
OUR CHOICE *James Doyle, Big Orange, Ascot Gold Cup*
Dynamic, decisive and driven, Doyle produced some ride to beat Ryan Moore

RIDE OF THE YEAR (JUMPS)
OUR CHOICE *Derek Fox, One For Arthur, Grand National*
The ride of a lifetime as Fox showed extreme coolness before striking late

RISING STAR OUR CHOICE *David Egan*
The 18-year-old's talent and tenacity took him to the British apprentice title

COMEBACK OF THE YEAR
OUR CHOICE *Arctic Fire*
Landed the ultra-competitive County Hurdle after 14 months off

MOST IMPROVED HORSE OUR CHOICE *Battaash*
Brilliantly handled by Charlie Hills to become Europe's best over five furlongs

FLOP OF THE YEAR OUR CHOICE *Douvan*
Supposedly unbeatable but lost Queen Mother Champion Chase at odds of 2-9

BEST TV RACING PUNDIT OUR CHOICE *Jason Weaver*
Former jockey has been the star of ITV Racing's coverage with his knowledge and delivery

BEST 'I WAS THERE' MOMENT OUR CHOICE *Enable winning the Arc*
WOW! said the next day's Racing Post front page. If you were there, count yourself lucky

BEST RIVALRY OUR CHOICE *Colin Keane v Pat Smullen*
The young challenger and wily champion rode like demons in their Irish title battle

Icons of the sport recognised in Royal Mail's 'racehorse legends'

RACING'S place in the British sporting fabric was recognised in April when the Royal Mail issued a commemorative set of stamps entitled 'racehorse legends' featuring eight horses including Desert Orchid, Frankel and Red Rum.

For more than 50 years the Royal Mail's stamps series has commemorated anniversaries and celebrated events relevant to British heritage and life, and the racehorse legends set was part of this year's programme alongside David Bowie, ancient Britain, Windsor Castle, songbirds, windmills and watermills, First World War: 1917, landmark buildings, classic toys and Christmas.

Illustrated by renowned equestrian artist Michael Heslop, the racehorse legends set featured original artwork of the eight horses achieving notable wins on British racecourses across six decades. A collector's set also featured a medal designed by engraver Laura Clancy featuring the outstanding racehorse and sire Hyperion, winner of the 1933 Derby and St Leger.

The four jumps horses chosen for the set were Arkle, winner of three Cheltenham Gold Cups and widely acknowledged as the greatest jumps horse in history; Grand National legend Red Rum, the only horse to win the sport's most famous race three times; four-time King George VI Chase winner Desert Orchid, who also won a Cheltenham Gold Cup; and Kauto Star, a modern-day great with five King Georges and two Gold Cups on his CV.

Three of the choices from Flat racing were unarguable: the mighty Frankel, unbeaten in 14 starts and regarded as one of the best of all time; Shergar, who bestrode the turf in 1981 with emphatic wins in the Derby, Irish Derby and King George VI and Queen Elizabeth

Stakes before being kidnapped from stud in 1983; and Brigadier Gerard, the 2,000 Guineas winner in 1971, who captured the King George the following year.

Yet, while greats such as Mill Reef and Dancing Brave were overlooked, there was surprise that the final Flat choice was the Queen's Estimate. Trained by Sir Michael Stoute, the mare's finest hour came in the Gold Cup at Royal Ascot in 2013 – her only top-level victory.

One man who was certainly not amused by Estimate's inclusion was Racing Post historian John Randall, who was consulted during the selection process.

He said: "How can the Royal Mail be so misguided? Its choice of Estimate as one of British racing's eight legends, along with seven authentic giants of the Turf, is embarrassing. For a sub-standard Ascot Gold Cup winner to be given this ultimate accolade at the expense of Mill Reef and Dancing Brave, just because she happened to be owned by the Queen, is absurd."

●Swell guy Hanagan put out of action by wasp sting

JOCKEYS suffer all kinds of injuries but one of the more unusual put Paul Hanagan out of action for a few days in September when he had a frightening allergic reaction to a wasp sting.

The problem occurred as the former champion Flat jockey was winning on Powerful Society at Carlisle. Soon afterwards he had severe swelling in his left hand and had to give up his remaining rides.

"I felt my hand throbbing when I was unsaddling and I thought I might have banged it coming out of the stalls," he recalled. "But I had to go to the stewards' room and as I stood in there I thought I was going to faint.

"I got all my gear off and my whole body came out in

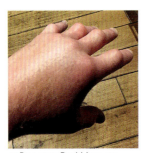
▶▶ Bite size: Paul Hanagan shows his swollen hand

blotches. There was a bit of a mark on my hand where I'd been stung and it was swollen up to the elbow. It must have happened during the race but I didn't feel it at the time with the adrenaline pumping.

"They gave me an injection at the races that seemed to calm it but as soon as I got home I took a really bad turn and I couldn't stop being sick.

So I went to hospital and they gave me antibiotics. It was frightening as my lips started to swell and I was worried it was going to go into my throat."

●Punter off target

SOCIAL media can be a minefield for jockeys and Paddy Bradley took some abuse for a losing ride at Ripon in April – even though he had nothing to do with it.

Bradley had been booked to partner favourite Quatrieme Ami but broke his wrist in a fall while riding work and Ben Robinson came in as a late replacement. After Quatrieme Ami was unplaced, one misguided punter took aim at Bradley.

The 22-year-old said: "My name was in the Racing Post

next to the horse at Ripon, but in the morning the jockey change came through that Ben Robinson would be riding it. And then I got an abusive message from a punter for the ride I'd given the horse. If he'd been paying attention he'd have seen there was a jockey change."

On the perils of online trolls, he added: "Every day you get them – even if you win. If you've won and they've backed something else they'll message you for costing them money. It's crazy.

"I don't open them most of the time as you see a name you don't know and the first word is a swear word, but with this one I thought, 'What could he be moaning at me for? I didn't even ride it'."

ALTERNATIVE

AWARDS

The Donald Trump Award *for making friends and influencing people*

Jockey Club Racecourses for its unpopular proposal to close Kempton Park

The Samuel Beckett 'Waiting for Godot' Award *for never showing up*

Faugheen, who did not run in the 2016-17 season despite several bulletins suggesting he was due back

The Bible Studies Award *inscribed 'So The Last Shall Be First'*

Jointly won by Arrogate (Dubai World Cup) and Fayonagh (Champion Bumper) for remarkable victories after all seemed lost in the early stages

The NHS Award *for premature jockey elation*

Frankie Dettori for his over-excited performance when almost winning the Nunthorpe Stakes on Lady Aurelia

The Chuckle Brothers Award *inscribed 'To Me To You To Me . . .'*

Might Bite, who had RSA Chase victory in his sights, threw it away, then took it back again

The Doctor Who Award *for incredible regeneration*

Sizing John, who turned from serial loser over two miles to golden hero once he went beyond three miles

The Julius Caesar Award *inscribed 'And You Brutus?'*

Buveur D'Air, who switched back from chasing to win the Champion Hurdle, leaving stablemate My Tent Or Yours in the runner-up position for the third time

The Premier League Football Award *inscribed 'What's Austerity?'*

The top-end yearling sales, where prices included

4,000,000gns (£4.2m) paid by Godolphin for a daughter of Galileo, the second most expensive yearling filly ever sold at auction

The Julian Assange Award *for hiding in plain sight*

Richard Melia, the well-known gatecrasher who evaded security to lead in Cheltenham Gold Cup winner Sizing John

The Boris Johnson Award *inscribed 'With Friends Like You, Who Needs Enemies?'*

Ryan Moore for his grinning aside to the stewards in a televised inquiry that Oisin Murphy wasn't strong enough to keep his mount Dark Red straight at Goodwood. Dark Red was duly demoted

A-Z of 2017

The year digested into 26 bite-size chunks

B

C

J

A is for Almanzor, remember him? The 2016 European Flat champion was kept in training at four but made only one appearance when a dismal fifth of six in a Deauville Group 3 in August.

B is for baffling as Douvan flopped at odds of 2-9 on his big day in the Queen Mother Champion Chase after carrying all before him until then.

C is for Chantilly and the Curragh. The Paris track earned a big *tres bien* as it deputised for Longchamp for a second year, not least on Arc weekend, but Ireland's premier Flat course faced much criticism as it clung grimly to all five Irish Classics with a greatly reduced capacity and the building work continuing apace.

D is for drainage, the failings of which meant the cancellation of the prestigious Ayr Gold Cup meeting in September. An area of waterlogged ground around two and a half furlongs from the finish was a persistent problem and – allied to poor communication from the racecourse – led to the loss of the three-day fixture.

E is for Enable, who lit up the Flat season with her power, professionalism and panache. And for excitement at the news that she is staying in training in 2018.

F is for four winners on one day at Cheltenham, shared on the Thursday by Willie Mullins and Ruby Walsh with Yorkhill, Un De Sceaux, Nichols Canyon and Let's Dance. Walsh became the first jockey in history to score four in a single day of the festival.

G is for Game on! After years of spurning the undoubted charms of rival Coolmore stock in the sales ring, Godolphin unexpectedly set Tattersalls alight with the purchase of several yearlings by supersire Galileo. It will be fascinating to see where this leads – on and off the racecourse.

H is for the heart on the sleeve of Rupert Bell, whose TalkSport commentary on the Ascot Gold Cup victory of Big Orange, trained by his brother Michael, evolved into a joyfully partisan rant reminiscent of every punter, everywhere. "Go on Big Orange . . . I think he's done it. Yes! You beauty! Un-be-lievable!"

I is for ITV Racing, whose performance in their first year since taking over from Channel 4 as sole purveyors of racing's terrestrial television coverage was seldom less than assured.

J is for Jo-Go: Josephine Gordon, the 2016 champion apprentice, thrived in her new role riding for Newmarket trainer Hugo Palmer, for whom she had a couple of Group-race winners en route to her best-ever total.

K is for King at last as Sizing John seized the crown in the Cheltenham Gold Cup that

had been denied him over shorter distances.

L is for Lizzie Kelly, who outdid Paddy Brennan and Cue Card to land the Grade 1 Betway Bowl at Aintree on her beloved Tea For Two. Kelly gave as good as she got in a driving finish, and just a little bit more.

M is for mistaken identity, a notorious case of which arose at Yarmouth in July when trainer Charlie McBride saddled the wrong horse to win. The 50-1 shot who won a two-year-old contest as Mandarin Princess was actually the three-year-old Millie's Kiss. The horse was disqualified and McBride was fined £1,500.

N is for nostalgia, sparked by the decision of Sheikh Mohammed to re-register his famous old maroon-and-white racing colours for his daughter Sheikha Al Jalila, in whose name (and silks) Royal Line competes. Oh So Sharp, Pebbles, Ajdal, Kribensis –

they all flashed before our eyes again.

O is for oneupmanship. No sooner had Sheikh Mohammed voiced his intention to increase the purse at the Dubai World Cup to regain top spot in the prize-money charts than those behind the usurper, the Pegasus World Cup, pledged an extra $4m to boost their prize fund to $16m.

P is for Poundland, the low-cost retailer that took over sponsorship of the Hill area at Epsom for the Derby meeting. Social media generally reacted badly – "please tell me this is fake news," said one Twitter user – but Rod Street of Great British Racing described it as "an elegant brand fit".

Q is for quick as a flash. In two of Europe's premier five-furlong dashes, Lady Aurelia scorched the turf again at Royal Ascot and Battaash left his rivals gasping in the Abbaye. Blink and you'd have missed 'em.

R is for right hook, as delivered by Davy Russell to his uncooperative mount Kings Dolly at Tramore in August. The 2014 Cheltenham Gold Cup-winning jockey was given a four-day ban. Eventually.

S is for Silvestre de Sousa, a byword for power in the saddle as he set about reclaiming the British Flat jockeys' title.

T is for Two Golf Widows, who showed there are better things to do than spending your time on the links – like owning a Grand National winner. Belinda McClung and Deborah Thomson, the 'widows' in question, celebrated as One For Arthur romped home at Aintree under Derek Fox.

U is for the umbrellas that were pressed hastily into service as the second day of 'Glorious' Goodwood was almost

washed out. It rained and rained from morning through to evening, prompting a flood of non-runners and a shock win for mudlark Here Comes When in the feature Sussex Stakes.

V is for valedictory as Many Clouds gave his all to defeat Thistlecrack in the Cotswold Chase but collapsed and died after his gallant effort.

W is for Winx, the Australian supermare whose winning streak lit up the racing scene down under. Maybe we'll see her at Royal Ascot next year; fingers (and everything else) firmly crossed.

X is for X-pensive, such as the Galileo

filly out of Dank who was sold for 4,000,000gns at Tattersalls to the bid of John Gosden on behalf of Sheikh Mohammed. Notionally named Gloam, she fetched the second-highest price of any yearling filly ever sold at auction.

Y is for Yikes! as Yorkhill frayed nerves on several occasions, most notably with his left-leaning tendencies in a dramatic Ryanair Gold Cup at Fairyhouse.

Z is for Zero to Hero, the trajectory taken by Padraig Beggy, rider of Derby winner Wings Of Eagles. Before his 40-1 success at Epsom, the Irishman had ridden only three winners since the beginning of 2015.

FLASHBACK

1997 The bomb-scare Grand National: evacuation and resurrection

By Scott Burton

TWENTY years on it remains a miracle on Merseyside: the evacuation of 60,000 racegoers, as well as more than 100 horses and their connections, following two calls with verified IRA codewords claiming a bomb had been planted at Aintree on Grand National day; and 48 hours later the resurrection of the event that the racecourse executive and the people of Liverpool refused to let die.

Such a triumphant outcome seemed a very long way off as the order was given to clear the course half an hour before the Grand National's scheduled start time of 3.45pm on Saturday, April 5, 1997. Those caught up in the drama still have clear memories of the day.

"I will always remember the policemen coming to the office," says former Aintree chairman Lord Daresbury. "When it turned out to be a hoax, people thought it can't have

been serious. But it was very serious at the time."

In the weighing room the National jockeys were embarking on their final rituals before heading out to the parade ring.

"There was a sense that it was like a fire drill and we'd be back in shortly," says Jamie Osborne, rider of Suny Bay. "I walked out in boots, breeches and colours, leaving behind car keys, wallet, the whole lot."

When reality dawned that the evacuation was for real, the jockeys were among the tens of thousands of people displaced on the streets while police conducted an intensive sweep of the racecourse. Even as the evacuation was in full swing, Aintree managing director Charles Barnett and Lord Daresbury went to meet Merseyside police with intent to resurrect the race. "All I was concerned with was 'when can we run this race again?'" says Barnett.

Less than 48 hours later the plans were in place and more than 20,000 people inched their way through tight

▶▶All was not lost: (clockwise from top left) Police evacuate the course on the Saturday; racegoers queue the next day to retrieve their cars and belongings; Lord Gyllene comes home well clear in the Monday National
Pictures: **PHIL SMITH & DAN ABRAHAM**

security into the immediate grandstand vicinity free of charge, creating something of a carnival atmosphere for the Monday National.

Joint-favourite when BBC's Grandstand programme went on air on Saturday lunchtime, Lord Gyllene was a drifting 14-1 shot by 5pm on Monday. But he was one of the most impressive National winners of modern times, making just about every yard under Tony Dobbin, who says: "About 20,000 people came and it felt like 120,000. I'm biased but for me the buzz was still there and it was fantastic."

Lord Daresbury is in no doubt about both the welcome afforded to Lord Gyllene and the wider significance of the Monday National. "It was a unique experience. People really rallied to be there on that day and it was just fantastic. Charlie Barnett did an absolutely amazing job because at five o'clock on the Saturday it didn't look feasible."

The Grand National, in the year of its 150th running, had been saved.